Gadamer's Dialectical Hermeneutics

Gadamer's Dialectical Hermeneutics

Lauren Swayne Barthold

LEXINGTON BOOKS
A division of
ROWMAN & LITTLEFIELD PUBLISHERS, INC.
Lanham • Boulder • New York • Toronto • Plymouth, UK

Published by Lexington Books
A division of Rowman & Littlefield Publishers, Inc.
A wholly owned subsidiary of The Rowman & Littlefield Publishing Group, Inc.
4501 Forbes Boulevard, Suite 200, Lanham, Maryland 20706
http://www.lexingtonbooks.com

Estover Road, Plymouth PL6 7PY, United Kingdom

Copyright © 2010 by Lexington Books

All rights reserved. No part of this book may be reproduced in any form or by any electronic or mechanical means, including information storage and retrieval systems, without written permission from the publisher, except by a reviewer who may quote passages in a review.

British Library Cataloguing in Publication Information Available

Library of Congress Cataloging-in-Publication Data
Barthold, Lauren Swayne, 1965–
  Gadamer's dialectical hermeneutics / Lauren Swayne Barthold.
     p. cm.
  Includes bibliographical references (p.   ) and index.
  ISBN 978-0-7391-3887-8 (cloth : alk. paper) — ISBN 978-0-7391-3889-2 (electronic)
  1. Gadamer, Hans-Georg, 1900–2002. 2. Hermeneutics. 3. Dialectic. 4. Plato. 5. Aristotle. I. Title.
  B3248.G34B37 2010
  193—dc22   2009036729

∞™ The paper used in this publication meets the minimum requirements of American National Standard for Information Sciences—Permanence of Paper for Printed Library Materials, ANSI/NISO Z39.48-1992.

Printed in the United States of America

For Pablo

The Gazer

I gaze at the trees in the storm,
Which after days grown mild
Are striking my anxious windowpanes.
And now I hear the voice of distant things,
Things I cannot bear without friends,
And cannot embrace in love without my sister.

The storm roars on—a veritable transformer—
Right through the woods and through time,
And everything seems ageless;
The landscape, like a verse from the Psalms,
Is earnest and compelling—and from Eternity.

What humans are able to conquer is miniscule,
And how large is that which wrestles with us!
So let us become like those small things out there
That are controlled by the great storm—
Then we will become vast and nameless.

What we ourselves overcome is small,
Even our successes only make us small!
For the Eternal and Exceptional
Does not want to be bent by us!
Like the angel in the Old Testament
Who appeared to all who wrestled.
And when his opponent in the struggle
Felt like flesh under his fingers, it is
Like strings sounding a deep melody.

The man who is overcome by this angel—
An angel who so often renounces all struggle with mortals—
Now goes forth justified and resurrected
Made great by that same hard hand
which, while forming him, also caresses him.
And victory now no longer attracts him.
The attaining of full maturity, for him,
Consists in being completely overcome
By that which is the Always Greater.

"Der Schauende" from Rainer Maria Rilke's *Buch der Bilder,*
Trans. Richard E. Palmer

Table of Contents

Acknowledgments	xi
Introduction	xiii
Chapter 1: Gadamer's Dialectical Plato	1
Chapter 2: Gadamer's Dialectical Aristotle	25
Chapter 3: The Dialectic of Understanding: *Theoria* and *Praxis*	47
Chapter 4: Truth's Dialectic	71
Chapter 5: Hermeneutics' Dialectical Ethics: Dialogue and the Good	99
Bibliography	129
Index	139

Acknowledgments

This work germinated as my dissertation written at the New School for Social Research under the direction of Richard Bernstein, whose passion for arguing about the strengths and weaknesses of Gadamer's hermeneutics inspired me along the way. Dennis Schmidt has provided much needed moral support and practical guidance over the years. David Vessey read the whole manuscript and offered sharp criticisms and philosophical insights that made the book stronger. Manny Gomez gave generously of his time and expertise to assist in formatting and indexing. Richard Palmer so graciously provided the very fine translation of the Rilke poem used in the book's epigraph. Beth Shotton not only kindly offered her art for the cover but also the listening ear of a friend. Josh Hasler helped proofread. Gordon College awarded me an Initiative Grant for time off to complete my manuscript. And my husband, Pablo Muchnik, a co-traveler in the exhilarating and excruciating process of a first publish, was always there cheering me on. To all these individuals (and institutions) I am truly and deeply appreciative.

Part of chapter 5 is a substantially rewritten version of "How Hermeneutical is He? A Gadamerian Analysis of Richard Rorty," *Philosophy Today*, vol. 49 2005: 236-244.

Introduction

All experiences are moral experiences.[1]

All living is interpreting; all action requires seeing the world as something.[2]

The way in which questions are put, the points of view assumed, presuppose a relativity of interest; all characteristics imply values, and every objective description, so called, implies an ethical background.[3]

From its earliest days, hermeneutics has concerned itself with distance: how are we to cope with the divide between the alien and the familiar? That such distance enables rather than disables hermeneutics can be seen in two common tropes that reflect the essence of hermeneutics: the hermeneutical circle, as marked by the constant movement between part and whole, and Hermes, the messenger between gods and humans. Hans-Georg Gadamer attests to the crucial role distance plays in hermeneutics when he writes: "Hermeneutic work is based on a polarity of familiarity and strangeness. . . . The true locus of hermeneutics is this in-between [Zwischen]" (Gadamer 1992b, 295). This book is an attempt to understand the significance of such "in-betweenness" for Gadamer's own hermeneutics.

To fully appreciate the extensiveness of in-betweenness for Gadamer, this work situates his later hermeneutics in light of his early work on the Greeks.

1. Nietzsche 1974, 114.
2. Nussbaum 1990, 47.
3. Beauvoir 1974, 9.

Gadamer himself explicitly attested to his general indebtedness to Plato and Aristotle: "So I have to say that the dialogues of Plato, even more than the works of the great thinkers of German Idealism, have left their stamp on my thinking" (Hahn 1997, 32); and: "The most fruitful impulses for my work came from [the Greek philosophy of Plato and Aristotle]" (Hahn 1997, 347). Catherine Zuckert also affirms this relation: "Gadamer's understanding of Plato with the help of Aristotle's conceptual analysis merges almost completely with his own understanding of the hermeneutical character of human existence" (Zuckert 2002, 218). Given Gadamer's indebtedness to Plato and Aristotle, throughout this work I will use the term "dialectic" to characterize the in-betweenness central to Gadamer's hermeneutics.[4] While my aim is to explicate precisely the sense in which Gadamer's hermeneutics is dialectical, a preliminary clarification of how "dialectic" will be used is necessary.

In its most general and pedestrian meaning, "dialectic" refers both to a tension between two opposite entities and to a logical inquiry into truth. While Gadamer's own desire to preserve the intimacy between dialogue and dialectic embraces both of these general meanings, I will use "dialectic" primarily in the first of these senses and even then more as a trope than a concept per se. Thus it will not refer to a "dialectical argument" that aims at achieving truth but to the way in which Gadamer's hermeneutics seeks not only to preserve (without overcoming) oppositional terms but also to reveal such a tension as productive of the very process of understanding. The use of "dialectic" evokes Gadamer's desire to preserve an in-betweenness characteristic of Platonic dialectic and to refuse the overcoming suggestive of Hegelian dialectic.[5] Furthermore, understanding "dialectic" as requiring the preservation of this in-betweenness reflects the fact that as long as we are not gods we require the service of Hermes. Such an in-betweenness demands that we accept, indeed embrace, and not try to eradicate or solve the "problem" of, the Platonic *chorismos*. As Gadamer insists, the *chorismos*, i.e., the separation between the transcendent and sensual realms, was never a problem for Plato but only became one due to Aristotle's misreading. Another way to put it is to maintain that such dialectic denies the viciousness and affirms the fecundity of the hermeneutical circle.[6] In other words, by refusing the Hegelian movement toward absolute knowledge, the dialectic of hermeneutics emphasizes the original Platonic meaning of a dialectic that renders un-

---

4. Paul Ricoeur also picks up on the importance of such a "dialectical" tension for Gadamer's work when he speaks of the "dialectic of participation and distanciation [sic]" in Gadamer's work (Ricoeur 1991, 73). However, Ricoeur ultimately sees this tension as problematic, an antinomy that needs to be resolved. I offer a criticism of Ricoeur's position in chapter 4.

5. On the superiority of Plato's "practical" dialectic over Hegel's conceptual one, see Griswold 1982.

6. Francois Renaud also links up Gadamer's rendering of Platonic dialectic with the hermeneutical circle: "Das Problem des Einen und Vielen ist also, so Gadamer, kein anderes als dasjenige des hermeneutischen Zirkels des Ganzen und der Teile" (Renaud 1999, 70).

derstanding inseparable from dialogue and is marked by a constant and productive "chorismatic" tension.

In thinking through the significance of dialectic for Gadamer's hermeneutics, one must also acknowledge how Gadamer attests to the way in which "'dialectical ethics' indicates an intention that remains throughout all of my later work" (Gadamer 1991a, 15). Yet in spite of this telling description, he remains practically mute about what this actually means. Furthermore, very little secondary literature addresses the significance of holding these terms together for Gadamer's thought as a whole.[7] And given Gadamer's own claim that his work is descriptive and not prescriptive in nature, it becomes even more challenging to grasp the meaning of his reference to "ethics."[8] For, it would be one thing to maintain that his work is "ethically dialectical"—which could be taken to refer to the ethics of understanding. But in what sense is Gadamer involved in elucidating not merely the *ethical* components of understanding but an ethics that is fundamentally *dialectical*? The question then becomes twofold: how is his work one of "ethics" and how is it "dialectical"?

On one hand, dialectical ethics can be understood in terms of Gadamer's claim that hermeneutics is "practical philosophy." "Practical philosophy" signifies the dialectical tension crucial to both Plato's and Aristotle's work, namely, that between *theoria* and *praxis*. Thus part of what it means to argue for a dialectical understanding of hermeneutics is to demonstrate how the *theoria-praxis* tension plays itself out in Gadamer's hermeneutics. For, as we shall see, Gadamer's hermeneutics is committed to the fact that the "theoretical" question of who we are as understanding beings is unanswerable apart from the "practical" question of what it means to live the good life. As will be demonstrated, the dialectical tension between *theoria* and *praxis* in Gadamer's own work reveals an ethical emphasis suggestive of practical philosophy. As Graeme Nicholson attests: "We can say that dialectic performs for hermeneutics itself the service which has fallen to philosophy ever since Socrates: it puts to hermeneutics itself the challenge: 'know thyself'" (Nicholson 2002, 502).

On the other hand, taking seriously Gadamer's dialectical ethics sheds light on the dual role of the good in understanding. Keeping in mind that Gadamer is too radical an interpreter of Plato to suppose that one can ever fully conceptualize the good enables us to adopt a more truly Platonic way of construing the good: namely, in terms of both the good-for-us and the good-beyond-being. Concerning the latter, it will be demonstrated that Gadamer advances a "hermeneutical" role for the good: it is that at which all "true understanding aims" (Gadamer 1991b, 3). But what can it mean that all true understanding aims at the idea of the good? I will argue that the good serves as a tacit assumption necessary for all understanding, and as a tacit assumption it "transcends" our capacity

---

7. While Foster 1991, Smith 1988 and 1991, Sullivan 1989, and Wachterhauser 1999 all take up the ethical or political potential of Gadamer's hermeneutics, none articulates this emphasis in terms of its relation to dialectic.
8. See his introduction to Truth and Method, in particular p. xxiii.

to fully conceptually grasp it. Its inability to be fully articulated ensures the ongoing nature of understanding. It is that which we look toward but can never quite get into focus. As such, the good-beyond-being incites all understanding while it itself lies beyond the grasp of our understanding. Gadamer's hermeneutics demonstrates that dialectical ethics is about neither the final articulation of the good nor the normative conceptualization of the good. According to Gadamer, to impute such a goal to Plato is to misunderstand him.

A second way of understanding the role of the good is by attending to the ethical implications of dialogue. We could say that the good-for-us refers to the dialogical ability to listen to and answer another. Hence the dialectical approach to the good that affirms the Platonic *chorismos*: all understanding presupposes the good-beyond-being and reflects an ethical comportment as found in dialogue. For instance, Gadamer tells us that "the dialectic of an absolutizing (in Hegelian terms) or a skeptical/historicist worldview is translated into the ethical dimension of the dialogue" (Gadamer 2004, 27).

Thus Gadamer's dialectical ethics maintains the vitality of both *theoria* and *praxis* that defines practical philosophy; at the same time it recovers a role for the good in understanding—both in terms of its assumptive role as beyond-being and in its dialogical role as a good-for-us. For, by privileging understanding as our fundamental way of being in the world we find both that the good emerges as necessary for understanding and that the dialogic nature of understanding that Gadamer esteems is "always already" ethical. As we shall see, dialogue, as the paragon of understanding, aims not to provide us with clear and distinct knowledge of the way the world "really is," rather, its aim is to reveal the reality of human solidarity. In other words, dialogue exposes the relational qualities of human existence, which serves as the basis for all human knowing. Dialogue's importance, then, challenges modern attempts to define knowledge as clarity about isolated bits of knowledge. Gadamer follows Socrates in insisting that our most basic understanding is self-understanding, one requiring an acknowledgment of our historical finitude that awakens our connectedness to others. The necessary tension between the good-as-transcendent, as the requisite provisional assumption for all understanding, and the good-for-us, as born out in the *ethos* of dialogue, reflects the dialectical ethics at the heart of Gadamer's hermeneutics.

Another preliminary point of clarification regarding dialectic is required here. Given the proximity of dialogue and dialectic in Gadamer's work, it is not uncommon in the literature to use the terms "dialogue" and "dialectic" more or less interchangeably.[9] In fact, it seems as if Gadamer does just this himself at times.[10] While it is not accurate to reduce one to the other, there is certainly a strong connection and similarity between the two, not the least reasons of which is the fact that, as P. Christopher Smith points out, "Plato's word dialectic derives from the Greek *dialegesthai*, which exactly translated means just this talk-

---

9. See, for example, Coltman 1998, Decker 2000, and Kidder 1995.
10. See Gadamer 1992b, 362-369.

ing something through" (Silverman 1991, 34). Rod Coltman also notes the "etymological relationship" in so far as both *dia-lexis* and *dia-logos* can be translated literally as "through speech" or "through language" (Coltman 1998, 45, 136 note 61). Without equating the two, Gadamer maintains that Platonic dialectic finds its true expression in Socratic dialogue. My aim is to demonstrate that while dialogue and dialectic are inextricable terms for Gadamer, there is, as I will detail below, more to the latter than the former.

Another caveat in approaching the role of dialectic in hermeneutics concerns the fact that while Gadamer demonstrates the necessity of both Platonic dialectic and Socratic dialogue to Plato's overall project, describing Socratic dialogue as "the container of Platonic doctrine" (Gadamer 1991b, 20), Gadamer not only is careful to distinguish between Platonic and Hegelian dialectic, he also makes a further distinction between early and later Platonic dialectic.[11] For example, in his later essay, "Dialectic and Sophism in Plato's *Seventh Letter*," Gadamer distinguishes among: 1) early, or "initial," dialectic, which is most closely fused with Socratic dialogue, 2) late Platonic dialectic, which is the one fused with the "logical concerns" of *dihairesis* and hypothesis, and 3) modern/Hegelian dialectic, which has its origin in Eleatic dialectic of contradiction (Gadamer 1980, 93). This distinction serves to clarify his suspicion of the tendency to equate language with propositions and to esteem dialectic as the paragon of language-as-statement. For, there is another way to conceive language: namely, dialogically, which is also Platonic/Socratic.

Such distinctions amongst different types of dialectic prove crucial for further understanding just what "dialectic" means for Gadamer and how it is related to dialogue. For while Gadamer himself admits that his own project "seeks to free itself from the embrace of the synthetic power of the Hegelian dialectic, even from the 'logic' which developed from the dialectic of Plato, and to take its stand in the movement of dialogue" (Gadamer 1992b, xxxvii), this does not entail, as some commentators suggest, a complete diremption between dialectic and dialogue. For example, James Risser (2002a) argues explicitly that we should not read dialogue and dialectic as synonymous terms since Gadamer endorses the finitude of the former but is wary about the infinitude of the latter. Risser bases his claim on Gadamer's statement made in his "Foreword to the second edition" that he wants to distance himself from the "synthetic power of Hegelian dialectic, even from the 'logic' which developed from the dialectic of Plato" and instead to privilege dialogue (Gadamer 1992b, xxxv-xxxvii). However, once we recognize Gadamer's insistence upon distinguishing amongst different types of dialectic it becomes clear that the Gadamer quotation Risser cites is meant only to distinguish what sort of dialectic Gadamer is *not* appealing to and to clarify that his dialectic in fact most resembles the early (non-excessively logical) Platonic dialectic grounded in dialogue. It is important to note, then, that Gadamer wants to distinguish the dialectical components of his project from the

11. See Gadamer 1991b, 21 where this specific distinction is made, and Gadamer 1976, 5-34, where he also mentions Kantian and modern dialectic.

extremes of either a Platonic or an Hegelian dialectic. His criticisms of Platonic and Hegelian dialectic in *Truth and Method* (Gadamer 1992b, 468ff.) are aimed at the propositional and sentential reductionism inherent in both. Language is not reducible to propositions, and a dialectic based on the logical requirement of the proposition fails to capture the full "dimension of the linguistic experience of the world" (Gadamer 1992b, 469). But this is not the same as saying that dialectic is non-dialogical. Gadamer's aim in this section in *Truth and Method* is to recover the speculative element of dialectic that illustrates what is essential to hermeneutical experience, namely, "an activity of the thing itself, an action that, unlike the methodology of modern science, is a passion, an understanding, an event that happens to one" (Gadamer 1992b, 465). Dialectic, in this instance, maintains a linguistic relation to what lies beyond being without attempting to capture this relation propositionally. Language expresses our relationship to being without insisting on the sufficiency of those statements for capturing all there is to being. As Gadamer puts it: "Someone who speaks is behaving speculatively when his words do not reflect beings, but express a relation to the whole of being" (Gadamer 1992b, 469). That language relates us to the whole (i.e., being) without ever fully articulating that whole suggests the kinship between hermeneutical experience and dialectic. Dialectic thus comes to demonstrate the in-betweenness of the hermeneutical condition, where the incompleteness of language is not a hindrance but the very impetus for understanding. That is why Gadamer looks to poetry as the exemplar of such speculative dialectic.

In spite of his criticisms of Plato's and Hegel's dialectic in *Truth and Method*, I will show in my first chapter that Gadamer does identify with the early dialectic of Plato, which was based on Socratic dialogue and provided a response to the failure of Eleatic dialectic to take into account the "*ti estin*," the "what," or what Gadamer calls, "*die Sache*." In addition to *die Sache*, Gadamer's reading of Socratic dialogue also emphasizes its requirement of *logos*, *arete* (the good-for-us), and the good-beyond-being. The final part of chapter 1 construes Gadamer's reading of Platonic dialectic as primarily concerned with its ability to hold in tension the one and the many. More specifically, we will see how Gadamer reads the "problem" of the one and the many through the lens of the productive and ongoing nature of the *chorismos* and the dual role of the good. The result will be to show that while it is accurate to avoid identifying Gadamer with either Hegelian or the later Platonic dialectic, this does not mean that Gadamer refuses dialectic altogether. Chapter 1 thus pinpoints three key features of Platonic dialectic that demonstrate its connection but irreducibility to dialogue: 1) its grounding in Socratic dialogue, 2) its productive and constant chorismatic tension, and 3) and its requirement of the dual role of the good (as both contributing to the solidarity of beings and as an assumption that lies beyond being). By delineating these three thematics, the first chapter prepares the way for grasping the dialectic found in Gadamer's own hermeneutics, which will be characterized by its productive and constant "chorismatic" tension that manifests itself in 1) the integrity between *theoria* and *praxis* (chapters 2 and 3), 2) the losing (marked by transcendence) and finding (marked by application) of oneself that the event of truth requires (chapter 4), 3) dialogue (chapter 5), and 4) the necessity of the dual role of the good (as both beyond-being and for-us) (chapter 5).

As the second chapter details, Gadamer's (early) interpretation of Aristotle serves as a bridge between his (early) work on Plato and his more explicitly dialectical hermeneutics. For, Gadamer shows us that while Aristotle ostensibly criticized Plato's appeal to the *chorismos* (specifically in terms of the problem between the good-as-transcendent and the good-for-us) a certain form of *chorismos* (and thus, as will be shown, dialectic) emerges in Aristotle's own thought. The tendency of Gadamer to read a continuity between Plato and Aristotle specifically in terms of a chorismatic tension constitutes Gadamer's dialectical reading of Aristotle. But let me first add that while I will rely heavily on *Plato's Dialectical Ethics* in this chapter, I do so in the light of Gadamer's later comment that "the basic theme of Plato's doctrine was pushed all too much into the background" (Gadamer 1980, 125). This leads me to emphasize Gadamer's original interest in reading a unity between Aristotle and Plato and in downplaying the differences. I will develop Gadamer's dialectical reading of Aristotle along three trajectories. First, Gadamer takes Aristotle's notions of *theoria* and *techne* to be extensions of, and not attacks on, Plato's thought. Second, Gadamer maintains that Aristotle, like Plato, concerns himself with the question of what it means that the good itself is common to all things that are good. And finally, Aristotle, like Gadamer's Plato, values the integrity of *theoria* and *praxis*.

The Platonic and Aristotelian origins of Gadamer's own dialectical ethics are demonstrated in chapter 3, which addresses the way in which Gadamer considered both *theoria* and *praxis* relevant for his hermeneutical project. Beginning with Gadamer's esteem of *theoria* and moving on to a discussion of hermeneutics' relation to both *phronesis* and practical philosophy, chapter 3 elucidates a similar tension between a life of *theoria* and life of *praxis* that undergirds Gadamer's hermeneutics. As stated above, another way of describing my overall project is that it takes seriously Gadamer's claim that hermeneutics is practical philosophy. As a reading of some of Gadamer's essays on this theme reveal, practical philosophy is to be distinguished from *phronesis* to the extent to which the former allows for theoretical reflection on human life. For, as we also learn, Gadamer takes care to distinguish between hermeneutical philosophy (akin to practical philosophy) and the universality of the hermeneutical experience that is part of all human attempts to understand (but that does not necessarily require the degree of theoretical distantiation implied by hermeneutical philosophy). Keeping this distinction in mind leads to a new appreciation for the role of *phronesis* in understanding, albeit a more limited one. The result of such an appreciation is to ward off charges that Gadamer's reliance on *phronesis* results in conservatism.[12]

That hermeneutics' dialectic, then, is primarily characterized by a productive and constant chorismatic tension (of the early form, rather than by Hegelian

12. See, for example, Bernstein 1983 and Figal 1995.

synthesis or (later) Platonic logic) bears significance for Gadamer's conception of truth. Chapter 4 delineates hermeneutics' dialectic of truth as the movement of distantiation (from the particulars of self) followed by a return to self. This way of construing hermeneutics' in-betweenness accords with Gadamer's own description of understanding as an "event," which will be shown to be characterized by moments of both loss of self as well as a return to self that entails an applicative moment. Beginning with an analysis of *Truth and Method*, I note this dialectical movement in several of Gadamer's concepts: *Bildung, sensus communis*, taste, experience, play, and transformation into structure. Gadamer's discussion of the truth of art also suggests a dialectical movement to the extent to which it is marked by a moment of being drawn away from ourselves (as exemplified by play) and a moment of self-understanding in which one must return to, i.e., understand for, oneself (as exemplified by application). Thus a further way of elucidating such a dialectical rendering of truth is in terms of Gadamer's own claim that "all understanding is self-understanding," meaning that all understanding requires one to understand anew for oneself. Finally, drawing on some of Gadamer's shorter essays on truth, we see that there is also a sense in which truth suggests the movement between the other and the familiar, as demonstrated by Gadamer's analysis of poetry. For, poetry's power comes from its ability to draw us out of ourselves, while at the same time (like Aristotle's *theoria*) making known the unfamiliar and bringing what is distant near. In spite of his plethora of images and tropes used to illustrate truth, we find a productive and ongoing chorismatic tension demonstrating the importance of "in-betweenness" for them all.

Chapter 5 moves us closer to the meaning of dialectical ethics for Gadamer's work by highlighting the way in which this term elicits a dual role for the good in understanding: for-us and beyond-being. The first part of the chapter offers a phenomenology of dialogue in order to demonstrate the dialectically ethical relevance of hermeneutics and its debt to Socrates. If dialogue is central to understanding, then we must pursue in more detail what it might mean to come together with another in seeking truth. Hermeneutical truth, i.e., the event of understanding, is an ethical affair to the extent it requires embarking on a common pursuit with another. Thus we could say that the "good-for-us" emerges out of a thick conception of dialogue. At the same time, the model of dialogue put forth here rejects the modern assumption that truth is something that can be secured by a lone individual. The purpose of offering a phenomenology of dialogue is not, however, to offer a method to guarantee, or a blueprint for how to achieve, understanding. Rather, the account of dialogue given in chapter 5 serves to clarify further what the event of understanding looks like and what assumptions are necessary for it. In addition, it provides a deepening of the sense in which hermeneutical truth is meant by fending off criticisms that hermeneutics lacks the possibility for critique.

As noted above, it is one thing to speak of the ethical implications of an understanding modeled on dialogue; it is another to figure out just what is "dialectical" about such "ethics." An answer to the latter query leads to an insistence on the relevance of the good-as-transcendent for understanding. How does such an ethical understanding aimed at the good reflect the dialectic so central to Gadamer's thought? Building on chapter 1's analysis, this section argues that Gadamer insists that the good-beyond-being must be tacitly assumed in order for understanding to get underway. We all speak, think, act, "as if" there were a good, even if we cannot fully articulate just what that good is. The tacit assumption of a transcendent good is thus shown to be present in all reasoning, and yet the good as such ultimately escapes full articulation, codification, conceptualization. To attempt to fully conceptualize the good is to diverge from the spirit of both Plato and Gadamer. For example, Gadamer insists that by "idea of the good" Plato does not mean "concept" of the good—something that can be fully explicated by means of thought. Gadamer argues that to develop *arete* "into an available and repeatable possession, by means of the *concept*" (Gadamer 1991b, 3) is the concern of an "emasculated philosophical ethics."

Refraining from an "emasculated philosophical ethics" not only avoids one snare of "traditional ethics" (e.g., exacerbating the theory-practice split), it also leads to a richer understanding of the importance of philosophy to the extent it acknowledges its source in human practice. Just as Gadamer's reading of Plato taught us that Plato rejected the commonly propounded philosophical belief of his day that the life of *theoria* excludes the life of *praxis* and *arete* or that the pursuit of *theoria* is completely removed from the political life, so taking seriously Gadamer's own commitment to a Platonically inspired dialectic shows us that a similar rejection of such a dualism underlies the whole of Gadamer's philosophical hermeneutics. The significance and meaning of hermeneutics' dialectic is reflected in Gadamer's acknowledgment that "it is precisely this that is Socratic in this dialectic: that it carries out, itself, what it sees human existence as. This is where philosophy's name comes from: it is not sophia—the knowledge that gives one disposition over something—but a striving for that" (Gadamer 1991b, 4). The good we pursue as understanding beings is neither possessable nor able to be converted into a moral code or prescription for human behavior. Furthermore, unlike the practices of scientific method, we will never be able to test our progress toward it: it will always, as Gadamer emphasizes, remain "dream-like," ever eluding us. Yet without it understanding would never get underway. The philosophical life and the pursuit of the idea of the good have in common that both are always on the way to something beyond human existence.

It is this commitment, I believe, that undergirds Gadamer's own project and makes his work on understanding distinct and weighty. And it is this commitment that leads to my claim that for Gadamer understanding requires the good, whose role is not to yield normativity, but to foster understanding, an understanding that is entrenched in dialogue. In other words, the Platonic influence on Gadamer's hermeneutics suggests that true dialogue requires both an ethical stance toward another and an acknowledgment of a transcendent good, where the latter reflects our continuous desire to want to say what can never exhaustively or definitively be said. The good is that which lies ever beyond full articulation, and as such, makes our yearning for understanding all the more urgent. It stands for that which can never be understood, and yet elicits all of our understanding. Maintaining a dual role for the good, as that which is reflected in the dialogical processes (the good-for-us) and as that which lies ever beyond our understanding (the good-beyond-being), allows Gadamer to preserve the *chorismos* in Plato, substantiating his claim about the significance of a dialectical ethics for his own hermeneutics. At the heart of Gadamer's insistence that philosophical hermeneutics is essentially practical philosophy lies the belief that without such a *chorismos* of the good understanding is impossible. This work attempts to make sense of this commitment by showing the way in which understanding is not merely ethical, but dialectically ethical. And acknowledging that Gadamer's hermeneutics preserves the tension between our finite, practical existence and our desire to transcend it causes us to see Hermes anew. He is no longer just an unknown messenger sent from on high, but our own kin: as understanding beings caught "in-between" we are the offspring of Hermes.

Chapter 1
Gadamer's Dialectical Plato

True to his hermeneutical commitments, Gadamer takes seriously what Plato was arguing against. Consequently, Gadamer notes how Plato revolutionized dialectic by basing it on Socratic dialogue in order to challenge the relativism of the sophists. According to Plato, unsubstantiated opinion and its lack of concern for the truth made the discourse of the sophists dangerous. Gadamer tells us that this drove Plato to attempt

> a new art which would promise deliverance from this danger, and this new art was that of leading a discussion in such a way as to remove the risk that all knowledge and insight would eventually be confounded. That any insight can be confounded has always been and still is the experience we have in discourse, in which medium alone, however, all philosophy must take place. Philosophy had to put itself on the very same basis from which the danger of sophistic verisimilitude arose and therefore finds itself in the constant company of its shadow, sophism. As dialectic, philosophy never ceases to be tied to its origin in Socratic discussion. (Gadamer 1980, 123)

In other words, Plato's solution was neither to deny the danger and precariousness of discourse nor to flee from it altogether but to propose a new form of it, one that is concerned more with truth than power. The result is a dialectical philosophy grounded in Socratic dialogue that remains savvy about the shadow of sophism. Might Gadamer's interest in Plato suggest a similar motivation at the heart of contemporary hermeneutics—namely, one that does not attempt to repress the shadow but respond dialectically to it? I contend that Gadamer's description of his own work both as "dialectical ethics" and "practical philosophy" invites us to do just that by helping us think anew Plato's proposed solutions and find their relevance for contemporary philosophy. For example, Gadamer's works can be read as suggesting that all that passes itself off as "truth" (as that which can be quantified, verified, measured, etc.) does not do justice to that concept. In fact, what is sometimes passed off as truth, due to its scientistic tendencies and underpinnings, is really only another form of power.[1]

This chapter, then, lays the groundwork for considering the hermeneutical significance Gadamer attaches to Plato, specifically his interest in Platonic dialectic. As such, the intent is neither to satisfactorily reconstruct Plato's conceptions nor examine the extent of the faithfulness of Gadamer's reading of Plato. Rather, the aim is to highlight three key features of Plato's dialectic that prove salient for Gadamer's hermeneutics: its grounding in Socratic dialogue, its productive and constant chorismatic tension, and its requirement of the dual role of the good (as beyond-being and for-us). While Plato's dialectic is itself a much richer and complex notion than what emerges in this chapter, my concern is primarily with Gadamer's interpretation and its impact on his more explicitly hermeneutical writings.[2]

The Ground of Dialectic: Socratic Dialogue

According to Gadamer, Plato's disdain for the "negative" dialectic of the Eleatics arose from the fact that it allowed one to defend any position without reference to the "*ti estin,*" the subject matter—what Gadamer calls "*die Sache.*" Its negativity was seen in the way that it began by positing one hypothesis and showing how it leads to contradictions; it then took up an opposing hypothesis and proceeded to negate it in the same way. The goal was to be able to assert something from all opposing sides and to perfect the art of developing to their conclusions the assumptions of every possible position. Empty refutation abounded. Eleatic dialectic, often referred to by Plato more generally as "eristic," was thus something that aimed to disprove any hypothesis; its objective was to defeat one's opponents via skill of argument rather than to arrive at truth. A contemporary example would be formalized debates as found in debating clubs where participants are expected to be able to argue for or against any position that is chosen for them. And one could argue further, as Richard Bernstein

1. See in particular Gadamer 1992a and 1992c.
2. Gadamer's work on Plato's dialectic, as a response to the seminal theories of Paul Friedländer, Paul Natorp, and Julius Stenzel, acknowledges the difficulty of coming to agreement on just what was Plato's dialectic—not to mention the difference between the dialectic that corresponds to each of the three periods of the dialogues. For example, Richard Robinson opines how "the word 'dialectic' had a strong tendency in Plato to mean 'the ideal method', whatever that may be" (Robinson 1953, 70) and goes on to relate how for Plato this means that dialectic is philosophy—not a tool for philosophizing as Aristotle later insisted (71ff).

has, that the "analytic" style of argumentation also shares a common method with Eleatic dialectic. Bernstein describes how the adversarial approach to argument (which is not without advantages) carries certain dangers: "For in being primarily concerned with exposing weaknesses, with showing the absurdities in what is taken to be mistaken, we can be blind to what the other is saying and to the truth that the other is contributing to the discussion" (Bernstein 1997, 399). I think this is precisely Gadamer's Socratic worry. While a more detailed account of what Gadamer means by truth will be given in chapter 4, the point Gadamer highlights in Plato's criticism of Eleatic dialectic is that by forsaking a focus on the subject matter it fails to elicit any positive knowledge or truth. As Gadamer puts it: although "refutation . . . succeeds in laying bare the object field, . . . in itself it does not have at its disposal any means by which to prove 'the appearance'. . . positively by reference to the object" (Gadamer 1991b, 19). In other words, Gadamer points out how Plato criticized the negative propensity of Eleatic dialectic that failed to make a gain in "true knowledge." It was Plato's disdain for the emptiness of such speech that drove him to propose an alternative dialectic, which he based on Socratic dialogue. For, according to Gadamer, Socratic dialogue alone could recover the focus of the subject matter, "*die Sache,*" which provided the positive and unifying factor Plato sought. Gadamer explains:

> The decisive fact . . . is that Plato, in his efforts to disclose the facts of the matter, recognized in Socratic dialogue itself the means—and the only means—by which to arrive at a really secure stance towards the things. Socratic dialogue, in particular, is distinguished from all disputation technique by the fact that it is not a disorderly disputatious talking back and forth, which takes up and plays off against one another whatever arguments happen to come to mind. Rather, Socratic dialogue has a stylized uniformity. It embodies, for the first time, what fundamentally distinguishes the logos of science, which is speech that exhibits the facts of the matter in a logical sequence. (Gadamer 1991b, 20)

It is important to note that on Gadamer's reading, Plato's challenge to the relativism of the sophists was based on dialogical constraint that eschewed epistemic criteria. This point is crucial for understanding that Gadamer's talk of "*die Sache,*" "true knowledge," "facts of the matter," etc., does not mean he is imputing to, nor deriving from, Plato any sort of realism, including the "perspectival realism" endorsed by Brice Wachterhauser (Wachterhauser 1999, especially 52-61; and 1994). Such a "perspectival realism" admits that we can only "know the things themselves (*die Sachen selbst*) in and through history rather than without or despite history" (Wachterhauser 1994, 150). While I agree with this general description, I do not grasp what Wachterhauser gains by maintaining the term "realism." For, if we acknowledge our finitude and the fact that we can never know absolutely, what work does the label "realism" do? No one denies that there is a mind-independent reality out there if all this means is that there are objects that exist when humans are not there to talk about them (not even Richard Rorty, for example, denies this). So once one accepts the embeddedness of all knowing, why continue to emphasize the epistemic or aletheic role this "reality" plays? We could put it another way and ask what Wachterhauser means that Gadamer's theory of truth reflects both coherence and correspondence but that neither of these functions as a "criterion" (Wachterhauser 1994, 153). Given that Wachterhauser aptly acknowledges that "word and thing 'belong together,' i.e., that although all access to reality is in terms of language," why does he go on to insist that "nevertheless, our linguistically mediated beliefs accurately reflect, for the most part, the way the world is" (Wachterhauser 1994, 154). How can there be any traction to the claim that our language accurately reflects "the way the world is" once we have accepted that "all access to reality is in terms of language"? If our only access to "reality" is via language, how can we ever speak about "accurate reflection" of the "way the world is" without referencing a standpoint external to our language? Even if what Wachterhauser wants to get at by his use of the term "perspectival realism" is a sort of fallibilism, this remains difficult to reconcile with Gadamer's rejection of an "epistemological concept of fallibilism" (Gadamer 1988, 258 and passim). For, Gadamer insists that realism's "application to Plato is then incomprehensible to me, as is likewise the application of this concept to the other great thinkers of tradition. Who is not a realist in the sense of believing that the reality of the world does not depend on us, our thinking, or our opinions? Only in the Kantian sense can the transcendental idealism stemming from Kant be designated as empirical realism" (Gadamer 1988, 264). It would seem, therefore, that one of the key appeals of Plato for Gadamer is his ability to take knowledge seriously without summoning the spirit of realism.

When we pay attention to the context in which "*die Sache*" is brought up, then, we see that its importance lies in its ability to unify and focus dialogical partners and not to provide epistemic constraint. To say that the use of "*die Sache*" in this context reflects an epistemological point—that what is "really there" must be directly perceived in order to count as knowledge—commits an anachronism. Namely, it is to saddle Plato with the "Cartesian angst" that is marked by fear of not conforming to a truth "out there."[3] Instead, Gadamer shows us that Plato's concern was not so much epistemic but ethical; he feared the empty dispute of the sophists would lead to moral relativism. Yes, *die Sache* provides constraint in order to foster positive knowledge, but the constraint provided by *die Sache* is primarily dialogical. As such, the constraint provided by dialogue's focus on *die Sache* does nothing to guarantee unencumbered access to "the way things really are" nor does it insure a clear and distinct view of the things themselves. For, such a demand makes its claims "after the fact," so to speak. Rather, and this is what Gadamer thinks Plato helps us see, without a focus on *die Sache* we are susceptible to the wiles of the majority and Thrasymachus would be proved correct: whatever the strong say is just is indeed just. There would be no recourse for staving off deception by the masses. Focus on *die Sache* helps pre-

---

3. See Bernstein's discussion of "Cartesian angst" (1983).

vent irrational persuasion in whatever shape it presents itself: via entertainment, majority rule, popularity, public relations, advertising, ideology, etc. We could say, then, that the agreement fostered by *die Sache* is not between proposition and world, but amongst members of the world. Catherine Zuckert describes the dialogical nature of such constraint in the following way: "The agreement Socrates sought was not, therefore, merely between word and thing; it was primarily an agreement between human beings taking part in the conversation about the way in which they viewed the things they confronted" (Zuckert 1996, 77-78).

Another way of putting it is to say that while *die Sache* orients the interlocutors in a dialogue, this does not mean it is an end in itself. This is the case in spite of the fact that the visual metaphor of getting *die Sache* "in focus" suggests that we use a lens to narrow down our focus in order to see better. This imagery is suggestive of the epistemological approach where we block out extraneous and obscuring items so that we can see something in its nakedness. Rather, what Gadamer shows us about Plato's emphasis is that by turning our attention to the subject matter all become equal partners in an interpretive endeavor. This can be seen in the way in which Gadamer wants to distinguish *die Sache*-as-*die Streitsache* (the thing in dispute) from Husserl's use of *die Sache*-as-intentional-object (Gadamer 2007, 416). And this means that Wachterhauser's attempt to derive Gadamer's essentialism from his use of *die Sache* becomes untenable. For example, Wachterhauser insists on the affinity between Gadamer's use of "*die Sache*" and Husserl's use of "*die Sachen selbst*" and maintains that this

> places Gadamer's hermeneutics in close proximity to the phenomenological tradition with its insistence that the things themselves, which thought attends to, are noetic or essential realities. . . . *Die Sachen* of interpretation pertain to the intelligible structure of reality, which is often found in the common eidetic components that unite temporally and spatially distinct particulars in common species and genera. In Husserl's terms, these things are "essences" (*Wesen*) and in Plato's terms they are called "Ideas." (Wachterhauser 1999, 56)

While in *Truth and Method* Gadamer discusses the "world in itself" as a Husserlian concept, his point is to emphasize that there is no "world in itself" over and against our view of the world or "beyond all language": "What the world is is not different from the views in which it presents itself" (Gadamer 1992b, 447).

The significance of *die Sache* for Gadamer, then, is its role in eliciting respectful and productive dialogue:

> The thing against which one struggles if one is intending *die Sache* is wishful thinking, and here one needs to defend the being of the other. This goal is especially of service when I and thou dispute with each other in a conversation. For the conversation depends on the other person participating in the dispute also realizing that he too has unconscious prejudices. This belongs to the nature of a fruitful conversation. When we do not listen with such clear good will that the

other recognizes in you his view of what he means, then we are merely sophists. (Gadamer 2007, 416)

The knowing subject's clear and distinct sight of the thing-in-itself is not the primary goal of understanding. As Zuckert insisted above, the aim is not to achieve agreement (or correspondence) between word and thing. Rather the goal is to come to a solidary agreement about *die Sache*. Solidary understanding as a form of knowing gets privileged over correct seeing. The solidary effort to understand is, however, neither an unimaginative "mirroring" of a thing "in itself" nor a capricious free-for-all in which interlocutors speak their piece with no regard for the common subject matter. That only this ongoing, rigorous, and solidary pursuit can properly be called truth comes to light in Gadamer's discussion of the role of dialectic in Plato's *Seventh Letter*:

> [W]here we are really concerned with the truth itself . . . we compel one another to get clear about what is right and to put up an argument. One should note that the text does not say "be compelled" but uses the active form, "compel." This way of putting it expresses the solidarity which binds us to one another in such cases when we all, as mathematicians for example, refute an unmathematical argument on the squaring of the circle. But above all it is in the momentous matters of living rightly, of right decisions in life, where we have such solidarity with one another that our concern is solely with "the thing itself," i.e., with that which is really good. (Gadamer 1980, 114-15)

While the importance of the roles of both solidarity and the good in understanding will be taken up in more detail later (chapter 5), suffice it to say here that *die Sache* has a positive effect on dialogue not just by constraining its focus, but by the way in which it invites all to come together around the thing. Gadamer's reading of Plato thus suggests that the way to confront sophism's shadowy power is to acknowledge that truth is a group project and, as with any group project, it behooves us to consider how we will treat the other(s). What might this look like?

The attentiveness with which we comport ourselves around *die Sache* brings us to the second component of Socratic dialogue central to Gadamer's reading of Plato, namely, *logos*. It is important to note how Gadamer emphasizes both the unifying and agonistic elements of *logos*: it allows for a plurality of voices to come together, to work themselves out together via a giving of reasons, resulting in a productive, rather than an ideological, unity. Gadamer writes, "After all, all knowledge of something claims an understanding of the facts of the matter [*der Sache*] which is such that, when it is articulated conceptually in the logos, every other person can also be brought into the same being toward the facts [*zur Sache*] that the knower himself has" (Gadamer 1991b, 114). Reversing the Eleatic tendency to negate perspectives, where the cleverest speaker exerts power over all other perspectives, Socratic dialogue invites a plurality of voices to aim together at a unified perspective. As the many gather around the subject matter, the subject matter is addressed by a multitude of perspectives, where the goal is not to win but to understand. The focus on the subject matter creates something positive: true understanding rather than either idle or ideological chatter. Gadamer thus describes the positive advance of Plato's dialectic:

> For the fact that this capacity of the logos for multiplying the one is a positive capacity is shown by the fact that the logos enables people to reach shared understanding. . . . It is from the perspective of this positive capacity that dialectic in the Platonic sense receives an unusual scope . . . . [And] everything that is defined by logos, and is thus within the realm over which a knowledge has disposition, gets its binding certainty from dialectic. (Gadamer 1991b, 19-20)

It becomes crucial for Gadamer to read Plato's account of *logos* as holding together both the one and the many without attempting to unify them in a way that occludes difference. In fact, as we shall see in the following section, Gadamer regards the ability to hold together the one and the many in productive tension as one of the distinguishing features of Platonic dialectic. For now, however, let us note how Gadamer insists that "in Plato the logos is thought of essentially as a being-there-together, the being of one idea 'with' another. In that they are taken together, the two of two separate ideas constitutes the one of the state of affairs expressed" (Gadamer 1980, 148). And how exactly is it that the two ideas can "be there" and remain together at the same time—without being taken up in an Hegelian *Aufhebung*? What Gadamer is getting at here is that Socratic dialogue holds in tension the one and the many by maintaining an ongoing dialogue that is silenced by neither the cleverest voice nor the clearest idea. Indeed, the way in which this emphasis becomes important for Gadamer's own work is suggested by Zuckert who tells us that

> Plato's dialogues provided an ontological and epistemological foundation for [Gadamer's] own doctrine of the fusion of horizons by showing the arithmological relation of all the differentiated parts to an indeterminate, ever expanding whole. . . . Gadamer's study of Plato convinced him not only that this distinctively human enterprise remains essentially the same over time but also that it is essentially open-ended and hence, in principle, unending. (Zuckert 1996, 100)

The appeal of Plato for Gadamer is thus the way in which the unending nature of dialogue helps prevent power struggles in which the voices of the many are silenced. For example, Gadamer reads Plato's discussion of the one and the many as reflecting the limitations of human cognition, not as guaranteeing "that we can attain unequivocal meaning in a classificatory structure" (Gadamer 1980, 110). In other words, Gadamer emphasizes how the very appeal to a single, final way of seeing things itself becomes a tool of ideology, one that masks our finitude. Gadamer reminds us: "Is it not always the case, as Plato so effectively teaches us here, that as human beings we can perceive the order of good and bad, order of reality as a whole, only in finite, limited attempts? Perhaps in the final analysis the indeterminacy of the Two is meant precisely to imply that for us there exists no clear, unambiguous structure of Being" (Gadamer 1980, 110). Thus the *logos* born of dialogue is always one that remains in process, on the way. Claims with the pretence of absoluteness deny the finiteness of human existence, pulling us into the shadows of sophism and making us more susceptible to power.

That avoiding ideology is something to be gained from dialogue can be seen by the way in which Socrates always aims to check the excess power of both *logos* and speaker by insisting that the speaker be accountable. Against the sophistic assumption that truth is whatever the powerful say it is, Socratic wisdom unfolds in the dialogical process of presenting reasons. Gadamer puts it this way: "Knowledge is no longer possible as the wise proclamation of the truth but has to prove itself in dialogical coming to an understanding—that is, in an unlimited willingness to justify and supply reasons for everything that is said" (Gadamer 1991b, 52). Dialogue is generated not by an abstract pursuit of truth— the attempt to find the true nature of the "thing itself," but by the request (made by another) to explain oneself, to offer reasons for one's own being.

But what sort of reasons is Socrates looking for? According to Gadamer, Socrates is not looking for a sophistical defense, that is, for any old reasons that have no satisfactory way of defending themselves against external inquiries. Neither is he looking for an abstract, timeless reason applicable to all humans past and present. This brings us to the third component of Socratic dialogue attended to by Gadamer. What interests Socrates is the examination of reasons in light of something specific to the individual, namely, one's *arete*. Socrates asks each individual to defend himself in light of his own *arete*. What does this mean and what sort of knowledge is entailed? According to Gadamer:

> It is not a knowledge by which only the "wise" are distinguished but a knowledge that everyone must claim to have and must therefore seek continually insofar as he does not have it. For the claim to this knowledge constitutes the manner of being of human existence itself; it is the knowledge of the good, of arete. Part of being human is the fact that one understands oneself in one's arete; that is, that one understands oneself in terms of what one can be. (Gadamer 1991b, 52-3)

Socrates is not looking for a privileged knowledge, something that only a chosen few (i.e., the inner circle, the educated, the powerful, etc.) have privy to, but he is asking for reasons based on knowledge that is available to all who are human beings. And what sort of knowledge is it that cannot be reduced to a possession in the hands of the powerful few? The knowledge that grounds the possibility of Socratic dialogue, and that is equally available to all, is, in Gadamer's terms, "self-understanding." As Gadamer construes it, "self-understanding" means being able to see oneself in light of one's own end, one's "for the sake of which," one's *arete*—what Gadamer refers to (and will be explicated further below) as knowledge of one's own good. This knowledge is available to everyone since it is a knowledge rooted in our being, our existence, and reflects the understanding we have of ourselves in light of our own end. Put this way, we are helped to see why it is that Plato and Socrates maintain that this is not a knowledge that can be taught but that must be engaged dialectically. Gadamer writes:

> [A]rete is something that one always knows already and always must know already. To use the fashionable word today, arete requires self-understanding, and Socrates proves to his partners that this is what they lack. Plato gives self-understanding a more general meaning: wherever the concern is knowledge that cannot be acquired by any learning, but instead only through examination of oneself and of the knowledge one believes one has, we are dealing with dialectic. (Gadamer 1986, 42-3)

Knowledge of our own end, our "*arete,*" is the most fundamental knowledge to the extent it "constitutes the manner of being of human existence itself." For, as Gadamer goes on to state: "All Dasein lives continually in an understanding of arete" (Gadamer 1991b, 53). This claim helps us grasp why Gadamer considers all understanding self-understanding: all understanding takes as its starting point one's *arete*.

What is the significance of Gadamer's insistence that *arete* is a requirement of the human condition? Drawing a parallel with Protagoras' claim that "it is sheer madness for someone to assert that he is not just" (Gadamer 1991b, 53) Gadamer maintains that there is no one who is human who does not have an *arete*. For, insofar as one is a human with rational capacities, one always thinks that what one aims at is good. Gadamer writes that *arete* "is self-knowledge, phronesis. In the end our behavior attains its unity when our actions are undertaken in regard to the good" (Gadamer 1986, 66). *Arete*, in other words, reflects the human tendency to justify oneself in light of one's own good. Gadamer's point is that no one thinks that she is ultimately aiming at a bad end. Where rationality reigns, one's own final end is necessarily taken as good. So long as one possesses even a minimal degree of rationality it is impossible to do things solely for the sake of being bad; one performs deeds because one thinks (no matter how horrific they may appear to others) they are (in one way or another) "good." This is not to say that one cannot do something simply to be bad, but to say as much is to admit either that one has no real reasons for doing so or that one is doing something "bad" ultimately to further some other end that one takes as good. Gadamer goes on to describe the relationship Plato advocates between the good and the ultimate cause in this way:

> The real reason or cause, on the other hand, . . . the reason or cause that is posited when he claims to act on the basis of reason, would be that it is good this way. . . . And thus, in general, one demands of a reason or cause that when it is assigned, the way the thing is, is understood—that is, the thing is comprehended as being good as it is or as being best as it is, as what it must be always

would imply. To understand the nature of the things in *this* way . . . is the only thing that Socrates would call "understanding". . . . (Gadamer 1991b, 70)

The final, sufficient reason is what is sought, and what qualifies as the final reason, is one's own *arete*: a thing's "for the sake of which" (as seen, Gadamer notes, in the *Republic* and in the *Phaedo*), which one ultimately deems good. We could infer from what Gadamer says that the very propensity to rationalize—i.e., the ubiquity of "rationalizing" our "bad" choices and actions—reveals that everyone aims at a good. Thus the danger, as Plato warns, is when we are mistaken about what is "truly" good, when our rationalizing takes on sophistic tendencies to justify power.

But how does acknowledgment of one's *arete*, as Gadamer is defining it here, provide a suitable opposition to sophism? In other words, how does justifying oneself in light of one's own good challenge the relativistic claims of sophism? Could not the fact that everyone has his or her own good in fact lend credence to relativism? Here a fourth requirement of Socratic dialogue comes to the fore: the good-beyond-being. Gadamer emphasizes the importance of the connection between the good-for-us (in terms of *arete* as self-understanding) and the good-beyond-being. We will return to the significance of this *chorismos* below, but for now let us observe how Gadamer reads Plato as maintaining that the justificatory appeal to one's own good is impossible without recourse to that which lies beyond the immediacy of the situation. Gadamer explains: "[E]veryone must also be willing and able to give an accounting as to why he acts and conducts himself as he does; he must be able to *say* what he understands himself to be, with his claim to arete, at least insofar as he is able, through the *logos*, to understand himself in terms of something—that is, to be toward something that is not present at the moment" (Gadamer 1991b, 53). In other words, the ability to provide an account that serves as a dialogic justification requires an orientation "to be toward something that is not present at the moment." It is precisely this ability to be toward something that is not present at the moment that defines what is unique about being human. For only with such an orientation are we able to have knowledge as opposed to mere sensory stimulation. Furthermore, Gadamer tells us that Socratic questioning, the goal of which is to confront one's *arete*, aims to elicit an accounting that goes beyond the merely acceptable, the popular, the immediately gratifying. An accounting stance requires more than being able to say what "feels good" or what everyone else is doing; it requires that one know the *why* of one's own actions. One must be able to justify one's knowledge in the light of that which lies beyond one's immediate situation. Thus self-understanding requires that we assume there is something (i.e., the good) that transcends what is immediately present. Gadamer explains the way in which such justification requires a pointing beyond to one's own end:

> Every Socratic conversation leads to this sort of examination of what a person himself is (*Laches* 187e). Even when the initial topic of the conversation is not

knowledge about one's own being but a claim to knowledge in a specific area, the Socratic testing of this claim leads back to oneself. In such knowledge, after all, one thinks that one possesses something that is good. But whether it is good is decided not by whether one really has this knowledge—whether one is well versed in a field or knows how to perform a task—but whether the use of this knowledge is guided by insight into the one thing that makes oneself and everything that one does good. No individual knowledge or ability is good in itself; rather, it needs to be justified in terms of an understanding of what one's own existence is for the sake of. One must be able to say why one behaves in a certain manner—that is, what the good is that one understands oneself as aiming at in one's behavior. (Gadamer 1991b, 54)

A more detailed discussion about the role of the good as necessary to understanding will be offered at the end of chapter 5. Suffice it to say here that Gadamer's point is that, according to Socrates, certainty of knowledge entails a claim that one's knowledge is "good," and this claim of the goodness of one's knowledge cannot be made except in the light of one's *arete*, the end of one's existence, or one's own "for the sake of which." However, this "for the sake of which," this "good for me," does not reflect transitory desires, i.e., whatever seems "good" to me in the moment. Being able to give an accounting of oneself means not just referencing whatever one holds as an end, but doing so in such a way that projects one's good as transcending what is immediately present to one. Without this ability one is left with a decrepit hedonism: "For if one is no longer really able to understand oneself in terms of arete, then the idea of the good, as the formal idea of all understanding of oneself, falls back upon the immediate and simply certain experience of 'feeling good'"(Gadamer 1991b, 55). There is no possibility of proclaiming "this is good" in regards to one's knowledge without assuming this "good" is irreducible to one's immediate feelings and proclivities. Every reference to our own good implies that this good "transcends," extends beyond, the dictates of the immediate situation.

One of the keys for understanding the significance of Plato for Gadamer's own hermeneutics is to note how Gadamer reads Plato as implying that justification requires an assumption of a good-beyond-being. This hermeneutical emphasis deriving from the relationship between *arete* and the good as "the formal idea of all understanding of oneself" comes out in the following statement by Gadamer:

Socrates makes visible what it is that this arete is sought as, namely, knowledge about the good. The good, then, is knowledge's object; that is, it is the unitary focal point to which everything must be related and in relation to which human existence in particular understands itself in a unified way. The general character of the good is that it is that for the sake of which something is and thus, in particular, that for the sake of which man himself is. It is in the light of it that human beings understand themselves in their action and being at any given moment, in terms of what they have to do and to be. In this self-understanding, Dasein finds its footing, its stance (*Stand*)—in so far as, knowing the good, it does everything that it does for the sake of this. . . . Knowledge of the "for the sake of which" of its own being is thus what brings Dasein out of the confusion into which it is drawn by the disparateness and unfathomableness of what impinges on it from the world into a stance toward that, and thus into the constancy (*Ständikeit*) of its own potentiality for being. (Gadamer 1991b, 59-60)

In other words, *arete*, as knowledge about the good, refers, on one hand, to our own "for the sake of which." But this "for the sake of which" is not any old end one happens to prefer in the moment. It is important to note how, on Gadamer's reading, *arete* also suggests more: what Plato and Socrates refer to as the good-beyond-being. The way to make sense of these two emphases is to take Gadamer to be making a hermeneutical point (and not a metaphysically dualistic one) about the relation between one's own good and the good-beyond-being. I will contend in the final chapter that just as Gadamer emphasizes that for Plato human understanding requires a good that transcends our immediate situation, so this commitment underlies Gadamer's own philosophical hermeneutics. Let us explore further Gadamer's dialectical rendering of *arete* as that which embraces both senses of the good.

One way to grasp the hermeneutical significance of this tension is to ask whether or not it is possible to evaluate or critique one's own *arete*. Is *whatever* one takes one's *arete* to be worthy of being identified as *the* good? On what basis can one critique it? In order to begin to scrutinize the meaning of the good-beyond-being in light of these questions, let us attend to Gadamer's analysis in the *Philebus*, where Socrates enters into a conversation about whether one is justified in identifying pleasure as the good. The key, as Gadamer describes it, is whether there is indeed something self-justifying in pleasure presenting itself as an end, since it does so so forcefully—in a way that we almost cannot refuse it. Is pleasure's strength a suitable defense? Gadamer argues that pleasure's presentation of itself as an end-in-itself is actually self-contradictory due to the peculiar role that such an end plays in one's own self-understanding. For, taking pleasure as one's good—as that which one lives for—requires one to rely on an end that is not defined solely in terms of immediate needs and pleasures. In other words, in order to answer the question, "why pleasure?", one must rely on something other than pleasure. Defending pleasure as one's end requires another end to justify it. Gadamer's point is that one must always defend the immediate (e.g., pleasure) in light of something non-immediate, i.e., something that one takes to justify and thus transcend the immediacy of the present moment. Thus, on Gadamer's account, in order to have self-understanding, one needs to refer to an end that transcends the immediate situation in order to process, evaluate, and make sense of this input.

Even when it comes to pleasure, then, we need to be continually making decisions as to which is the "real" pleasure. For, as we shall see below, Gadamer stresses that there is no pure giveness of pleasure. Gadamer writes: "If Dasein's ultimate 'for the sake of which' is its own well-being, then the fact that it wants to *understand* itself in terms of its well-being means that it must have disposition over that well-being through knowledge" (Gadamer 1991b, 60-1). That is to say, as soon as one claims anything about understanding one's own end, then one betrays a commitment to something beyond the immediate giveness of pleasure. For to appeal to pleasure-as-an-end is to assert that we understand ourselves in light of that pleasure and we then must make decisions about which of the immediate pleasures are more conducive to our overall goal of pleasure. Pleasures do not come to us as "raw feels"; we must interpret them. Gadamer writes: "However unambiguously good one's own well-being may seem to be when one experiences it—as the 'for the sake of which'—immediately, this does not provide a unified point of view for human Dasein as it wants to *understand* itself. For if Dasein wants to understand itself as good, the 'for the sake of which' of its own being is not the way it feels at the moment but its well-being as a *constant* potential that it possesses" (Gadamer 1991b, 61).

Gadamer's interpretation of the *Philebus* shows that as soon as one asserts that one makes choices based on pleasure, one must have some way of ordering and prioritizing the different experiences that one finds pleasurable. One must be able to make some sort of reasonable judgment about which pleasures are to be followed, which are beneficial, and which are harmful. After all, at any given moment, one is confronted with a myriad of pleasures: eating, sleeping, drinking, reading, playing, conversing, etc. So long as one wants to understand oneself as good, one must reflect on the benefit of following one's immediate pleasures. Accordingly, one shows a propensity for thinking beyond the moment, and has thus demonstrated a capacity for reflection that relies on something external to the supposed giveness or immediacy of pleasure. One has, in other words, assumed a "good," a standard by which to evaluate and order one's pleasures. Gadamer takes Socrates' point in the *Philebus* to be that even the most die-hard hedonist must distinguish between an immediate pleasure and one that is more worthwhile to pursue. Even the hedonist must ask: which is the pleasure more worth pursuing? And this means that the life of hedonism requires reflective choice, the ability to decide what is best in an overall sense. In order to answer questions such as: "Why do I prefer this pleasure over that one?" even the hedonist must measure herself in light of the good, a good, that is, that transcends the immediate pleasure of any given situation. Gadamer wants us to see that as soon as we posit any end, we are assuming a justification for it that necessarily relies on something beyond the immediate: hence the justificatory role of the good. E.g., even the hedonist must reach beyond the immediate pleasure to explain why such a pleasure counts as his end.

Gadamer's discussion of *arete* has shown that it is not problematic to maintain that one way of understanding the good is as a transcendent end: that which is not fully articulable but nonetheless functions as the ground of our justification. Given the fact that it lies beyond the immediate situation and is something required for reasoned defense and argument, we can make better sense of what Plato may have meant by referring to it as a form without which knowledge is impossible. Gadamer explains:

[It] is not an entity any longer, at all, but an ultimate ontological principle. It is not a substantive determination of entities but the thing that makes everything that exists understandable in its being. It is only in this universal ontological function that the idea of the good is in fact the ultimate basis of *all* processes of coming to an understanding—not as a highest-level, universal eidos but as the formal character of everything that can really be called "understood," which means, however, as the angle of vision to which the claim to understanding itself submits itself. In this respect, the idea of the good is nothing but the ideal of complete cognizability and cognition. (Gadamer 1991b, 77)

In other words, the good has direct relevance for us as the very possibility of understanding; it is what allows the dialectical movement of understanding to occur at all. I thus take Gadamer to be insisting on a hermeneutical role for the good, a move that is possible so long as one reads Plato metaphorically and not literally (as Gadamer complains Aristotle was wont to do). Chapter 2 will detail how such a metaphorical reading of Plato frees us from the problems bequeathed to us by Aristotle. But in the meantime, let us focus on how a further ramification of Gadamer's reading is that if the good is a "form" that transcends the immediate moment, this also must mean that wherever understanding occurs, one must fill in the specific and substantive "content" of what this good is. In other words, only where one also makes the good one's own, i.e., one's own *arete*, can understanding occur. This means that, on the one hand, the good-as-transcendent, as form, accords with Socrates' insistence that the good cannot be grasped in and of itself; we can neither gaze directly at it nor speak comprehensively of it. But to say that we cannot grasp with the hands of being what is beyond being is not to render it useless. On the other hand, it means that one can, in fact, must be able to, give reasons for one's own end/s. We could say that such an effort, relying on one's *arete*, entails supplying the content to the form. But doing so is a creative act: the content, as language bound, is created and not found by us. The content is thus akin to the interpretation we supply. I believe that Gadamer's interest in Plato is due to his insight that the good is beyond being and yet implicated in all our human understanding.

My intention has been to show Gadamer's struggle (against the tide of a traditional "Platonism") to reclaim the productive legitimacy of the "good-beyond-being." As such, Gadamer's take on Socratic dialogue directs us toward understanding the relevance of the good for understanding. The reciprocity between the good's transcendence and its hermeneutical relevance for us becomes even clearer in the following statement by Gadamer:

[A]n understanding of Dasein must understand present things in terms of non-present ones and can grant them goodness only in such a relation. Thus this Socratic course of argumentation allows us to see what the good must (in any case) be sought as: namely, the central thing on the basis of which human being can understand itself. So the positive point of Socratic refutation consists not only in achieving a positive perplexity but also—by the same token—in explaining what knowledge really is and what alone should be recognized as knowledge. It is only in the concept of the good that all knowledge is grounded; and it is only on the basis of the concept of the good that knowledge can be justified. The ultimate possibility of arriving at a shared understanding depends upon having in common a pre-understanding of the good. (Gadamer 1991b, 63)

This quotation delineates the need for a transcendent good as a hermeneutical concept, one, as will be more fully propounded in chapter 5, that is necessary for understanding. But what does this have to do with our dialogical stance toward others? For Gadamer "having in common a pre-understanding of the good" is a requirement for understanding to the extent that without it we would have no incentive, urge, or reason to dialogue with another. Just as we assume a good in our own lives, so we assume one in the life of another. In order to reach agreement with another, we first must assume that the other is able to give reasons. Thus our willingness to dialogue with another implicitly attributes to the other an assumption of the good.

Earlier we saw how Socrates expects an individual to offer reasons in light of her own *arete*. We can now see that this does not render justification a purely individualistic affair. To the contrary: Socrates is not asking about private reasons relating only to the individual. For, since giving reasons occurs in language, and since language emerges from a community, then *arete* is not just a private matter, but concerns who we are in relation to others. We are required to do more than provide justification to ourselves, we must be able to justify ourselves to others. Gadamer thus highlights the fundamentally ethical implications of such an aretic justification: "What the good citizen must be and how he must act are prescribed for everyone in an explication that dominates the entire public understanding of Dasein: in what is called 'morals'. So the concept of arete is a 'public' concept. In it, the being of man is understood as a being with others in a community (the *polis*)" (Gadamer 1991b, 53). *Arete* is not something available to the mythic "lone individual." Accordingly, the fact that *arete* is something that can only be understood communally suggests the ethical implications of dialogue. The successful or truthful dialogue requires an ongoing process that elicits reasons and responses from all involved. Ethical considerations are already part of the practice of dialogue: we cannot truly speak with another without treating her as one worthy of being listened and spoken to. Gadamer's account of Socratic dialogue shows that from its inception its concern with truth is inseparable from ethical concerns.

I will return to the role the other plays in Gadamer's account of truth in chapter 4, but suffice it to say here that what the foregoing analysis reveals is that the *logos* of dialogue is a speech that demands accountability both to oneself (to the extent that "only in the logos is Dasein itself" (Gadamer 1991b, 64)) as well as to others. And only by responding to the justificatory demands of a dialogical partner can we reach understanding of the subject matter. Thus the uniqueness Gadamer finds in Socratic dialogue is that it, more than eristic reasoning, is able to reach true, as opposed to distorted, understanding. Furthermore, we have seen how Plato's attempt to stem the tide of sophistic relativism, while making an appeal to what lies beyond the immediate, at the same time demands a working together with another to achieve the agreement that really matters: the understanding with another.

That Gadamer takes the clarification of *arete* as serving as the very possibility of dialogue returns us to Plato's concern that discourse not succumb to an ideology of power. The truth strived for in Socratic dialogue has nothing to do with winning people over to one's side. Socrates' own motivations were not to get his interlocutor to mimic his (Socrates') life or to accept a prefabricated ideal but to examine his own life in light of his own *arete*. The starting point of all understanding is Socrates' claim that he "knows that he doesn't know." As such, he does not maintain that he can know ahead of time—prior to the dialogical justification—what his interlocutor "should" be doing with his life. The conditional "should" (if this is my end then I *should* do X) emerges from the process of working out and clarifying what one is about. Accordingly, we find the hypothetical nature of Socratic dialogue to be that its strength derives not from what can be secured in advance, but what is reached through "its substantive accomplishment of grasping a manifold reality in its unitary selfsame being" (Gadamer 1991b, 65). The sophists "know" in advance; Socrates, on the other hand, "knows he doesn't know." Gadamer describes how this claim is made by Socrates not simply to defeat his interlocutor, but to get him to question his own presuppositions, requiring his interlocutor to be as ready to be refuted as Socrates himself. For only once one knows one doesn't know, is one on the way to knowledge. Another way to put it is that knowing one doesn't know serves as the only suitable motivation for dialogue. And it is the willingness to not just offer up reasons for one's position but to also take seriously the questions and challenges of the other that, on Gadamer's reading, distinguishes Socrates from the sophists. Although Gadamer does not deny that sometimes Socrates himself appears to adopt the practices of the sophists, Gadamer reasons that this is due to the fact that Socrates engages in a live conversation and therefore must make use of, at times, the tools of his conversants. For Socrates cannot but help rely on his own sense of what will get his point across most effectively. However, unlike the sophists, Socrates always stands ready to be refuted; his concern is more with truth than with winning.

Thus Gadamer is careful to offer a reading of the significance of Socratic dialogue for Plato that takes seriously the historical and rhetorical context. We are now in a better position to see the way in which the following statement by Gadamer is anything but an endorsement of "Platonic realism": "through the refutation, what the thing that is sought after is sought *as* is laid bare; and second in that from this understanding a methodical conduct of research and questioning emerges, and with it the steadiness of progress toward a shared understanding, which distinguishes Socratic conversational procedure from the eristic technique of refutation" (Gadamer 1991b, 59). This section has looked at the significance Gadamer attaches to *die Sache*, *logos*, *arete*, and the good for

Plato's account of Socratic dialogue. Since dialogue proves a central feature in Gadamer's understanding of dialectic, the bulk of this chapter has been devoted to Gadamer's account of Socratic dialogue. To gain insight into why Gadamer takes dialogue to serve as the best expression of dialectic, we now turn to consider his reading of Plato's dialectic.

Platonic Dialectic: Embracing the One and the Many

The inextricability of dialogue and dialectic for Gadamer himself is evinced by his claim that dialectic is "the art of questioning and of seeking truth" (Gadamer 1992b, 367). The section in *Truth and Method*, "The Model of Platonic Dialectic," from which this statement comes, describes dialectic in terms of its directed openness, an openness that knows how to keep the dialogue going by asking the right questions.[4] In other words, Gadamer's account of Platonic dialectic in that section, like that found in his *Habilitation*, is defined primarily in terms of its association with dialogue. However, unlike his earlier account, the section in *Truth and Method* provides little substantive discussion of Platonic dialectic per se. Therefore, the following analysis will primarily draw on Gadamer's earlier analysis of Platonic dialectic. Doing so will allow us to further clarify the way in which Gadamer sees dialogue and dialectic related in Plato's work and subsequently allow us to come to terms with the role they play in Gadamer's later hermeneutics.

In his *Habilitation*, Gadamer describes the aim of dialectic as "*a care for the unity and sameness of the thing* that is under discussion" (Gadamer 1991b, 64).[5] Above we saw how this commitment manifests itself in dialogic constraint that goes beyond epistemic concerns: namely, dialogue's care for unity must take into account the concomitant multiplicity. Thus it is not, as some critics of Gadamer have charged, that the concern with unity rules out the possibility for difference.[6] This section addresses the concern for unity at the heart of dialectic by examining Gadamer's esteem for Platonic dialectic in terms of its ability to embrace both the one (unity) and the many (difference). This commitment is seen in Gadamer's summary of the purpose of the dialectic of the *Parmenides*:

> It shows that the idea of unity does not exclude, but posits together with itself, the idea of multiplicity. So this is the positive intention of this dialectic, which seemed so lacking in direction: to show that the Ideas, as things in regard to which there is unity, do not need to be absolutely one but can embrace a multi-

---

4. I will return to the theme of openness in chapter 5.
5. See also Gadamer 1991b, 73 and 88.
6. See for example John Caputo's Derridean critique along these lines (Caputo 1987, 2000, and 2002).

plicity of things in regard to which there is unity. . . . The one is shown to be many, but not as the undefined manifold of things that are coming to be but as a definite—which means comprehensible—multiplicity of unities. (Gadamer 1991b, 97-98)

In other words, as Gadamer insists, dialectic becomes the key for clarifying the core of Plato's thought: namely, how to hold in tension the need for unity and multiplicity. In what follows below, Gadamer's analysis of the "one and the many" in Plato will be explicated specifically in terms of the *chorismos* between the good-beyond-being (i.e., the requisite assumption of the good) and the good-for-us (i.e., that which engenders solidarity).

When Gadamer insists that the *chorismos*, the separation between the realm of the forms and the sensible realm, is an "essential component of true dialectic" (Gadamer 1986, 20), he means that dialectic gains its productivity as a result of the *chorismos* not in spite of it. It is, as will be demonstrated, the chorismatic tension that serves as the very possibility for understanding. At the same time, Gadamer also uncovers the ethical implications of the *chorismos*. The following quotation bears this out:

> The distinction between justice itself and what is considered (*dokei*) to be just is anything but an empty conceptual abstraction. On the contrary, it is the truth of our practical consciousness itself, the truth as Plato saw it graphically before his own eyes in the person of Socrates: true and just behavior cannot be based on the conventional concepts and standards to which public opinion clings. . . . This severance of the noetic from the sensory, of true insight from mere points of view—this chorismos, in other words—is the truth of moral consciousness as such. (Gadamer 1986, 18)

How does the *chorismos* imply the truth of moral consciousness? By suggesting the need to transcend the following: the efficacy of public opinion, the immediacy of our desires, the demands of the social world, sophistry, sensual urges— any or all of which could obstruct the possibility for dialogue and understanding. For if the good is only a matter of what the majority says it is, then *the* good as such is an empty concept. It is the necessity of our appeal to something that transcends our immediate situation that saves the good-beyond-being from vacuity. But this is not to say that in turning to something transcendent we must ignore our immediate and sensual needs. The conflict between transcendence and immanence is not one that we should attempt to vanquish. That such a tension is not a hindrance to but productive of understanding is what Plato saw and Gadamer embraces. As human beings, we live in the tension of trying to grasp intellectually a concept that always eludes our firm grasp. To deny the *chorismos* is to deny one part or another of reality, of our human condition as beings caught in-between. It is to forget that our in-betweenness is ultimately productive of understanding, of knowledge. Plainly put: as Gadamer reads Plato there is no knowledge without the *chorismos*.

Thus the tension born of the *chorismos* does not just produce empty reverberations. Rather, it leads to knowledge precisely because such movement allows us to get at the ground of a thing, what Gadamer refers to as the good. An important component to reaching this ground is *dihairesis*, which Gadamer describes as the "core of the art of dialectic" (Gadamer 1980, 102). This claim reveals the need for *logos* to give way to, to be transformed into, dialectic, in order to avoid distortion. In breaking down the one into many, the point is not simply to smash it into pieces, but to break it up into its essential number of pieces, answering the question of: how many is it truly? The breaking up is not destructive, but ultimately constructive (Gadamer 1991b, 120). Recalling Plato's disdain for the negativity of Eleatic dialectic can help us grasp his intention to transform dialectic into that which could get at *die Sache*. Platonic dialectic aims at true understanding, not merely the negative Eleatic procedure of breaking apart for its own sake. Gadamer tells us that

> true dialectical division must always arrive at unities again, and necessarily comes to an end (with the atomon eidos) at the point at which a cutting up of the unity (into individual cases) would cease to produce unities—that is, concepts in which the entity is grasped. . . . So when a final, indivisible eidos is arrived at, part of what is arrived at is that, in it, the thing that it sums up in a unified way is comprehended in a logos that fixes the thing, and only it, in what makes up its selfsame being. (Gadamer 1991b, 121)

But what exactly does it mean that dialectic is a breaking down that does not result in a multiplicity but in a unity? To grasp this is to see the relationship between *dihairesis* and the process described above as self-understanding that requires justification in light of one's *arete*. *Dihairesis* breaks down the steps of justification in order to bring us to an ultimate ground or reason, what Gadamer and Plato refer to as the "good." The unity that results from breaking down reflects "what makes up its selfsame being." Only *dihairesis* allows us to reach "the final, indivisible *eidos*" and provides us with the certainty that we have reached an understanding of the thing. But in light of the preceding discussion about the ungraspable nature of the good, what can it mean that only this "final, indivisible *eidos*" (which we have above seen named as the good) shows what a thing "always is"? Again, to grasp Gadamer's meaning here requires we lay aside our realist aspirations. It is not that dialectic primarily (or only) yields clarity and distinction about an isolated essence, rather it helps us situate and contextualize what we are attempting to know. Gadamer tells us:

> So what dialectic accomplishes . . . is not only that the sense-perceptible manifold of entities is defined in terms of genus and species (that is, in what it always is and what constitutes the being of each entity) but also that this definition gives us a disposition over it. Insofar as it is known in what it always is, the individual and the particular is seen, just as certainly, *in its potentiality for being with other things. This* is what the dialectical comprehension of entities in their being accomplishes which makes that comprehension the precondition

of all concrete coming to an understanding about something. (Gadamer 1991b, 124)

Here we learn that this seeing something as it is "in itself"—far from implying only an isolated seeing that would suffice for knowledge—actually suggests that knowledge only becomes complete when we are able to see something "in its potentiality for being with other things." For when it comes to standing firm, not being swayed, and thus knowing something, Gadamer notes the importance of being able to see something in terms of something else. Understanding a thing's situatedness becomes the goal of knowing—not clarity of focus, per se. The division of *dihairesis* results not in isolation but always maintains a view toward something else, what we could call (and will be developed further in chapter 3) an "horizonal" seeing that places a thing in context. In other words, that Gadamer's interpretation is not a candidate for essentialism can be seen to the extent that seeing what is does not mean isolating a thing in order to perceive it "clearly and distinctly." The point is not to hone in on one thing, but to see it in perspective, what it is connected to. When Gadamer tells us that Plato's preference for dialectic is due to the fact that only dialectic provides access to the "logos of the thing itself" he is not endorsing a form of essentialism. Instead, dialectic is described as an ongoing process made possible by the assumption (hypothesis, even, as we shall see below) of the good that does not aim at grasping the final *eidos* but at seeing "what is" in its context:

> Only dialectic goes to the archai (principles) of what exists, ultimately to the Idea of the Good—that is, to that in relation to which everything that exists is to be understood as remaining unchanged in its being. It represents the most certain knowledge because its object is fully revealed in what it is. Something that is understood as good is understood in what makes it what it is and has to be. So the fact that dialectic is the highest science is due to the fact that its object— the "Ideas"—really is entirely discovered by it. It has disposition over the logos of the thing itself—for example. (Gadamer 1991b, 202-3)

That Plato "uses only the word *idea* and never *eidos*, for the *agathon*, surely has something to do with that transcendence" (Gadamer 1986, 27), Gadamer tells us, and that *idea tou agathon* "implies not so much the 'view of the good' as a 'looking to the good'" (Gadamer 1986, 28). This means that the good is not something to be grasped, but that which orients us; the point is not to see the good in order to obtain it but to see in light of it. The element of transcendence must be preserved, for (to extend the metaphor) we cannot benefit from light if we gaze directly at it. The inaccessibility of the good is precisely the point of the discussion of the good in the *Republic*, wherein Socrates asserts that the significance of the good can only be grasped by analogy to the sun and not directly. Just as we become blinded and unable to see anything when looking directly at the sun, so would the ability to finally grasp the good foreclose the possibility of understanding. When Gadamer remarks that dialectic is "unending and infinite"

(Gadamer 1980, 152), he is suggesting an indirect reliance on the good, whereby we aim at but never fully achieve the final *eidos*. For, he insists: "If it were possible, through the dialectic, for me to come to knowledge of the good as the ultimate ground of being, then I would be God" (Gadamer 2004, 33).[7] But how, then, can we speak about reaching understanding if the *eidos*, strictly speaking, is never fully obtained? Is any positive knowledge achieved as a result of dialectic? How can we make sense of a process that is both "unending and infinite" *and* that arrives at true understanding?[8]

The only way to make sense of this apparent *aporia* is to deepen our understanding of what it means that the good functions as the final *eidos* and how this ultimately bears itself out in a theory of understanding. Recalling the above discussion, we can posit that to the extent it allows us to see better, to situate ourselves within a horizon, we thus have a gain in knowledge. Making an analogy between the good and horizon, we could say that the good, as the end of dialectic, serves as an orientation (like an horizon) for continual movement. Yet in and of itself it is something that can be neither achieved nor fully comprehended—just as we can never reach the horizon since it always moves with us. In the same way, saying that all dialectic aims at the ultimate *eidos* does not mean that it ever actually reaches the final *eidos*. Rather, Gadamer stresses that all dialectic is done in light of, or based on, an assumption of the final *eidos*, which is named as the good. Chapter 5 will explicate further what it means to speak of assuming the good. In the meantime, let us consider how Gadamer refers to such a dialectical process as one of hypothesis: "Thus the procedure of hypothesis, and of dialectic in general, has the goal of comprehending entities, through the logos, in their being, so as to be able to have disposition over them in their ability to be together with other things" (Gadamer 1991b, 68). Again, the reference to hypothesis reiterates that, on Gadamer's reading of Plato, the point of knowledge is not to strip bare a single entity but to see it "as" something in the context of its horizon.

The movement implied by the hypothetical and "horizontal" nature of dialectic has further significance for Gadamer's hermeneutical reading of Plato. For, the fact that we aim at but never achieve the good is reminiscent of Gadamer's insistence that a true philosopher is one who is on the way toward wisdom. Socrates' claim that "he knows he doesn't know" stands in stark opposition to the sophists' claims to already possess knowledge. The good, Gadamer tellingly writes, is "an expression for this thing that is never quite attainable" (Gadamer 2004, 36). Describing the way in which the unattainability of the good provokes understanding Gadamer remarks, "I think it is precisely what justifies hermeneutics" (Gadamer 2004, 36). Hermeneutics, after all, would be of no use were everything immediately and fully understood. Hermes is not needed where

---

7. Gadamer takes a distinctly anti-Plotinus stance. See The Enneads I:2:6 where Plotinus insists that our goal is, indeed, to become God.
8. See Decker 2000 that raises just this point.

there is no distance between gods and mortals. But that it is unattainable does not mean it is empty or irrelevant. The ineffable remains a crucial element in the lives of the finite, enabling us to know anything at all. And this is precisely what Gadamer meant earlier when he remarked that "the idea of the good is nothing but the ideal of complete cognizability and cognition" (Gadamer 1991b, 77).

Thus the Platonic dialectic that attracts Gadamer is one that, although aiming at, never attains the transcendent good. By now it should be clear that far from a shortcoming, the ultimate inaccessibility of the good is what fosters understanding. The striving after the elusive good is no Sisyphean task. For while the one-way ascent to the ideas is not enough to provide us with understanding, the Platonic implication is that we must also make our way back down the darkening slope of the cave. As Gadamer remarks, "the ascent to the presuppositionless arche is for the sake of the descent" (Gadamer 1991b, 76). Here Gadamer reveals his hand. The role of the ideas, in particular the idea of the good, is for the sake of our understanding here and now. To speak metaphorically: the ideas are not our final stop, but are a resting place, we might say, to gather strength for the descent. To be human is necessarily to return down the dark slope of the cave. As Gadamer has reminded us, only the gods can remain in the transcendent realm. To be human is thus to be in perpetual motion between the constraints of our finitude and our desire for the infinite, between immanence and transcendence, between the good-for-us and the good-beyond-being. And it is just this ongoing movement—born of the *chorismos*—that fosters the dialectic of understanding. In fact, Gadamer insists that to the extent that we are understanding beings, we are also dialectical beings, since dialectic aims at

> possibilities of human existence whose being and nature is in dispute. So the dialectical clarification of these existential possibilities, the gaining of their oikeios logos, means giving an accounting in regard to what man claims to be. This general sense of dialectic as man's giving an accounting regarding the existential possibilities to which he lays claim and regarding his claim to knowledge of entities in general makes dialectic important, at the same time, in a way that reaches beyond each particular object of investigation and accounting: it makes us, in general, "more dialectical," by grasping the possibility (which is inherent in human existence) of understanding ourselves and of justifying the claim to knowledge wherever it is made. (Gadamer 1991b, 100)

We thus see how our dialectical attempt to uncover the fundamentals of human existence, to give and solicit reasons for our very being, necessarily engages us with others and awakens our solidarity. And thus the answer to the question of why Socratic dialogue was so appealing to Plato in working out his conception of dialectic should now be clear. Socratic dialogue recovers for dialectic not just the possibility of positive, unified knowledge; it also uncovers a dialectically ethical component of understanding that is based on the exigencies of multiplicity. As understanding beings we find ourselves caught in-between the desire for the one (i.e., the good at which we aim) and the many (i.e., the multiplicity defining human solidarity). It is precisely the precarious nature of understanding that when dialectically construed confronts us with our dual longings: to transcend our finitude and to connect with others. The following statement by Gadamer echoes Plato's hope for dialectic, with which this chapter began, and returns us to the integrity of dialogue and dialectic: "What is mere talk, nothing but talk, can, however untrustworthy it may be, still bring about understanding among human beings—which is to say that it can still make human beings human" (Gadamer 1980, 123).

The aim of this chapter has been to draw attention to three key features of Gadamer's early reading of Platonic dialectic: its grounding in dialogue, its productive and constant chorismatic tension, and the requirement of the dual role of the good (as both contributing to the solidarity of beings and as an assumption that lies beyond being). While Plato's own conception of dialectic is more multifaceted than the account given here, my interest has been to extract these basic components of dialectic that prove essential to Gadamer's interpretation of Plato in order to see how they play out in Gadamer's more explicitly hermeneutical work. In the chapters that follow, hermeneutics' dialectic will be developed in terms of its productive and constant chorismatic tension that manifests itself in 1) the integrity between *theoria* and *praxis* (chapters 2 and 3), 2) the losing (marked by transcendence) and finding (marked by application) of oneself that the event of truth requires (chapter 4), 3) dialogue (chapter 5), and 4) the necessity of the dual role of the good (as both beyond-being and for-us) (chapter 5).

Chapter 2
Gadamer's Dialectical Aristotle

No account of Gadamer's hermeneutics is complete without an understanding of his reliance on Aristotle. Yet while most of the literature on Gadamer's interest in Aristotle has focused on the significance of *phronesis*[1] (which certainly proves to be an important concept for Gadamer, one that will be treated of in chapter 3), this chapter highlights three additional aspects of Aristotle's thought that remain important for Gadamer's dialectical hermeneutics. As with the first chapter, my concern is not to assess the accuracy of Gadamer's reading of Aristotle but to highlight how Gadamer's unique rendering of Aristotle undergirds his hermeneutics. The argument here focuses not on the specifics of Gadamer's attempt to read a continuity between Plato and Aristotle in terms of the good (as is a now well-established Gadamerian move[2]) but the way in which his account of the similarities between the two thinkers leads him to emphasize a dialectic between a distanced knowing (as exemplified by *theoria*) and an embedded knowing (as exemplified by *praxis*) that proves crucial for understanding his hermeneutics in general. As explained in my Introduction, I am not using "dialectic" in the sense of "argumentation"—as Aristotle himself used it—and so will not be referring to Aristotle's dialectic, per se, but to Gadamer's dialectical

---

1. Of the thirty plus works devoted to the importance of phronesis and/or practical philosophy some worthy of mention are: Baracchi 2000, Bernstein 1983, Dobrosavlejev 2002, Figal 1995, Foster 1991, Poole 1995, Risser 2002b and 1984, Schmidt 1995 and 2003, and Shuchman 1979.

2. E.g., *Die Idee des Guten zwischen Plato und Aristotle*, Gadamer 1978. See Renaud 1999, 78-81 for a brief account of the intellectual origins of Gadamer's arguments.

reading of Aristotle.[3] My use of "dialectic," then, demarcates the productive and ongoing chorismatic tension that issues forth from the refusal to overcome opposites.

The first section examines Gadamer's argument that Plato's dialectic ultimately leads to Aristotle's notion of *theoria*. Showing the importance of *theoria* for Gadamer's interpretation of Aristotle thwarts criticisms that Gadamer "neglects almost completely the importance attributed by Aristotle to theoretical philosophy" and that Gadamer "[downplays] the role of *theoria*" in Aristotle (Berti 2004, 287, 300). While it is true that Gadamer, as Enrico Berti maintains, "undervalues the primacy of *sophia*" (Berti 2004, 286) and privileges practical wisdom, this need not be detrimental to Gadamer's interpretation of Aristotle. For example, Christopher P. Long argues (based on the spirit although not the letter of Aristotle's thought) that the "conception of *phronesis* has an advantage over *sophia* because it is capable of critically considering the concrete conditions under which it operates" (Long 2002, 37). Long further insists that "an ontology directed by *phronesis* rather than *sophia*, would be one that recognizes itself as inherently ethical" (Long 2002, 37).

In *Plato's Dialectical Ethics*, Gadamer tells us that Plato's dialectic led not to Aristotle's dialectic per se but to Aristotle's *apodeixis*, the pinnacle of Greek science. As Gadamer explains: "the intention of the sketch that follows is to make intelligible the derivation of the Greek concept of science (which reached its mature form in Aristotle's apodeictic) from Plato's dialectic by showing its substantive origin in the specific form of the Socratic conduct of conversation" (Gadamer 1991b, 21). In other words, one important connection between Plato and Aristotle for Gadamer is their mutual esteem of "scientific" forms of knowing, or "scientific speech," as Gadamer calls it. By "scientific" Gadamer is referring to the pre-modern sense of that term: a knowing that is focused on getting clear about *die Sache* (as developed in chapter 1) but does not deny such a pursuit's rootedness in the life-world. Consequently, Gadamer provides an explication of *theoria* by way of its origins in Aristotle's conception of *techne* and shows how it relies on both a rich conception of experience and a distancing of oneself from one's environment. He then demonstrates how distance is a defining factor for both *techne* and *theoria* but in a slightly different way. That the latter emerges out of the former is due to the increasingly generalized distance characterizing *theoria* and leads Gadamer to detail the similarity between Aristotle's notion of *theoria* and Platonic dialectic. It is not, of course, that Gadamer sees Plato and Aristotle as being in accord at all points. Gadamer admits: "obviously there was a decisive difference between Plato and Aristotle regarding one crucial point, namely, the prevalence of mathematics in Plato, in contrast to the predominance of the model of the living body, of life, in the approach of Aristotle" (Gadamer 1979, 79). Chapter 3 will take up the importance of *theoria* for Gadamer's hermeneutics in general.

---

3. For a definition of Aristotelian dialectic proper see Witt 1999, 170.

The aim of this chapter, then, is to highlight Gadamer's reading in which Aristotle is taken not as rejecting *theoria* in favor of *praxis* but as reinterpreting the former in light of the latter by showing its origins in *techne*. Furthermore, the productive dialectical tension between *theoria* and *praxis* esteemed by Plato can be seen in the emphasis Aristotle places not only on scientific (theoretical) speech but also on pre-scientific speech, which refers to the practical origins of speech in the life-world. Gadamer's Heideggerian analysis maintains that all forms of speech derive from the fundamental concern of human beings to cope in the world.

The attention Gadamer draws to the dialectic between a distanced and embedded knowing paves the way for grasping Gadamer's truth-oriented understanding that rejects modernity's obsession with method as the only way to truth. Understanding that admits of truth certainly requires the distance afforded by *theoria*, but it never forgets its origin in, and homecoming to, *praxis*. What proves important for Gadamer's reading of Aristotle is the fact that both scientific and pre-scientific forms of speech are deemed legitimate. This means that illegitimate speech, the topic of the second section, comes to be construed in terms of degenerative forms of both of these types of speech. Gadamer's analysis laid out in this chapter will prove fruitful for chapter 5's distinction between "dialogue," as a true form of speech, and other forms of "conversation" not marked by truth.

The third section explores Gadamer's interest in the continuity between Plato's and Aristotle's conceptions of the good. Gadamer's point is that just as Plato productively embraces the tension between the good-for-us and the good-beyond-being, so a similar chorismatic tension emerges in Aristotle. Consequently, the *aporia* of the universal (i.e., transcendent good) versus particular (the practical good) that Aristotle believes is unhappily bequeathed to him by Plato is revealed to be as non-problematic in Aristotle as it is in Plato. This section prepares the way for a closer look, in the fourth and final section, at the way in which Gadamer takes Aristotle's ability to hold in productive tension *theoria* and *praxis* as demonstrating his own appropriation of the chorismatic tension upheld by Plato. It is in light of such a tension, it will be argued, that we are better able to grasp the appeal of *phronesis* for Gadamer's hermeneutics. The aim throughout this chapter is to emphasize how Gadamer sees an extension of Platonic dialectic in Aristotle's reliance on the productive tension between distance and familiarity, transcendence and embeddedness. It is in this sense that I speak of the dialectic Gadamer elicits from Aristotle: affirming the productive and ongoing nature of the chorismatic tension between the distance offered by *theoria* and the embeddedness of *praxis*.[4]

---

4. See Nussbaum 1996, chapter 2, especially 71-5, for a similar, although more cursory, use of Aristotle's "dialectic."

Legitimate Speech:
Scientific (Theoretical) and Pre-Scientific (Practical)

When Gadamer tells us that Aristotle maintains (in *Metaphysics* A 1-2) that "the genesis of the idea of science . . . is rooted in an original motive of Dasein" (Gadamer 1991b, 21), his interest is to emphasize how for Aristotle science depends upon us already having a world through which we understand. He observes that for Aristotle, "this world in which Dasein lives is not just its surroundings; it is more like the medium in which it implements its own existence" (Gadamer 1991b, 22). Accordingly, Gadamer tells us, Aristotle surmised that as understanding beings, our desires in relation to this world are twofold: to forge a practical relation with the world, i.e., to survive and cope, and also to achieve a "pure seeing of what is," i.e., *theoria* (Gadamer 1991b, 22). Humans desire not just to cope, but also to have comprehensive vision. Although we certainly want effective, successful relations with our world, we also want more: "To ensure that nothing unknown or unfamiliar is within the horizon of [our] vision" (Gadamer 1991b, 22). In Gadamer's construal of Aristotle, *theoria* primarily reflects the desire to avoid the unknown. While chapter 3 will further explore Gadamer's esteem of *theoria* and its relation to *praxis*, suffice it to say here that Aristotle emphasizes vision as the preeminent sense in overcoming unfamiliarity. Sight, according to Gadamer's reading of Aristotle, is the preferred means for humans to overcome their estrangement from the world.

In order to clarify *theoria*'s significance for Aristotle and to show its rootedness in the "original motive of Dasein," Gadamer begins with a discussion of *techne*, which serves as the origin of *theoria*. For, while our fundamental desire to overcome strangeness becomes refined via *theoria*'s emphasis on sight, Gadamer depicts how it originates in *techne*'s privileging of experience—but not experience in a passive, impoverished sense. What exactly is the nature of such true "experience"? In his analysis of experience (that predates and gives insight into the one in *Truth and Method*),[5] Gadamer compares *techne* to "genuine experience," *Erfahrung*, emphasizing that just as experience does not always mean passively "going through" something, so *techne* does not mean merely being a practitioner or "knowing how" to get the job done. *Techne* is not about improving one's performance or becoming a skilled practitioner, where what counts is passively following the steps set out in advance. Rather, it refers to the active engagement that yields knowledge of the why of an event: namely, why one deed is more effective than another to achieve a desired result. Gadamer stresses that this sort of knowledge is only possible given a certain degree of distance gained by reflection (which is what will ultimately connect it to *theoria*). Just as *techne* requires more than going through the motions of a practice— what occurs in imitation, for example—so "being experienced" demands more

---

5. See Gadamer 1992b, 345-362, which is discussed in my fourth chapter.

than merely "going through" an experience. Both true experience and *techne* require the ability to reflect on the experience itself. It is not enough to merely follow rules—something an automaton or non-rational animal could do by responding to mere stimuli. One first must be able to gain distance in order know where, how, and when the rules are applicable. *Techne* thus entails the type of experience that allows one not only to be able to choose in a particular case, but to know how to choose in every case. And what ensures the richness and activity of this sort of experience is memory, which allows one to generalize beyond a single, isolated experience: "From the multiplicity of memories the unity of an ability, a state of having experience, emerges. So the essential thing about having experience is that through our retention of what is the same in every same case, our having made something many times before leads to a wider circumspection" (Gadamer 1991b, 23). To be experienced means to possess a know-how that results from the ability to relate previous experiences to new ones. An experienced physician knows how to relate her experience of disease to a range of specific cases she has not yet encountered. This stands in contrast to a surgeon whose experience (i.e., *Erlebnis*) leads only to the ability to perfect his technical performance. Gadamer emphasizes that this is due to the fact that *techne* means that one not only knows what *is* the case (e.g., the surgeon's "know-how") but *why* it is the case (e.g., the physician's ability to diagnose). *Techne* thus implies knowledge of a thing's cause and the ability to "know why" something is the case. "In other words," Gadamer writes, "one has disposition over the production of these things because one's knowledge extends beyond the question of how one should act in each case" (Gadamer 1991b, 24). *Techne* thus links experiences together with reason. For, with the true experience of *techne* one is able to justify this knowledge based on reasons and causes; one's justification does not just result from the success of a performance. Justifications of the sort, "I am doing this because it has always worked," are not sufficient. The importance of being able to spell out the reasons and causes reveals *techne*'s connection with Plato's dialectic to the extent that

> this disposition over the reason or cause is primarily a knowledge of what one performs the task "for the sake of"; but this reason or cause also contains the cause in the sense of the *eidos*, or form (the appearance of what is to be produced), the cause in the sense of what it is to be made from (the material), and the cause in the sense of the beginning of the process of production (where one must begin in this process). (Gadamer 1991b, 25)

Gadamer, here referring to Aristotle's fourfold theory of causality, argues that *techne* means knowing what to do in light of a thing's ultimate for the sake of which. Humans do not simply build shelter from the storm; they know why they are doing so, can reflect upon the very need itself, and can intentionally and reflectively work toward an ideal. It is this ability to gain reflective distance that is expressed in what Gadamer refers to as both "anticipatory knowledge" and "care" and is what, as we will see below, provides the link between *techne* and *theoria*. For, according to Gadamer, Aristotle's

> concept of techne is already governed by an idea of knowledge which, in its most characteristic sense, goes beyond what techne accomplishes in producing things and performing tasks, so that techne already represents a new mode of Dasein's care.... This care about certainty manifests itself primarily in techne, as an anticipatory disposition over what is to be produced, a disposition that is characterized in its execution by knowledge of the reason or cause unfolded in the fourfold way. (Gadamer 1991b, 26)

Gadamer borrows Heidegger's conception of care to explicate the way in which humans have the potential to distance themselves from their environment. Gadamer's use of "care" in this Aristotelian context refers not only to the ability to get around in the world practically but also the ability to distance oneself from the immediate. As we have seen, Gadamer's point is that *techne* is not just about having the know-how to produce new things (bridles, health, etc.) but, by requiring knowledge of causes, reflects a distanced knowing. We can stand back and reflect on the best way to build a house, what worked before and why, what we would like to improve, and new strategies that may or may not work, etc.

It is the distance required by "care" or "anticipatory knowledge," then, that provides the connection between *techne* and *theoria*. For, Gadamer shows how when one takes the distanced knowing of *techne* even further one arrives at the universal knowledge of *theoria*. Whereas *techne* aims to produce things and achieve specific results, *theoria* refers to a more general conception of knowledge, namely, knowledge for knowledge's sake. Whereas *techne* seeks out causes of particular things, *theoria* seeks out the cause of being in general—with no interest in the practical at all. Gadamer describes how what began in terms of *techne*, as the "anticipatory disposition over what is to be produced," leads to *theoria*, which seeks "disposition in the same way over the being of everything that exists—that is, . . . to understand entities on the basis of that reason or cause as what they always and necessarily are" (Gadamer 1991b, 26). Thus while it is important to emphasize that both *techne* and *theoria* are marked by the ability to distance oneself from one's immediate situation, the crucial difference between the two is in terms of their ends: *techne* aims at achieving "practical" results, while *theoria*, to the extent it pursues knowledge for knowledge's sake, is its own end. Gadamer remarks that *theoria* further distinguishes itself from *techne* by the fact that it is marked not by production but by the tendency for lingering and leisure. Gadamer writes: "Theoria, is itself a specific way in which the care of being-in-the-world is put into effect. Its precedence over the *technai* (arts) is due to the fact that the knowledge sought in it is not sought for the sake of anything else at all, but purely for the sake of its ownmost accomplishment of discovery and knowledge, because it is not applicable in any practical performance" (Gadamer 1991b, 26, 27). It is, then, as Gadamer will show, the "why" extended to existence in general that defines *theoria*.

Yet in spite of the underlying difference between *techne* and *theoria* Gadamer insists there remains an important similarity: namely, that both *techne* and *theoria* require one to know what one performs the task "for the sake of." This insight is what leads Gadamer to emphasize the connection between *theoria* and Platonic dialectic. For example, recall the discussion of *arete* in chapter 1 where we learned that all knowledge presupposes the ability to offer justification to another in light of one's own *arete*. So, too, *theoria* requires justification, or what Gadamer refers to as "answerability in the *logos*," which means being able to state the reason or cause and to make known a thing's essence, addressing it as "something that necessarily is as it is" (Gadamer 1991b, 27). It is crucial to clarify that this does not reflect an essentialism on Gadamer's part, however. For, when Gadamer refers to the logos-embedded *theoria* allowing us to address "something that necessarily is as it is" he has in mind the ability to grasp a thing's *arete* (as was seen in Platonic dialectic). Gadamer insists, "Thus the care that goes with knowledge is a care that has to do with giving reasons or causes. As such it presupposes the primary understoodness of the entity as something that is given together with the understanding of the world which is part of our understanding of Dasein itself" (Gadamer 1991b, 28).

Gadamer ends his account of *theoria* by discussing the way in which its propensity for relying on reasons and causes not only classifies it as "scientific speech," but puts it in proximity to Socratic dialogue, which is "*a speech that lets the other person speak too*" (Gadamer 1991b, 28). In scientific speech the aim is to expose the fact of the matter—disagreement and agreement give rise to each other concerning the fact of the matter. In other words, the orientation around a common theme in which reasons are given by all—what Gadamer takes as the defining characteristic of "scientific speech"—has its roots in Socratic dialogue, which privileges *logos* and *arete*. Gadamer's reading of Aristotle's notion of *theoria* emphasizes its similarities to Platonic dialectic to the extent to which both emerge out of the life-world (i.e., *Dasein's* original motivation), strive for a degree of distance from the life-world, and then return us to the life-world (i.e., the need to dialogue with others).

But this is not the only legitimate form of speech for Aristotle. Gadamer tells us that speech has another role apart from giving an account that aims to clarify the subject matter; it also aims to draw others into an understanding that fosters productive functioning. This practical concern is what Gadamer terms the "pre-scientific" form of speech. Gadamer, again following Heidegger, is making the point that our primordial way of being in the world is to be able to get around, and to achieve a successful functioning together, in the world. We are fundamentally practical and involved beings who initially seek out a thing in order to see what it is for—not to expose its timeless essence. This is the apophantic moment where we understand something "as" something, "for" something. He gives the example of how when someone hammering exclaims, "This hammer is heavy!", the desired response from the hearer is not to ask, "How heavy?", but to look around for a lighter hammer. In other words, the most fundamental and primitive intent of speech is to get the job done. Speech is thus "a circumspect interpretation of the circumstances, [which] has the character of giving direction; that is, it serves to direct the other person not to what it exhibits, as such, but to an actively productive use of what it exhibits. As a mode of circumspection, then, the declaration reveals the entity in the existential mode of being ready-to-hand in a way that is plain to circumspection" (Gadamer 1991b, 31). The emphasis on speech's ability to foster productive use distinguishes it from a way of encountering entities as "present-to-hand," Heidegger's term for things looked at from a distance, in "carefree regard." In the "present-to-hand" relationship, we disengage ourselves from the activity associated with using a thing. With such a gaze, we "rest from the care of producing" (Gadamer 1991b, 32) and thus Gadamer describes our attitude as characterized by tarrying, resting. He gives an example of game playing—where one forsakes a seriousness towards life by transcending immediate concerns. For, in order to truly play, we must allow ourselves to be swept away; we must relinquish our purposiveness towards immediate concerns. Here, in Gadamer's nascent formulation of play he brings out the paradox of play: to be overcome by and drawn into something that has no direct purpose for us. Gadamer remarks that a similar comportment marks our pre-scientific engagements: "Something becomes the object of care and effort without being something that would be the object of such care 'in earnest.' The object of the player's effort is something that is of no concern in itself: the game exists for the sake of playing" (Gadamer 1991b, 32).

While this early discussion of play focuses on its link to *theoria*, his later discussion in *Truth and Method* relies on play to help explain how truth is possible in art. What unites the two descriptions is the fact that in play one encounters something bigger than, transcendent to, oneself that ultimately draws one out of and away from oneself. Chapter 4 discusses the significance of such a movement for Gadamer's notion of truth, but for now let us consider how Gadamer notes the similarity between our playful attitude and another way of regarding—not that found in *theoria* but one that involves the "communication of how one is faring." What distinguishes the "communication of how one is faring" from *theoria* is that the former does not have as its goal the reification or objectification of a thing, but rather concerns the sharing of what we see with another, the sharing of our way of being toward this object with another. Such tarrying or regarding, as a rest from the making of provisions, connects us with others in a way that puts on hold the desire to communicate about a thing, and instead we communicate directly about our being:

> In its resting and tarrying, this attitude has a characteristic tendency to want to be with others. Speaking with one another, which is a way in which this being together can be accomplished, is not so much one's being toward the object (taking that as something to be communicated) as the sharing of this being to-

ward the object. Thus speech is essentially expressing oneself; that is, it is *communication of how one is faring*. . . . In this way of explicating the world by only regarding it, speech and expressibility do not have an importance that modifies one's comprehension itself; nor does one avail oneself of the other person with whom one speaks in the special function of someone who shares in constituting the explication and its implied claims. (Gadamer 1991b, 33, emphasis added)

Gadamer's point has been that although not "scientific" in its aim (since it is not directed at *die Sache*), "pre-scientific speech" nonetheless remains for Aristotle a genuine form of speech in that it opens a space for another, promoting the expression and communication of one's own being. Even when *logos* is not focused on *die Sache*, given its practical roots it requires a response from another to the extent we are seeking to cope in the world. At the same time, pre-scientific speech also involves a sort of withdrawal, where the immediate cares are left behind, exemplified, as Gadamer notes, by the playing of games. This form of carefree withdrawal and resting regard thus stands opposed to what Gadamer characterizes as the scientific form of speech which aims at the fact of the matter, and does not concern itself with the self-expression found in the "communication of how one is faring." For, Gadamer states that in the "communication of how one is faring" one's own comprehension of the world is not necessarily modified. Thus the fact that pre-scientific speech leaves one's self understanding fundamentally unchanged (since it restricts itself only to self-expression) distinguishes it from the *logos*-orientation of scientific speech. The implications of this claim for an understanding of truth, as that which necessarily changes us, will be addressed in chapter 4.

Degenerate Forms of Speech

In order to grasp what constitutes illegitimate speech, it is helpful to clarify what the two forms of legitimate speech discussed above, in spite of their differences, have in common. Gadamer tells us: "This subordination to the idea of simply opening up access to the facts of the matter entails a characteristic restriction of the function of speech itself. For in speaking about something, Dasein always expresses *itself* at the same time" (Gadamer 1991b, 36-7). In other words, "what is common to all modes of understanding"—the object of Gadamer's investigation in *Truth and Method*—can be identified as the self-expression of *Dasein*. Chapter 4 will examine in more detail the nature of such self-expression in terms of language and its relation to truth, specifically the way in which the practical concerns of the self are implicated in all understanding. The focus in the meantime is on how all understanding, whether "pre-scientific"/practical or "scientific"/theoretical, remains grounded in the original motive of *Dasein* and thus can never thoroughly transcend human interests and practice. Demonstrating this insight was the aim of Gadamer's account of the dependence of *theoria* on *techne*. Yet, while such self-expression of *Dasein* is present in all forms of speech, the degree to which this occurs varies within, and thus defines, the two different forms of speech. In pre-scientific speech there will be more self-expression, in scientific speech, less. While *Dasein* plays a role in both types of speech, it does so to a greater degree in pre-scientific speech and to a lesser degree in scientific speech. Both entail restrictions and limitations. Pre-scientific speech has as its goal not the clarification and exposure of the thing, but the clarification of oneself: to make visible oneself to another. However, Gadamer notes how this "genuine way of being with another" can devolve into degenerative speech in instances when we think we have understood someone while we still disagree with her. For, in these cases, by having "protected [ourself] from the other person's contradiction" (Gadamer 1991b, 37) we block true understanding. Gadamer's point is that claims to have fully understood oneself or another, which all too frequently occur in pre-scientific speech, always result in simplifications and reifications of other and self:

> In understanding oneself—an understanding that essentially always involves contrasting oneself with others in this way—one rigidifies oneself in ways that make one, precisely, unreachable by the other person. Genuine being with one another can hardly be based on an understanding that pushes the other person away like this but must be based on a way of being with him that refrains from claiming this kind of understanding of the other person and of oneself. (Gadamer 1991b, 38)

Gadamer presumably has in mind here a "pseudo-agreement" born of frustration, impatience, or a desire for agreement at any costs. For example, when one rests content with explaining away disagreement as due to the fact that both interlocutors hold different assumptions and therefore nothing further can be productively pursued, one eliminates one's interlocutor as a true partner in dialogue. One jettisons one's desire to really hear the other anew and to work to expose false prejudices about the position of the other and/or oneself. For, dialogue entails both partners helping one another to come to an understanding. Agreeing to disagree is not a form of understanding. Therefore, to avoid the self-deceptive misunderstanding that occludes dialogue one must guard against both thinking that one has understood when one has not as well as accepting differences without further desire to understand them. This is not to say that we should never "agree to disagree"—for sometimes this may be the most pragmatic thing to do. But Gadamer would say: just do not call this understanding. In other words, to proclaim that understanding is ruled out ahead of time based on the "difference" between one's beliefs and those of another is to blind oneself to the real reason of the blockage: namely, the inadequacy of one's own desire to understand and the failure to question one's beliefs. Understanding requires a good will even more than it requires similar points of view.[6]

It is telling how Gadamer maintains that it is not just pre-scientific speech that can succumb to degeneration; scientific speech is also prone, in fact, to two different forms of degeneration. The first concerns speech that places more weight on the person speaking than on what is said, i.e., the subject matter. This is illustrated by situations where there is an excessive influence exerted by the authority of a speaker, for example, where the reputation or authority of the speaker trumps all other concerns and serves as the sole "reason." It is the authority of the speaker alone—with little regard for actual content—that convinces one. For this reason, concerns about the other person's personality or contingent motivations must be restricted in scientific speech in order to preserve the focus on the subject matter. As Gadamer writes, "a real conversation itself already requires one to attend to the substantive intention of what is said and not to what the speech expresses, along with that, about Dasein. . . . [T]he conversation's claim to be substantive is satisfied as long as the substantive reasons, and not these contingent motives, are the object of the argument" (Gadamer 1991b, 42).

But there is another form of degenerate speech to which scientific speech is particularly susceptible to succumbing, namely, "the refutation of others for the sake of refutation" (Gadamer 1991b, 49). This is exemplified by the desire of the sophists to privilege winning over truth. The important consideration is how Gadamer's reading of Aristotle and Plato suggests that scientific speech—here defined as "eristic"—implies no guarantee of arriving at truth. In other words, the effort to restrict the self-expression of *Dasein* is in itself not enough to guarantee distortion-free communication. For, as Gadamer maintained, Plato's opposition to Eleatic dialectic affirmed that degenerate speech can be due to an unbalanced emphasis on the strength of *logos*. Where invincibility is taken to be an end in itself, i.e., where winning is the sole goal, the importance of the subject matter is diminished. Where a certain *logos* or speaker claims omnipotence the result is the same: the silencing of the conversation. Where the only goal is winning, dominating the conversation, or presenting one's own *logos* as the most powerful, one stymies dialogue and in its place appears monologue, yielding an excess of power to the speaker. As we learn in the *Gorgias*, monologic speech aims to win, whereas dialogue aims at understanding the subject matter. For only by coming together with another can we achieve true *logos*. Gadamer's point is that the real power of *logos* is due to its emergence from the back-and-forth of a dialogue aimed at *die Sache*. Thus even scientific speech requires input from another subject and is not achieved by attempting to reduce itself to the purely objective. The danger of such a *logos*-dominant approach is that it denies the legitimacy of *Dasein's* socio-historical embeddedness.

---

6. This is not to say that goodwill alone is enough for understanding. See chapter 5 of this work as well as Michelfelder and Palmer 1989 for a discussion of the role of the "good will" in understanding.

What is interesting to note here, however, is that if scientific speech can succumb to degeneration and distortion, then engaging in *logos*-centered speech, where subjective influences are restricted, does not guarantee truth. The point, in other words, is not to try to elevate pre-scientific speech to the level of scientific speech by restricting subjective influences. Gadamer exposes the flaws in the Cartesian belief that a restriction of the life-world, i.e., of the subjective elements of speech, is the most reliable way to guarantee certainty, truth, or distortion-free understanding. Gadamer is not endorsing modernity's hierarchy. Rather, Gadamer suggests that both scientific and pre-scientific speech can lead to truth, and that both can be subject to distortion. But if method is no guarantor of truth, neither is it necessarily opposed to truth. Gadamer's account shows us that the solution is not found in privileging either the theoretical or practical, the distanced or embedded, the scientific or pre-scientific forms of knowing. Both are valid and productive and both are subject to distortion. Gadamer's point is that, like Plato, Aristotle does distinguish better from worse ways of arriving at truth, where the better is marked by the shared pursuit of truth. Even scientific speech must not forget its rootedness in the life-world. For, as Gadamer puts it, if "[a]ll speaking has the character of 'speaking with someone'" (Gadamer 1991b, 35), then all truthful understanding must keep in mind it is a "speaking-with." (And even where thought is not expressed in speech directly toward another, it is still speech to the extent that "the other person with whom I speak is in this case myself" (Gadamer 1991b, 41).) The significance of this for Gadamer's own conception of truth will be discussed in chapter 4. What proves important for the present discussion, however, is the way in which Gadamer highlights in Aristotle a tension similar to the one he sees in Plato: namely, the necessity of both a theoretically oriented distance and a practically oriented dialogue. We now turn to Gadamer's analysis of the way in which just such a tension is in fact preserved in Aristotle's "criticism" of the role of the good in Plato.

The Good(s)

When we turn to Gadamer's later writings on the Greeks (nearly 60 years after his *Habilitation*) we find an even stronger insistence on a dialectic that begins with Plato and is carried over into Aristotle. This section explores the nature of such a dialectic between *theoria* and *praxis* that emerges from Gadamer's reading of a continuity between Plato and Aristotle concerning the good. As such, my concern will be not to examine all the details of Gadamer's argument found in *The Idea of the Good in Platonic-Aristotelian Philosophy*, but to bring out those aspects that help us understand the chorismatic tension Gadamer reads into Aristotle's thought.

In explicating Aristotle's conception of the good, Gadamer acknowledges that his concern is neither to assess the faithfulness of Aristotle's criticism of actual arguments made by Plato nor to uncover whether it was really Plato himself who made such arguments. Rather, his aim is to assess how Aristotle interpreted the problems bequeathed to him by Plato and the significance of his "solutions" (Gadamer 1986, 127). This also means that Gadamer avoids getting caught up in debates over the differences amongst Aristotle's three ethical works and instead explicates the single problem common to them all: namely, the way in which each argues against Plato's universalizing of the idea of the good that ostensibly renders it irrelevant for human practice (Gadamer 1986, 128). Such a criticism is only "ostensive," in Gadamer's eyes, however, since he reads Aristotle as ultimately extending Plato's conception of the good.

Gadamer sees in Aristotle's thought a preservation of the Platonic *chorismos* between the good-beyond-being and the good-for-us. Explaining Aristotle's emphasis on the practical good, Gadamer tells us that

> Aristotle, the creator of physics and founder of practical philosophy, holds fast to the Socratic heritage in Plato: the good is the practically good. On the other hand, as the creator of physics, Aristotle also fulfills the demand made by Plato's Socrates, that is, that we understand the world starting with the experience of the good. The good thus appears in Aristotle's physics as well as his practical philosophy—in his physics as the hou heneka, in his practical philosophy as the *anthropinon agathon*. (Gadamer 1986, 128-129)

Yet at the same time, Gadamer (citing textual evidence from all three treatises) argues that Aristotle, again just like his predecessor, does advocate (although to a more limited and general extent) an idea of the good that goes beyond practice (Gadamer 1986, 129-30). As an example, Gadamer goes on to explain that

> the *Magna Moralia* comes close to granting the argument that what is most good, *to malista agathon*, the good itself, must be an idea, which is to say, the good of all ideas. . . . And the mutilated closing sentence of the critique in the *Eudemian Ethics* virtually seems to demand the investigation of the multiple meanings of agathon with an eye to the ariston panton (the best of all things), once the ariston ton prakton (the best of the practical) has been treated (1218a25). (Gadamer 1986, 129)

Thus in spite of Aristotle's explicit comments to the contrary, Gadamer sees Aristotle as insisting on the importance of a "good-beyond-practice," leading Gadamer to ask whether it is "not possible that what Plato truly intended becomes visible in Aristotle's discussion, nevertheless—against the latter's will, as it were?" (Gadamer 1986, 133). What proves crucial for the present argument is the way in which Gadamer refuses to accept the dichotomy that pits the "theoretical Plato" against the "practical Aristotle" and instead reads both thinkers as maintaining elements of both *praxis* and *theoria*. The result is a chorismatic tension that serves as a key component in Gadamer's dialectical reading of Aristotle.

The most fruitful way of understanding Gadamer's interpretation of the continuity between Plato and Aristotle is to acknowledge Gadamer's faithfulness to the hermeneutical principle of needing to understand the question to which a given statement is an answer. That is to say, for Gadamer, the primary similarity between Plato and Aristotle is demonstrated by the fact that they are both driven by the same question, namely: What does it mean that the good itself is common to all things that are good? Gadamer argues that, in spite of Aristotle's critique of "the universal ontological claim which Plato makes for his idea of the good" (Gadamer 1986, 128), Aristotle ultimately (and albeit unwittingly) "cannot ignore" the very same question driving Plato: i.e., "How is the good, as that which is in common, to be thought of?" (Gadamer 1986, 156). In other words, although Aristotle emphasizes the common good at the expense of the transcendent good, he still directs his energies towards figuring out what it means that the good is that which is held in common in all instances. Gadamer takes this as playing straight into the hands of Plato.

If Plato and Aristotle are joined by a single, fundamental question about the good, what accounts for the imputed differences between them? For Gadamer the main difference is one of style: even though both Plato and Aristotle affirm both a transcendent and practical good, Plato's metaphorical style emphasizes the former (particularly in his use of such terms as presence/*parousia*, participation/*methexis*, and similarity/*homiotes*), while Aristotle's conceptual style, relying on attributive analogy, emphasizes the latter.

Gadamer demonstrates how the tension between their fundamental similarities, on one hand, and their differences in style, on the other, means we are left with an Aristotle who attests to the importance of the role of the good in all areas and yet "must play down the 'transcendence of the good'" (Gadamer 1986, 132). Thus it is not, as Gadamer points out, that Aristotle wants to deny that the good is common to all good things—i.e., to the extent to which it has universal relevance, but rather that he does not want to place the idea of the good in a class apart from the other ideas. Yet, Gadamer argues, this is a conclusion that Aristotle ultimately cannot refuse. According to Gadamer, Aristotle does in fact "[insist] that like other ideas the idea of the good exists for itself separately (*choriston*)" (Gadamer 1986, 132). What does Gadamer take to be the source of this commitment?

Gadamer's point here is a subtle one and in order to make it he draws our attention to the fact that there were two senses to "*choriston*": "On the one hand, it refers to a thing's being *separate* and, on the other, to its consisting in [*existing in*] itself" (Gadamer 1986, 132, emphasis added). It is the latter that heightens the difference between Aristotle and Plato: according to Aristotle, the ideas do not *exist in* themselves, whereas the "things which are by nature" do. Relying on a helpful footnote by translator P. Christopher Smith, we could say that for Aristotle, no idea of the horse exists apart from the instantiation of the horse, but a horse does exist apart from its accidents like grey, Arabian, etc. "But," writes Smith, according to Aristotle, Plato is guilty of a misplaced concretion, so to speak, insofar as he assigns precisely this being choriston to the ideas themselves, as if they too were realities, while in fact only a this-something (*tode ti*) is real and choriston. When Aristotle comes to the idea of the good in Plato, he finds the same mistake that Plato makes with all the ideas: Plato, he says, treats the good as if it were a thing in itself, and that leads to an empty abstraction. (Gadamer 1986, 133)

Gadamer thus maintains that Aristotle's insistence that "the *physei onta* [things which are by nature] *are inseparable* from their *ti estin* what-it-is" (Gadamer 1986,132, emphasis added) leads to his doctrine of *ousia* which reveals that the "eidos is not to be separated from its phenomenal appearance" (Gadamer 1986, 132). However, Gadamer accuses Aristotle of putting a spin on Plato's account, the result of which creates a straw man. As Smith tells us, "Plato's aim is to make just Aristotle's point: the idea of the good is precisely not another thing alongside things that are good; rather, it is the structural order in any thing that is good. We call the good, insofar as it exists, the beautiful—a shining forth in things, an appearance. Aristotle's intended criticism thus actually reinforces Plato's point" (1986, 133, note 6). Let me quote at some length Christopher Long who sheds further light on this complex issue:

> In this *aporia* concerning the separate existence of principles, Aristotle begins as would be expected by suggesting that knowledge requires that there is something that exists apart from the singulars, for if there were no such thing, the singulars would be sensible, but not knowable, for [episteme] requires a separately existing one according to which the many are determined. However, immediately thereafter, Aristotle leaves off the epistemological concern and suggests that even on what may be considered a purely ontological level, it seems that some ungenerated, stable principle separate from and capable of ontologically grounding the identity of the plurality of composite individuals must exist if there is to be anything at all. Thus, the *aporia* of separability, which itself is intimately intertwined with that of the universal and singular, emerges not only as a result of the conflict between epistemology and ontology, but also as a problem inherent to any attempt to account for the ontological identity of beings that must submit to the process of generation and decay. (Long 2003, 124)

In other words, if Plato never intended that the *eidos* be separated from its phenomenal appearance, then the *aporia* of separation in Plato is not as stark as Aristotle suggests. The real factor contributing to a perceived difference between Plato and Aristotle is, Gadamer tells us, due to Aristotle's tendency to literalize what Plato intended metaphorically.

Further reflection on the philosophical significance of their different styles leads Gadamer to explain Aristotle's use of "participation" (*methexsis*) as a Platonic move. Gadamer observes: "it is applied to the good, whose presence (*parousia*) is said to cause all things that are good to be good (EE 1217b5). Precisely this formulation is used to introduce the idea of the good in the *Republic* (book 6, 505a)" (Gadamer 1986, 136). Gadamer goes on to remark that "we can now see there [in the *Eudemian Ethics*] Aristotle is striving for the least metaphorical exposition possible of what is meant by the idea of the good. Being primary among all those things that are good and being the cause of everything other than itself by virtue of its presence—these are obviously two aspects of Plato's methexis metaphor" (Gadamer 1986, 137). Gadamer's argument ultimately aims to show that Aristotle's criticism of the good is an "[unintentional confirmation of] the special status of the idea of the good" (Gadamer 1986, 139). To further make his point, Gadamer notes that while Plato maintained both that the good is first (*proton*) and that it is the cause of all things (via participation), Aristotle countered that the good cannot be taken as a genera of species and that the notion of the *eidos* of the good is useless for practice. But the problem Gadamer finds with Aristotle's line of defense is that in order to defeat Plato, Aristotle insists that no "being-for-itself" (*choriston*) of the idea of the good is possible. Yet Gadamer notes that this argument goes too far since it prevents saying the same about being—which would defeat Aristotle's whole project. Thus Gadamer finds the following contradiction in the *Eudemian Ethics*: "The point is that the good cannot be both something in common and something for itself. . . . But it seems to me that the line of thought here is incoherent and cannot be followed out to a logical conclusion" (Gadamer 1986, 140).

Gadamer's reading demonstrates that in trying to use Plato's argument against him Aristotle misconstrues Plato's position. That is to say, in trying to answer whether a universal (like good or being) can exist by itself, Aristotle himself ends up "hypostasizing . . . the good as the thing common to all virtues" (Gadamer 1986,142). Aristotle thus takes Plato's reference to "in common" to mean "existing eternally and for itself." But once we go this far, according to Gadamer, there is no returning to what they indeed have "in common"—for the many have disappeared in the glare of the "eternally existing." Gadamer's point is that it is Aristotle—and not Plato—who made the misleading deduction from the good-as-common to the good-as-eternal and existing for itself. Gadamer explains:

> To start with, the good is nothing other than the common logos (expression) and now the Platonists proceed to call it "itself" (*auto*), by which they must mean "eternal" (*aidion*) and "for itself" (*choriston*). This line of thought appears to end in a conclusion which Aristotle draws: if it is "itself," then it is "for itself," and in that case it is not something "in common." For what is in common is an attribute not of a particular individual thing but of all individual things (*EE* 1218a15 = *MM*1182b13). Now if one considers all those things that argued for the fact that Plato himself also had in mind no other presence of the good than its presence in all good things, the deduction of its being for itself (*choriston*) from its being eternal (*aidion*) is, to say the very least, quite misleading. This deduction is more an expression of what in Aristotle's view is an unavoidable consequence than of what Plato intended. (Gadamer 1986, 142-43)

Gadamer thus maintains that it simply makes no sense for Aristotle to claim that Plato's argument was that the good as the unity of number means that this "unity of an order of things [is] separate from the order itself" (Gadamer 1986, 143). For, Gadamer suggests that Plato's usage was metaphorical, and that this is something Aristotle disregards. In other words, according to Gadamer, Aristotle, in his reading of Plato, is a literalist who misses the subtleties of the latter's metaphors.

Gadamer also describes the way in which Aristotle assumes too quickly that when Plato says that "the good is found in orders of things and in numbers" he means that "the unity of an order of things is separate from the order itself." But Gadamer maintains that such a claim ultimately makes no sense since Plato was just using "a metaphor, and Aristotle, in his familiar fashion, makes things easy for himself when he takes this metaphor of the striving of the numbers literally and then finds that the numbers ought to have soul(s) but do not" (Gadamer 1986, 144). And because he takes Plato literally, Aristotle is forced to "resolve" a problem he himself contrived. Gadamer thus avers:

> The dialectical perplexities . . . are contrived. They are designed to introduce Aristotle's own solution: there can be no "good itself," no "good in itself," *except* in the functional sense of the telos (goal) or hou heneka (that for the sake of which). . . . His arguments are based on a literal reading of Plato's metaphorical statements within the framework of his own conceptual apparatus. But for just this reason they miss what Plato intended. (Gadamer 1986, 144-45, emphasis added)

Gadamer's point in rehearsing Aristotle's argument (which I am not covering in detail here) is primarily to show that the question that drove Plato continues to motivate, and ultimately remains unresolved in, Aristotle's own inquiry. Gadamer, asking what it means that the "good itself" is common to all things, concludes: "In the end, does it not mean that 'it itself' is nothing other than what is common to all things?" (Gadamer 1986, 145). Ultimately, Gadamer shows how the attempt to answer this question leads Aristotle to work out how the "practical good" relates to the "best of all things." That is to say, when Plato's metaphor of "what is held in common" is taken literally by Aristotle, the latter can only explain it in terms of a "for the sake of which," which is to elevate the practical over all else. This is the only way he can "solve" the problem he himself created. Gadamer summarizes: "Hence the foundations of ethics are provided by a kind of narrowing of the question about the good to the prakton (practical). Within the range of 'practical' problems, the question of what is good and, at the same time, one and unifying is easily answered, and in all three treatises it received the same answer: 'that for the sake of which' (*to hou heneka*). In each case the for-the-sake-of-which is the good" (Gadamer 1986, 145-46). In other words, although it is ultimately the practical good that is deemed to be the "best of all" (Gadamer 1986, 146), note how Gadamer reveals that the practical good is to be defined in terms of the "for the sake of which." The "practical good," then, is rendered close to the definition of the good we encountered in Plato, namely, the good as one's own "for the sake of which," or more specifically, one's *arete*.

Gadamer's argument aims to make the following hermeneutical point: in spite of his contention with the Platonic tradition, Aristotle remains driven by the very same questions that he seeks to dispel. Gadamer insists that

> although there is no mistaking the anti-Platonic turn [Aristotle's work] takes, it nonetheless remains an answer to the Platonic problem of the good and being. It is remarkable how much the Platonic problem of the universal dialectic in being—particularly as that dialectic occurs in the *Sophist* and *Parmenides*—evidences itself in many parts of Aristotle's *Metaphysics*, for instance, in the aporiai of Beta and in Gamma. When one compares the way in which the question about being is put there with the context in which the agathon comes up in Plato's *Republic, Philebus*, and indirectly, in his *Timaeus* too, one is struck by the identity of the problem, and the idea of analogy profers [sic] itself. (Gadamer 1986, 156)

Gadamer goes on to tell us that "[w]hat Aristotle rejects as such in Plato's philosophy is not the structural order of the whole but the derivation of that structural order from the hen (one) and the ontological primacy that Plato gives to mathematics as a consequence" (Gadamer 1986, 156). A genuine difference between Aristotle and Plato, in Gadamer's view, is the fact that Aristotle emphasizes physics while Plato focuses on mathematics. Aristotle was not so concerned with structure as with movement and this led him to posit the unmoved mover as the highest reality—as opposed to the "one." But what this unmoved mover nonetheless suggests is not just a specific order of being but that there is "a good existing apart for itself (*kechorismenon ti agathon* [a separated good])" (Gadamer 1986, 157). Writes Gadamer:

> When everything is ordered toward this primary reality, that is indeed "the best of all". . . , and this highest being is at the same time the fulfillment of what being means. Thus, Aristotle puts the Platonic heritage, which the question about the good represents, on the ground of physics. And starting there, he develops his doctrine of being in the conceptual form of an attributive analogy which has a highest *terminus* (end point). (Gadamer 1986, 158)

Thus we are brought back to Gadamer's original point that bears import for the argument of this book, namely, that Aristotle does not deny the *chorismos* but conceptualizes it differently than Plato did (Gadamer 1986, 158). That the *chorismos* remains crucial for Aristotle's own line of thinking also can be seen by turning to Gadamer's analysis of Aristotle's positive conception of practical philosophy, which has the effect of changing the focus from the tension between the idea-of-the-good and the good-for-us to the tension between *theoria* and *praxis* more generally. In other words, Gadamer's reading of Plato as holding in productive tension the good-beyond-being with the good-for-us parallels Gadamer's reading of the *theoria-praxis* tension in Aristotle.

Aristotle's "Dialectic"

While it is commonly accepted that Aristotle affirms that there can be no science of the good in general, but only of what it is good to do in practice, nonetheless, as Gadamer points out, Aristotle at the same time assumes that "practical philosophy has the character of theory. . . . He claims explicitly that such theoretical instruction as his enhances arete itself" (Gadamer 1986, 160-61). Just what is Aristotle's attitude toward *theoria,* given that his criticism of Plato's privileging of *theoria* does not include a rejection of *theoria* altogether but in fact affirms its legitimacy? In attempting to answer the question of the exact nature of the relation between *theoria* and *praxis* in Aristotle, Gadamer is wary of formulating the question in such a way that would betray our own modern bias about theory. For example, modern science (as over and against an ancient Greek conception) assumes a basic separation between theory and practice where we first derive theory that, in a separate step, is to be applied. In other words, modernity is characterized (according to Gadamer) by its assumption about the opposition between *theoria* and *praxis*. Consequently, Gadamer maintains that if we reject modernity's claim to pit theory against practice, then we will not be so hard-pressed to find a "solution" to the alleged theory-practice "problem." It is our modern obsession with objectivity that skews our approach to this issue, exacerbating the tension between the *theoria* and *praxis*. As was seen above, when one assumes that theoretical objectivity requires a complete suspension of subjective influences, which includes practice, one is forced to conceive of practice as a separate and secondary step of "application." Gadamer makes an effort to remind us, however, that the bifurcation between *theoria* and *praxis* was not part of the mindset of either Plato or Aristotle.

But if both Aristotle and Plato were committed to the integrity of *theoria* and *praxis* then what accounts for the perceived difference between the two philosophers and how are we to understand Aristotle's embrace of *theoria*? Gadamer insists that the difference between Plato and Aristotle lies in the way in which each privileged a different starting point. For example, Gadamer describes how Aristotle, unlike Plato who begins with an ideal (utopian) city and grounds this in mathematical harmony, begins from the practice in which we are now engaged. For Aristotle, *theoria* must be rooted in practice and not, as Aristotle thinks Plato insisted, the other way around. Gadamer explains: "The true arche (starting point), as he says with startling radicality, is the 'that,' *to hoti* (*EN* 1095b6, 1098b2)" (Gadamer 1986, 162). Aristotle's insistence on the priority of the "that" stands opposed to Plato's construal of the good in terms of mathematical harmony. For Aristotle, we begin with our own practice and not with an idealized structure in order to discern what is good. Thus, it is not that *theoria* has no role to play for Aristotle. To the contrary: Aristotle values *theoria* but insists it must be born out of *praxis*.

How exactly are we to understand the practical, though, if it is not to be divorced from the theoretical? Gadamer refers to Aristotle's opening example in the *Nicomachean Ethics* where an archer is esteemed as a good example of one living according to a practical philosophy which at the same time requires *theoria*: we need to know not only what our mark is (which requires the distance of *theoria*) but practically how to achieve it. The practical, though, cannot be reduced to the mere application of theory (i.e., rules) to practice. Perusing an *Archery for Dummies* book, for example, to find the rules for archery will not allow one to hit the mark. We need more than rules; we need "know-how," which involves training, experience, and habituation. Gadamer remarks:

> One has to have learned how to handle the bow, and in the same way, whoever wishes to profit from practical philosophy must be trained for it in the right way. Only then is practical philosophy of use in decision making. It assists our concrete, practical ability to size things up insofar as it makes it easier to recognize in what direction we must look and to what things we must pay attention. (Gadamer 1986, 164)

Thus we learn not only that all *theoria* is born out from and aims at *praxis* but also that *theoria* cannot be reduced to a set of rules that we then apply.

The productive tension between *theoria* and *praxis* can also be seen in Aristotle's appeal to *phronesis*. For, as Gadamer remarks, *phronesis* "is displayed not only in knowing how to find the right means but also in holding to the right ends" (Gadamer 1986, 165). *Phronesis* requires not just that one know how to reason in an instrumental way, but that one know how to choose the right ends. And in order to choose the best end, we must be habituated. Habituation requires having been able to have learned from our experiences, which requires not only *praxis* but the distance provided by *theoria*. For, becoming mature means fighting against one's immediate desires by appealing to something beyond the moment. We must have some distance in order to see beyond our immediate passions. We must learn to transcend our immediate needs and desires in order to make good decisions. Thus in spite of his desire to focus on the good-for-us and to refute Plato's idea-of-the-good, Aristotle embraces the integrity of both *praxis* and *theoria*. Both the immediacy of practice and the need for transcendence, then, present themselves as important features of Aristotle's account of human nature. We are neither purely animal nor purely mind. And it is these dual aspects of human nature, Gadamer thinks, that are brought together in his notion of the good: "Doubtless, for Aristotle too, the structural order that is to be attributed to this whole of things can be conceived of in reference to the good. That it can may be deduced from the fact that Aristotle finds his teleological cause (*aitia*) missing in all his predecessors. The teleological cause, together with the doctrine of the eidos, is Platonic inheritance" (Gadamer 1986, 174). Aristotle and Plato together share a commitment to affirming both "the ontological superiority of [*theoria's*] objects" and the reality of the "world of *praxis*" (Gadamer 1986, 174) without privileging either one. For, Gadamer tells us, "both dispositions of knowing and reason are something supreme. Practical reasonableness, phronesis, as well as theoretical reasonableness are 'best-nesses' (aretai). That which is highest in the human being—which Aristotle likes to call 'nous' or the divine—is actualized in both of them" (Gadamer 1986, 174-75). In other words, a close reading of Aristotle reveals a dialectic between two "bestnesses" (Gadamer 1986, 175).

But how are we to make sense of the two "bestnesses"? Gadamer offers an explanation that draws on both Plato's and Aristotle's views of the divine. Concluding his essay, "The Idea of Practical Philosophy," Gadamer writes: "With that a final and substantive similarity between Plato's philosophy and Aristotle's practical philosophy comes into view. It turns on the relationship [of human life] to the divine, a relationship which both take as the starting point for their thinking on the finite, conditional, and limited nature of the human being" (Gadamer 1986, 176). What is the significance of this claim? It highlights a central motif in ancient Greek thought: namely, that in thinking about our relationship to the divine we confront the finitude of human knowing, which modern philosophy, with its obsession with certainty, denied. Gadamer cites Hegel as the modern philosopher who represents the polar opposite of the ancient position, since he advocates the possibility of actually achieving, not just pursuing, wisdom. Gadamer suggests that the happiness of the practical life, although "second best" when compared to the highest form of happiness gained from *theoria*, is still actually a "best." For, humans are finite, given to practical considerations, and do have a nature different from the gods. Therefore, when we ask about what is the best for us, any answer must take into consideration our practical nature: "And precisely for this reason the practical happiness of human beings is not second rank, rather precisely what has been apportioned to them" (Gadamer 1986, 177). As Gadamer's reading of Aristotle helps us see, there are indeed two bestnesses: there is a best-overall and a best-for-us. As humans we are not condemned to choose one over the other but must live in the dialectical tension between both.

While Gadamer does not deny that Aristotle provides an important criticism of Plato, the main focus of this chapter has been to consider Gadamer's claim that Aristotle indeed "[carried] out what Plato intended to do—indeed, even go beyond it in fulfilling it." For, as Gadamer continues, "there are basic truths that the Socratic Plato did not lose sight of any more than did the Platonic Aristotle: in human actions the good we project as hou heneka (that for the sake of which) is concretized and defined only by our practical reason—in the euboulia (well-advised-ness) of phronesis. Furthermore, every existent thing is "good" when it fulfills its telos (purpose, goal)" (Gadamer 1986, 177).

I have been trying to show how Gadamer's reading of Aristotle emphasizes the continuity between Aristotle and Plato not only in terms of their similar accounts of speech/dialogue but also in terms of the way in which Plato's chorismatic tension gets played out both in Aristotle's criticism of Plato's idea of the good, as well as in Aristotle's affirmation of the need for *theoria* and *praxis*. Gadamer sees Aristotle as affirming both the importance of distancing ourselves from our immediate situation and the importance of affirming our practical existence. And these core Aristotelian themes are precisely what Gadamer defined as central to Plato's philosophy (particularly about the good)—although they were expressed in a different (i.e., more metaphorical) way. It is, then, the productivity of the chorismatic tension between transcendence and immanence, between *theoria* and *praxis*, between our longing for infinity and the reality of our finitude that Gadamer insists impacted both thinkers, albeit in different ways. In the chapters that follow we will see the way in which a similar dialectical tension motivates Gadamer's more overtly hermeneutical writings.

Chapter 3
The Dialectic of Understanding: *Theoria* and *Praxis*

Building on the previous two chapters that emphasized the dialectical tension at the heart of Gadamer's interpretations of Plato and Aristotle, this chapter argues that a similar productive tension between *theoria* and *praxis* emerges in Gadamer's own hermeneutics. The result will be to further elucidate the meaning of dialectical ethics in light of Gadamer's claim that hermeneutics is practical philosophy.

The interpretation offered here will present a direct challenge to positions that take Gadamer as emphasizing *theoria* to the exclusion of *praxis*. Gianni Vattimo, for example, accuses Gadamer's hermeneutical ontology of being unable to "bring out [a] mediation" between practice and theory and goes on to describe how, as a result, "every historical happening may become equivalent to a legitimation of all theoretical activity insofar as it is always already *de facto* practice" (Vattimo 1993, 26-27). In other words, Gadamer's alleged lack of mediation between theory and practice means that the latter is reduced to the former and there is no possibility or motivation for real change to occur. According to Vattimo, Gadamer's hermeneutics is marked by pure description and for that reason fails to elicit practical change: "Thus Gadamer has no wish to teach us anything that we cannot and do not in fact already do: he is content to make explicit what happens in every kind of knowing, starting with historiographical knowing, and ending with a redefinition of experience *in terms of what it already actually is*" (Vattimo 1993, 27). However, if we take Gadamer's hermeneutics seriously, then we are forced to reject the Marxist assumption that interpreting and changing the world are two separate activities. The dialectical account of Gadamer's hermeneutics set forth in this chapter demonstrates that true interpretation will always produce change and that hermeneutics itself is practical philosophy.

Acknowledging Gadamer's insistence on the productive relation between *theoria* and *praxis* also offers a corrective to secondary literature that has emphasized the importance of the practical element in Gadamer, particularly in terms of *phronesis*, to the exclusion of the theoretical.[1] While I refuse such a one-sided emphasis on *phronesis*, it has nevertheless been important for two reasons. First, it served to correct an earlier view that maintained that understanding could be achieved (indeed must be achieved) apart from any practical interpretation—that somehow a law, for example, has a "theoretical" (i.e., essential and timeless) meaning apart from all instantiations of it. Second, it paved the way for a discussion on the ethical and political relevance of hermeneutics.[2]

Without minimizing the work done along either of these two trajectories, I begin here with an exploration of the significance Gadamer attaches to the role of *theoria* in understanding, specifically its propensity to free us from the immediate demands of human needs.[3] But while the freedom implied by *theoria* suggests a withdrawal from the care-strewn life, I will show how on Gadamer's reading this is a withdrawal that assumes both prior and subsequent engagement with others and hence ultimately finds affinity with *praxis*. The productive interrelatedness between *theoria* and *praxis* can be seen in the following statement by Gadamer: "We have the ability to become so absorbed in something that we totally forget ourselves in it; this is one of the great blessings of the experience of art, as well as one of the great promises of religion. Indeed, this is ultimately one of the basic conditions that will allow us human beings to live together in a human way" (Gadamer 2007, 120). The absorption in something greater than ourselves, which allows us to lose ourselves, promotes increased solidarity and thus *praxis*. In distinction from modern conceptions of theory, which reduce theory to technique and attempt to eradicate all subjective and inter-subjective influences, Gadamer shows us how *theoria* yields what I referred to earlier as an "horizonal seeing" that reveals to us the situatedness of our being.[4] In other words, the understanding that results from *theoria* is not one that seeks to over-

---

1. Baracchi (2002), for example, reasons that Gadamer privileges the practical over the theoretical. And while Smith (in his introduction to Gadamer 1986 (especially p. xxviii)) mentions the importance of the integrity of theoria and praxis for Gadamer's interpretation, to my knowledge, Walter Brogan (2002) is the only one to adequately develop the role theoria plays for Gadamer's hermeneutics. See chapter 2 footnote 1 for a list of other literature that focuses exclusively on phronesis.

2. See Smith 1988, 1991; Foster 1991; and Warnke 1987, 1990, 1993 for more favorable discussions; and Bernstein 1983 for a more critical one.

3. Throughout I use the Greek "theoria" in order to distinguish it from a modern view of "theory" which Gadamer takes to exclude the very possibility of praxis.

4. See pp. 20-21.

come our thrownness, unnaturally distancing us from our engagement with the world and with other understanders, but one that gains traction from the very conditionedness of our being. An appreciation of such an "horizontal seeing" leads to an emphasis on our engagement with the world (and with others) as opposed to an idealized withdrawal from it. This reading of *theoria* affirms that as humans we are indeed caught in-between two "bestnesses."

Hermeneutics and the Joy of Being: The Significance of *Theoria* for Human Understanding

Gadamer, following Plato and Aristotle, sees *theoria* as being indelibly wedded to our human nature: without involvement in theoretical pursuits, life would simply be less than human.[5] This implies, first and foremost, that devotion to *theoria* renders one free, free from immediate cares, seriousness, and usefulness. Plato was the first to insist on the negative component of freedom, which, as Gadamer notes, caused a rupture in the meaning of freedom. Gadamer points out how for the ancient Athenians freedom was primarily conceived as freedom for, specifically *for* political involvement. To be free in that context meant to be a political being. However, Plato, according to Gadamer, emphasized the negative freedom resulting from devotion to *theoria*—specifically, freedom from the political, seriousness, use, etc.[6] As a result, *theoria* suggested retreat and flight from the world. As humans, we find ourselves drawn to something higher not because it will immediately aid our care-strewn life, but because there is something pleasant about it in and of itself. *Theoria* thus allows us to engage in wonder for wonder's sake—simply because it is in our "nature" to do so. We pursue knowledge for knowledge's sake—not because there is any justification for its usefulness. It is this freedom from our own propensity to control, manipulate, and use the world around us that renders *theoria* significant for Gadamer's hermeneutics.

The so-called "negative" freedom wrought by *theoria* manifests itself in several of Gadamer's concepts and helps us grasp its centrality to understanding. For example, we might note the affinities between the Platonic emphasis on freedom gained by *theoria* and Gadamer's conception of "play." Gadamer writes, "the word 'theory' already tells us something about the thing it refers to, about the concept itself: its proximity to mere play, to mere looking and wondering at something, far removed from all use, profit, and serious business" (Gadamer 1998b, 17). In play, as in *theoria*, we find ourselves caught up in something greater than ourselves and able to step back from immediate needs; the ensuing surrender of our will ultimately leads to the enrichment of life.

---

5. See in particular Gadamer 1998b and 1986.
6. See Gadamer 1998b, 16; and 1986, 68-70.

Theoria also suggests the importance Gadamer attaches to *Bildung*: "'Bildung' still retains something of the expectation that a theoretical occupation with things that 'do not concern' one, that are 'free' from any calculation of use or utility, should be part of professional training and belongs with the practical abilities required for it" (Gadamer 1998b, 18-19).[7] Such a commitment, for example, is reflected in the idea of a liberal arts education, which stands opposed to practical, "vocational," or technical education. Hermeneutical philosophy, then, as the study of what it means to be understanding beings, restores the importance of engaging in "pure theory," i.e., philosophy, in the academy, without having to justify its usefulness (which is not to say that philosophy remains irrelevant). In fact, Gadamer comments: "In the paradox of the philosopher king, Plato articulated a lasting truth: being fit to rule over others or to carry out any official function can mean only knowing what is better and knowing how to perform the demands of one's office. So the ideal of the theoretical life does have political significance" (Gadamer 1998b, 19). In the end, however, because the pursuit of *theoria* reflects something of our human nature, specifically its propensity to make us happy, this is reason enough to pursue it.

Gadamer also notes how the freedom found in pursuing "theory for theory's sake" connects it to the beautiful. For, the realm of *kalon* is beyond justification in terms of usefulness or purposiveness. Gadamer writes: "The clever, deliberate creations of free human being [sic] bring a constant surplus into human life: play, initiation, rite, ceremony, and all those things that, unnecessary as they are stimulating, we call the beautiful" (Gadamer 1998b, 116). Theoretical pursuits, then, are beautiful to the extent that they are chosen for their own sake—not for the sake of any use—reflecting what is essentially human. Yet to speak of the "essentially human" is not to speak of an "essential" property whose a priori presence qualifies an individual as human. Rather, Gadamer envisions the essence of humanity as emerging from society as a whole, specifically where society is an outcome of the pursuit of freedom rather than needs. What it means to be human then is to be part of a society of freedom. He writes: "Is human society possible at all when work produces only the necessities? It is worth considering how to what extent what the Greeks called *to kalon*, the beautiful in the broad sense of a free surplus and superfluity, is that whereby human society satisfies itself as human" (Gadamer 1998b, 105). But if *theoria* is of the beautiful, and thus of the ideal that transcends this world, then we need to clarify exactly how Gadamer can link up *theoria* with society.

In order to explore this further, let us consider how Gadamer endorses Aristotle's position that our penchant for *theoria* defines us as human beings, and as such is connected to our happiness. Gadamer explains this happiness by taking up the connection Heidegger makes between seeing and the there-ness of our being. Gadamer explains: "Man's greatest joy is in 'pure theory.' This is attested

---

7. See pp. 76-78 for a discussion of the significance of *Bildung* for Gadamer's conception of truth.

to by the very fact that we are awake, that miracle of our vegetative rhythm that means we can see and think, and so that we are 'there'" (Gadamer 1998b, 20). I think what Gadamer is trying to get at here is that when humans are able to find relief from achieving we are able to connect with our "beingness" and that this is what provides the joy of existence. The confrontation with our own "being-there" means we are able to realize that we are truly human *beings* and not human *doings*. There is a joyful freedom in being able to experience one's own being when one ceases from the busyness and needs of daily activities. However, as will be explored in more detail below, the joy, in part, comes not just from the (negative aspect of) freedom *from* striving but also from a freedom that allows us to realize our being-there *for* (and hence connectedness to) others. We can only really enjoy another when we cease to use her or him.

For now, however, let us consider Gadamer's claim that only when we are freed from necessities are we able to see what is. We should not read this as a variation on modern scientific method that aims to be free from subjective influences to "see what really is." Gadamer wants to avoid such subjective-objective dualisms, as well as any sort of essentialism or realism: "seeing what is . . . does not mean merely determining what is in fact present. Even in science, a 'fact' is not defined as what is merely present-at-hand that can be fixed by measuring, weighing, and counting; 'fact' is rather a hermeneutic concept, which means that it is always referred back to a context of supposition and expectation, to a complicated context of inquiring understanding" (Gadamer 1998b, 31). What is the positive sense, then, of "seeing what is"? The original meaning of *theoria* does not imply a disengaged (much less disembodied) seeing but an engaged one. Gadamer tells us that *theoria*

> means observing (the constellations, for example), being an onlooker (at a play, for instance), or a delegate participating in a festival. It does not mean a mere "seeing" that establishes what is present or stores up information. Contemplation [the Latin for *theoria*] does not dwell on a particular entity, but in a region. Theoria is not so much the individual momentary act as a way of comporting oneself, a position and condition. (Gadamer 1998b, 31)

Inasmuch as *theoria* is an involved and connected gaze, it allows us to be present. It is as if it "throws" us into, catches us up in, a situation, a region. Thus while presence is connected with seeing, notice how Gadamer's emphasis here is not on the neutral seeing of an isolated object, but on the way in which we see ourselves as situated, connected, regional beings.[8] Engagement in *theoria* permits us to be more present, and thus more fully involved in being. In contrast to modern assumptions, hermeneutics insists that it is our involvement, our situatedness, that allows us to see, to understand. It is a seeing based squarely in a region—as opposed to the infamous "view from nowhere." The point of *theoria*

---

8. This theme of a "seeing that situates" also comes up in my discussion of the relation between poetry and truth in chapter 4.

is not to achieve an objective seeing of a "particular entity," as Gadamer puts it, but to grasp the conditionedness and the positionedness of the understander. We could therefore speak of the joy of knowing that depends upon the acknowledgment of finding ourselves within the world—not jettisoned from it to a "god's eye view." Furthermore, we could say that in refusing a "god's eye view" *theoria* emphasizes our finitude and it is in this knowledge of our limits that we find relief, and thus joy. The benefit of *theoria*, is, paradoxically, both to free us from pressing needs and to reveal us as engaged more fully with our world. Walter Brogan also expands Gadamer's point in terms of its relevance for community: "*Theoria* was originally the term for the role of the one who officially represented the *polis* at the performances of the tragedies, and whose presence bore witness to the transformation of this individual event into an enactment of the universal bond of community. The viewing of the divine proceedings is not participationless establishing of some neutral state of affairs or observation of some splendid demonstration or show. Rather it is a genuine sharing in an event, a real being-present" (Brogan 2002, 11).

That such freedom does not mimic the modern dream of depriving knowledge of its "subjective" components leads me to describe *theoria* as an "horizonal" seeing. While the ancient sense of *theoria* suggests a regional seeing—where our very involvement in a situation is what allows us to see—a modern scientific conception of theory privileges the microscopic view, where clarity of vision is secured by eliminating extraneous and subjective elements. Thus the use of "horizon" implies a seeing that makes us aware of our own connectedness to and situatedness within a region. As such, only an horizonal seeing allows us to fully grasp the meaning "for us," recalling our earlier discussion of Gadamer's emphasis on self-understanding. And this is not one option among many, but our fundamental way of seeing, of understanding. For, as Gadamer demonstrates in *Truth and Method*, it is only in relation to a horizon that we are able to see anything at all. Thus an horizon, as that which extends beyond the near and the immediate, gives perspective to the same, and aligns itself with the motivation of *theoria*: i.e., only by going beyond the immediate can we see. Furthermore, the horizonal vantage of *theoria* implicates the seeing itself with being-thereness. As we look, our own thereness is made manifest. We find out who we are not by plumbing the depths of some inner physiological or psychic core but by being involved with other beings. This is the paradox of *theoria* that an explication of horizon effects: in looking away from ourselves we get more in touch with who we are, namely, understanding beings alongside others. In drawing us away from our individual cares, *theoria* frees us to experience our connectedness with others.

If *theoria* means that we do not look "objectively," as isolated subjects, but are involved with, implicated in, our seeing, then we could also say that there is a certain degree of intimacy entailed thereby. The intimacy of *theoria* is made clear by Gadamer's reliance on the Augustinian distinction between *uti* (use) and *frui* (enjoyment). Whereas the gaze of modern science is marked by utility, and thus always attempts to remain completely distinct from its object, the gaze of *theoria* is full of love and praise. The loving engagement of *theoria* prevents it from devolving into curiosity, which Gadamer describes as "the mindless gaping that is always drawn in by the newest thing and never dwells on or gets absorbed in anything" (Gadamer 1998b, 22). This is particularly evident in the German word for curiosity: *Neugier*, literally, greediness for what is new (Gadamer 1998b, 22). The curious gaze is obsessed with the new and thus anxiously searches for another object, whereas the loving gaze, as exemplified by *theoria*, is content just to be.

Given Gadamer's readiness to associate *theoria* with freedom from daily cares and needs, might not some argue that this joyful gaze, akin to the beholding of beauty, is a privileged stance that can occur only after all of our pressing needs have been met? Is this an elitist philosophy for the few, well-fed philosophers who have no worldly cares? What about those who do not have the privilege of being able to take the needed time for theoretical pursuits since they are living, literally, hand-to-mouth? Is the "enjoyment of being" a luxury granted only to those whose material needs have already been met? To answer these important questions, first let us attend to the way in which Gadamer follows Plato in attesting to the fact that needs and desires "belong to a class of the *apeiron* (limitless)" (Gadamer 1998b, 33). If needs and wants belong to a class of things that have no limit, then we will always be in the state of wanting and needing more. That we will always have more needs than we can satisfy should serve as a warning that we should not take the satisfaction of our needs as the requisite step for pursuing that which transcends our immediate concerns.

We could think here, for example, of Jesus' statement, "the poor you will always have with you," offered as a rebuke to those who criticized the "waste" of an expensive oil in anointing him when it could have been sold and the money given to the poor.[9] His incisive words—far from being a denial of human suffering—suggest that appealing to needs can be just as politically motivated as ignoring such needs. It was, in other words, highly unlikely that the critics were really interested in feeding the poor; most likely they were incensed that a religious leader would allow a woman to do something so sensual, so abundant—and in the presence of others. Gadamer seems to be making an analogous point: the presence of needs should not mean abstaining from *theoria*, for our needs we will always have with us. We can always use the presence of needs to justify why we should not do something. What Gadamer would have us remember is that our neediness should not blind us to the joy of being.

On the other hand, that there is no end to, and thus no possibility of satiating, all of our needs and desires, is of course neither an argument against their importance nor a defense against trying to meet (at least some of) them. Is Gadamer overemphasizing *theoria* at the expense of being concerned with use-

---

9. Matthew 26:11; Mark 14:6; and John 12:8 (which provides a slightly different take).

fulness or practicality? To answer "yes" is not to impute any inadequacy to Gadamer's thought, rather we must remember that if it seems that he is bending a stick too far in the opposite direction in order to straighten it out then this is precisely his intent.[10] In other words, Gadamer is committed to showing how *theoria* can help us find joy in our humanity by looking beyond, and thus taking a respite from, our immediate cares. Specifically, this means that he wants to illuminate how (in Aristotelian fashion) humans are concerned with more than survival and this is what makes us human; humanity's urge to pursue the beyond defines our humanity. This is born out by the fact that we are not concerned solely with self-preservation "but [we] are also [thinkers]. Each of us asks himself how he should live. He seeks his fulfillment in a happy life—and that is not something that is exhausted by acquiring things and being successful; life is also devoted precisely to what is, to what is to be seen and what is beautiful to see" (Gadamer 1998b, 34).

Theoria, then, paradoxically returns us to the most practical of all questions: how should I live? That this is fundamentally a hermeneutical question is attested to in the following comment by Gadamer: "What is . . . all the more difficult to achieve, is for each individual in his practical life to see what is, instead of what he would like to be" (Gadamer 1998b, 31). The task of hermeneutics, which *theoria* aids us in, is to see "what is" in an horizonal manner. "Seeing what is" serves as the launching point for all understanding and defines our human quest as primarily practical and not epistemological: we are to figure out how to live. But the question of how to live cannot be answered by pointing to the immediate needs that surround us. In order, therefore, to answer the question of how we should live, we must engage in *theoria*, which allows us to transcend and break free from our addiction to utility that robs us of freedom. As beings who are concerned with more than survival, with more than just a life of pursuing immediate needs, the question of how to live better always looms on the horizon. In line with Plato and Aristotle, hermeneutics insists that only a life engaged (to some degree) in *theoria* is able to achieve the joy of being human.

To return to the earlier point about the relevance of *theoria* for the communal life: *theoria* in its ancient conception, unlike the modern theory of scientific method, does not imply an isolated and individual pursuit. The awareness of our situatedness that horizonal seeing effects fundamentally means being able to experience our connectedness to others. Gadamer describes the ancient Greek conception of *theoria* in terms of its relevance for community and how it suggests

> [having] been given away to something that in virtue of its overwhelming presence is accessible to all in common and that is distinguished in such a way that in contrast to all other goods it is not diminished by being shared and so is not an object of dispute like all other goods but actually gains through participation. (Gadamer 1992c, 77)

10. Gadamer 1992b, 555.

Theoria, then, has a unifying effect to the extent that we as finite beings can all engage in it without depleting it. In fact, Gadamer describes *theoria* as a good that is not only unable to be used up but increases the more we engage in it. We do not need to fight over our share of *theoria*; we can allow its pursuit to unite us with others. And the universality that connects us with others, according to Gadamer, takes on a specific form: "In the end," Gadamer writes, "this is the birth of the concept of reason: the more what is desirable is displayed for all in a way that is convincing to all, the more those involved discover themselves in this common reality; and to the extent human beings possess freedom in the positive sense, they have their true identity in that common reality" (Gadamer 1992c, 77). The common appeal to reason is made possible, then, by the freedom found in *theoria*. The beauty of reason lies in the fact that it is available to all, and the more who participate in it, the more it grows.

There is another way to describe how *theoria*, although a looking beyond, far from isolating us from others, reveals what we all as humans share in common. As Gadamer inquires:

> Is theory ultimately a practice. . . or is practice, if it is truly human practice, always at the same time theory? Is it not, if it is human, a looking away from oneself and looking out toward the other, disregarding oneself and listening for the other? Life, then, is a unity of theory and practice that is the possibility and the duty of everyone. Disregarding oneself, regarding what is: that is the behavior of a cultivated, I might almost say, divine, consciousness. . . . It does not need to be a consciousness cultivated by and for science; it only needs to be a humanly cultivated consciousness that has learned to think along with the viewpoint of the other and to try to come to an understanding about what is meant and what is held in common. (Gadamer 1998b, 35)

A helpful way of grasping in a concrete manner what it means that *theoria* draws us, ultimately, towards human community and not away from it is to attend to some of Gadamer's comments in *Truth and Method* that speak to the way in which language does the work of helping us rise above our mere "environment" in order to achieve freedom in the "human world." In these pages, Gadamer insists that language permits such a rising above not in the way a tool does—objectifying our world—but in allowing us to see more of our situatedness within the world. Our situatedness is more fully realized due to the fact that it is through language we gain this new "orientation," one that ultimately yields "freedom from the environment" (Gadamer 1992b, 443, 444). It is not that a withdrawal from our environment and the pressing cares of existence leads us to a heavenly, inhuman realm. For, we never fully sever our ties but we gain a more authentic relationship, a freer one, toward our world that is, as Gadamer puts it, "always realized in language" (Gadamer 1992b, 445). And the power of language resides in the fact that it not only allows us to connect with others but also to foster creativity, which serves as the very possibility of human freedom. Engaging in language is not to pick up a tool with which we objectify the world.

Rather, it entails world making, whereby the world becomes more fully present to us (Gadamer 1992b, 443). As Gadamer puts it: "Man's freedom in relation to the environment is the reason for his free capacity for speech and also for the historical multiplicity of human speech in relation to the one world" (Gadamer 1992b, 444).

Thus to be fully human is to be concerned with what lies beyond: both in terms of the transcendent and the human other. Achieving a theoretical gaze is not something that is a luxury, but is central to the joy of existence that emerges with understanding. For, in order to understand we need to look away from ourselves, and this draws us into solidarity with others, allowing us to find what is held in common. *Theoria* does not isolate us from others and their needs. In fact, it can have just the opposite effect: in being less ensnared with our own needs, we are free to meet those of others—and not out of political motivations (e.g., because we need them) but because we are free to see their humanity as well. Unlike the Cartesian dream, this does not mean suspending or denying our embeddedness in history, culture, tradition, society, etc.—we never lose sight of our point of departure, which is ultimately our returning point. In other words, *theoria* calls us to look away from ourselves, to what is universal, and the result is that our relationship with others is changed. By pursuing what lies beyond, we develop the mature stance of being able not just to be, but to be for someone else. Such a withdrawal away from the particularities of self toward the universal is also reflected in *Bildung*, which suggests the "cultivated" ability to be able to look beyond one's parochialism toward the other. Chapter 4 will examine the importance of this reading of *Bildung* for Gadamer's conception of truth. Suffice it to say in the meantime, however, that perhaps this is the secret hermeneutics uncovers: although humans are characterized by the penchant to want to know, this desire is ultimately inseparable from the desire to want to be known—not as a specimen under a microscope but known through the sharing of communal life. Thus we return to where we began: the freedom inherent to *theoria* is not purely a negative freedom; it is also a freedom that realizes our "being there" for others.

The *Praxis* of Understanding: Practical Reason and Practical Philosophy

If the above discussion reminds us of the essential role Gadamer takes *theoria* to play in the human life, then we also need to come to terms with what Gadamer means when he speaks of "practice" and how it is to be understood in relation to *theoria*. As noted above, most commentators have interpreted the "practical" bent of hermeneutics solely in terms of *phronesis*. This section attempts to understand the significance of *phronesis* by examining it in conjunction with other related terms. For example, a close examination of the nature of the "practical"

The Dialectic of Understanding: *Theoria* and *Praxis*

in Gadamer's work reveals that he speaks of: 1) practice (*praxis*), 2) practical reason/reasonableness (*praktische Vernunft* (Gadamer 1992c, 81)/*praktische Vernunftigkeit* (Gadamer 1992c, 117)) or *phronesis* (Gadamer 1992c, 115), and 3) practical philosophy (*praktische Philosophie*), which he renders close to Aristotle's "political science" (Gadamer 1992c, 89). I will use the English word "practice" and "practical" to refer to the general practical nature of understanding which lumps together the following terms: *praxis*, practical reason (*praktische Vernunft*)/*phronesis*, and practical philosophy (*praktische Philosophie*). In spite of the family resemblances amongst these terms, it will ultimately be important to distinguish amongst them. For example, in his essay, "What is Practice [*praxis*]? The Conditions of Social Reason" (Gadamer 1992c), Gadamer contrasts *praxis* with both *techne* and *poesis*, and develops its connection to practical reason (*praktische Vernunft*). In "Hermeneutics as Theoretical and Practical Task" (Gadamer 1992c), Gadamer distinguishes "practical reason" from "practical philosophy," where the latter offers a more theoretical reflection aimed at the "the problem of the good in human life" than the former.

These terms will be developed along the following trajectories. "*Praxis*," his most general term, is used primarily in his discussions of the way in which "practice" has been deformed. Gadamer thus takes an interest in restoring a fecund sense of *praxis* which requires that we pay attention to how modernity drove a wedge between it and *theoria*. In order to restore a more original and vibrant sense to *praxis*, Gadamer invites us to think anew the importance of both *phronesis* (practical reasoning) and practical philosophy. As it will be shown, *phronesis* reflects the practical reasoning of an individual who must make a concrete decision in the moment, while practical philosophy reflects a more generalized and distanced reasoning. Although both are necessarily connected to *theoria*, they are so to differing degrees: we could say that *phronesis* stands closer to the practical life of an individual and practical philosophy closer to *theoria*. It is therefore important to grasp how Gadamer wants to distinguish practical philosophy from *phronesis* and to define hermeneutics as itself practical philosophy. That is to say, *phronesis*, as operative where an individual must make a choice about what to do, is illustrative but not defining of hermeneutics-as-philosophy, which affords one the luxury of not having a pressing decision to make. As philosophers (primarily oriented towards theory) we do not have to choose; as individuals (primarily oriented towards practice) we do. (In fact, this leads Gadamer to warn of the temptation present in all philosophical thinking: namely, since it can afford to postpone deciding, it too easily can remain in the theoretical to its detriment.) And if *phronesis* is not to be understood as practical philosophy, then it cannot capture all there is to hermeneutics. This point proves significant to the extent it challenges criticisms that attempt to deny a degree of theoretical (and thus critical) reflection to Gadamer's hermeneutics based on his appeal to *phronesis*. For, such criticisms misunderstand the scope of *phronesis*: *phronesis* cannot be equated with hermeneutical philosophy, which, as akin to practical philosophy, does require a more theoretical level of reflection. Therefore any attempt to assess whether Gadamer's hermeneutics is critical enough must distinguish between *phronesis* as it relates to the individual *qua* individual and practical philosophy as it relates to hermeneutics *qua* philosophy.

To begin, then, for Gadamer, "practice has to do with others and codetermines the communal concerns by its doing" (Gadamer 1992c, 82). But what does "having to do with others" entail? That all "acting" involves a thinking that is influenced by, and directed at, not only the practices of the life-world but also its inhabitants implies a fundamental connection between *praxis* and solidarity. As Gadamer describes it: the general orientation of *praxis* is "conducting oneself and acting in solidarity," where solidarity serves as the "condition and basis of all social reason" (Gadamer 1992c, 87). The significance of *praxis* for Gadamer, in other words, is not just its capacity to bring about change in the world but its impact on social reason. For Gadamer, this means that the quality of "practice" (understood as solidarity) determines the quality of social reason. Consequently, when practice becomes debased, the same will happen to social reason. Hence Gadamer finds more than theoretical concerns at stake in returning us to a premodern sense of practice. As Gadamer reminds us, whereas ancient Greek science (as chapter 2 delineated) was marked by a unity of *theoria* and *praxis* (both of which were considered a form of knowledge), modern science rends the two apart so that we have "science and its application" (Gadamer 1992c, 89). In other words, while for the Greeks, *theoria* was itself a practice (Gadamer 1992c, 90), modernity sought to completely divorce theory from human experience and, as such, "practice" came to mean the "application" of an abstracted theory. Consequently, practice-as-application was taken to be a separate task from theory, which alone counted as true knowledge. The result, according to Gadamer, of this bifurcation between theory and application ultimately lead to the instrumentalization of the world through the dominance of "technique." Gadamer describes this process: "In prescinding from the primarily experienceable and familiar totality of our world, [science] has been developed into a knowledge of manipulable relationships by means of isolating experimentation" (Gadamer 1992c, 70). In other words, science is no longer primarily about investigating being in the world, but about manipulating it by means of ever-improving techniques.

The pervasiveness of technique resulting from *theoria*'s emaciation, Gadamer opines, deprives us of dealing with two crucial questions pertinent to human practice: "For whose benefit is the work being accomplished? And how much do the achievements of technology serve life?" (Gadamer 1992c, 71). The inability to deal with these two questions that ask about a purpose that goes beyond mere functioning leads to the undermining of social reason. He goes on to conclude: "From this there arises in a new way the problem that has been posed in every civilizational context, the problem of social reason" (Gadamer 1992c, 71).

As an example of such neglect, Gadamer describes the way in which in the twentieth century the technique of manipulation becomes extended beyond nature to the social world. This leads, as Gadamer describes it, to the esteem of the "expert," who is expected to know how to solve a vast array of problems from communicative to political. Gadamer writes, "the more rationally the organizational forms of life are shaped, the less is rational judgement exercised and trained among individuals" (Gadamer 1996a, 17). A fecund social reason, as Gadamer sees it, requires a happy marriage between *theoria* and *praxis*; when a divorce between the two occurs, the social component of reason becomes feeble and technique (as reason run amok) comes to dominate. Consequently, the esteem of the expert and technique means that the individual feels increasingly helpless and powerless in mass society. Quantity of information is preferred over quality of "craft" in the political and social realms. This means that "[t]he individual in society who feels dependent and helpless in the face of its technically mediated life forms becomes incapable of establishing an identity" (Gadamer 1992c, 73). Consequently, rather than engaging in the practical task of seeking one's identity or forging a creative life, the individual thinks that the only way to survive is to appropriate techniques for survival. When fitting in replaces forging, functionaries result. And "functionaries," as Gadamer calls them (Gadamer 1992c, 74), lose their ability for "social" reason: "the more strongly the sphere of application becomes rationalized, the more does proper exercise of judgement along with practical experience in the proper sense of the term fail to take place" (Gadamer 1996a, 17).

The significance of *theoria*, as the first part of this chapter detailed, reflects what is fundamental to human existence: our ability to think beyond our immediate cares and needs, to open up spaces where survival and functioning are not our sole concerns. Gadamer writes, "This special human dimension is the inbuilt capacity of man to think beyond his own life in the world, to think about death. . . . [Such a capacity] is a matter of the fundamental constitution of human being from which derives the specific sense of human practice" (Gadamer 1992c, 74-75). What Gadamer seems to be implying here is that a rich sense of the social is only possible when we give space for a proper exercise of *theoria*. Loss of an appreciation for *theoria* severs our social ties. And why is this? Because without a sense of the beyond, there is no way of ordering the complex needs of human life which ultimately demand "enlightened choice, just deliberation, and right subordination under common ends" (Gadamer 1992c, 76). Gadamer continues:

> We have to keep in full view the entire range of the human—from the cult of the dead and concern with what is just, to war—in order to apprehend the true meaning of human practice. It is not exhausted in collective and functional adaptation to the most natural conditions for life. . . . It is precisely the excess beyond what is necessary for the mere preservation of life that distinguishes [a person's] action as human action. (Gadamer 1992c, 76-7)

Gadamer's account demonstrates the way in which the divorce between *praxis* and *theoria* results in a profligate form of both, into application and technique, respectively. The result is an undermining of social reason. Practice, to reinvigorate itself (and thus social reason) and to avoid reduction to efficiency and technique, must, like the ancient conception, reclaim its roots in *theoria*. It is in this context (i.e., that of stressing the importance of the recovery of the dialectic between *theoria* and *praxis*) that Gadamer turns to *phronesis* as the paragon of the practical. For, it is the Aristotelian notion of *phronesis*, practical reason, that provides a model for understanding to the extent to which it embraces the dialectic of the theoretical and practical elements of human existence and thus refuses the reach of "technical control" (Gadamer 1975, 312).

What is the nature of *phronesis*, then, and what is its significance for hermeneutics? In his section, "the hermeneutic relevance of Aristotle," in *Truth and Method*, Gadamer tells us that "what interests us here is precisely that [Aristotle] is concerned with reasons and with knowledge, not detached from a being that is becoming, but determined by it and determinative of it" (Gadamer 1992b, 312). In other words, *phronesis* illustrates how a concrete individual can exercise reflective choice: not via a rejection of one's social and historical determinations but based on them. The good life is one that is shaped out of the particularities of a lived life—not one modeled on a theoretical ideal. For this reason, Gadamer takes such "phronetic" knowledge as illustrative of hermeneutics: "*For the hermeneutical problem too is clearly distinct from 'pure' knowledge detached from any particular kind of being*" (Gadamer 1992b, 314). Hermeneutics is not, and does not aspire to be, pure method removed from practical concerns. Since the literature on Gadamer's appeal to *phronesis* is well established, I will focus on drawing out its significance for the present discussion by examining the way in which Gadamer develops it as a particular form of choosing that stands in contrast to both wishing and instrumental reasoning. Second, I will discuss the role tradition plays in Gadamer's appeal to practical reasoning. Finally, I will defend Gadamer's conception of *phronesis* against those who see it as lacking resources for refusing ideology. This invites a discussion of practical philosophy and how it must be distinguished from *phronesis*.

Gadamer tells us that "practice means not only the making of whatever one can make; it is also choice and decision between possibilities. Practice always has a relationship to a person's 'being'" (Gadamer 1996a, 3-4). Gadamer's emphasis here stands in contrast to the dominance of the practice-as-application model that emerges out of modern science, which defines knowledge as what the experts possess. Gadamer directs our attention toward the need for choosing based on one's lived (and thus limited) experience. The practical reasoning defined in terms of the know-how born of experience is a creative act, albeit one fraught with uncertainty. Yet relinquishing the certainty provided by experts and/or method, we nevertheless have to choose. Our skepticism cannot protect us from the exigencies of life: in spite of the incompleteness of practical knowledge the individual finds herself pressed to act. The significance of the creative power of choice (here contrasted with mere wishing) of *phronesis* also comes to the fore in Gadamer's reflection on Plato's use in the *Republic* of the notion of utopia. It is not enough merely to wish for such a utopia; we must make it real, which can only come about by our choosing it. It is in this context that Gadamer emphasizes reflective choice as distinct from mere desire. He explains, "wishing is not willing, it is not practice. Practice consists of choosing, of deciding for something and against something else, and in doing this a practical reflection is effective, which is itself dialectical in the highest measure" (Gadamer 1992c, 81). The dialectical nature of practical reason Gadamer describes here thus serves as a paragon of the dialectic between the *theoria* and *praxis* in general. We choose deliberatively, reflectively, appealing to something beyond our immediate needs and desires.

But if practical reason is not a matter of mere wishing or desiring, neither is it a matter of simply choosing the best means for an end. Practical reasoning involves thinking through the consequences of one's actions both for oneself and for others. Thus the reflective capacity of practice stands in opposition to the clever analysis of the best means for an end: practical reason, as rooted in *theoria*, is never instrumental. Gadamer writes:

> For practical reason does not consist simply in the circumstance that one reflects upon the attainability of the end that he thinks good and then does what can be done. Aristotle distinguishes very explicitly the mere resourcefulness that for any given ends finds the right means with almost inhuman skillfulness (which means lying whenever necessary, deceiving wherever possible, talking one's way out of anything). The sharpness of the operator is no real "practical reason." (Gadamer 1992c, 81)

"Technical rationality" is not enough; one must be able to see the whole and evaluate it in light of one's particularity. It is thus not any sort of activity or movement that counts as practice, but one that comes forth from reflection. This claim returns us to Gadamer's point about Plato's use of utopia: "in this way, too, is the practical meaning of utopia filled in. It, too, is not a guide for action but a guide for reflection" (Gadamer 1992c, 82). In other words, Plato's use of utopia is not to provide an ideal that we then unthinkingly imitate, but to provide a stimulus for reflection and thus practical reason. Gadamer sees in Plato's appeal to utopia the possibility for theoretical reflection which raises us above our immediate needs and concerns so that we might better be able to make practical decisions that escape the dictates of technique.[11] And thus in spite of the negative examples Gadamer gives for the way in which practice is being replaced by technique, he does not lose hope that the recognition of our solidarity will allow us to recover a richer conception of practice. Gadamer writes:

> Just as we, in our overstimulated process of progress of our technological civilization, are blind to stable, unchanging elements of our social life together, so

---

11. In chapter 5 pp. 116-17 I note that the role of utopia is analogous to that of the good-beyond-being: that which allows understanding to get underway but which is never meant to be fully or finally grasped.

it could be with the reawakening consciousness of solidarity of a humanity that slowly begins to know itself as humanity, for this means knowing that it belongs together for better of for worse and that it has to solve the problem of its life on this planet. And for this reason I believe in the rediscovery of solidarities that could enter into the future society of humanity. (Gadamer 1992c, 86)

But what does this practice-embedded choosing look like? An answer to this question requires acknowledging the importance Gadamer assigns to the philosophical role played by tradition. Gadamer explains, "We are always dominated by conventions. In every culture a series of things is taken for granted and lies fully beyond the explicit consciousness of anyone, and even in the greatest dissolution of traditional forms, mores, and customs the degree to which things held in common still determine everyone is only more concealed" (Gadamer 1992c, 82). True practice, in other words, not only implicates itself theoretically (as we have seen) but also acknowledges its prejudicial inception and in so-doing reveals its rootedness in social reason. A thinking that aims at pure objectivity attempts to remove itself entirely from all interest—not just of the individual but of society as well.

Gadamer's point is that the way to avoid the manipulation of a technologizing reason (whether as born out in the practices of genetic modification or torture) is to acknowledge the efficacy of our socio-historical tradition. But as Gadamer clarifies elsewhere, his point is not to elevate tradition to a normative role—to have us preserve or conserve past practices in order for them to dictate present practices. Instead, he desires to help us "see through the dogmatism of asserting an opposition and separation between the ongoing, natural 'tradition' and the reflective appropriation of it" (Gadamer 1977, 28). In fact, where Gadamer speaks of "normativity" at all, he speaks of the "normative character of practice" (Gadamer 1992c, 83) which offers an antidote to the excesses of a theory removed from practice.[12] That is to say, Gadamer believes that the "common experiences" of our tradition will serve as a resource for helping us refuse the domination of an instrumentalizing technique. Tradition is the expression of human solidarity without which we would be susceptible to ideology:

> I am concerned with the fact that the displacement of human reality never goes so far that no forms of solidarity exist any longer . . . [For] if it were the case that there were not a single locus of solidarity remaining among human beings, whatever society or culture or class or race they might belong to, then common interests could be constituted only by social engineers or tyrants, that is through anonymous or direct force. (Gadamer 1983, 264)

His point is to illuminate the significance of tradition in general and not to esteem one tradition over another, which would reduce tradition to a set of iden-

---

12. See, for example, Lafont 1999, whose emphasis on the normative nature of tradition I discuss in chapter 4, pp. 89-90.

tifiable practices that we could then apply: "Tradition is not a privilege of Western culture; the dialogue between tradition as well as the dialogue between our past and our tradition is expanding beyond any pregiven limitations. . . . In all these things, we no longer pretend any form of exclusiveness and share with everybody our human task of contributing in the modest proportions which are ours to the well-being of human life" (Gadamer 1979, 85). Examining the significance of Gadamer's appeal to tradition, then, in light of the *theoria-praxis* dialectic helps us avoid reductionistic and normative renderings of this term. Such an approach allows us to appreciate tradition as a rich resource of interpretations that reflects what we as humans hold in common. As such, it is the appeal to tradition, to what we have taken ourselves to be and how we have understood ourselves, that holds the possibilities for freeing us from the snares of reductionistic technique. For example, he sees the abhorrence to genetic modification and to the torture of persons as arising from our shared tradition that has not yet been fully overtaken by technique. The very fact that there is repulsion against them signals that a voice from our common humanity is still audible. And yet, at the same time, the danger remains that the natural human desire to conform may ultimately contribute to the undermining of social reason. I take him to be suggesting that sooner or later it becomes easier just to go along with the "crowd" (or at least the pseudo-crowd manufactured by corporate or political marketers) and accept genetic modification or torture rather than to fight against them. In such instances our approach to tradition is marked more by technique than *phronesis*. And only the latter fosters solidarity.

The practice-embedded choosing so important to Gadamer's construal of *phronesis* requires solidarity, where solidarity reflects a willingness to listen to the other, to come together with the other to work on a shared problem, to engage in a common quest. But are there limitations to such solidarity? It has been suggested that the foregoing talk of the appeal to solidarity neglects the fact that our social reason itself might be distorted. Richard Bernstein, for example, notes: "But what, then, is to be done in a situation in which there is a breakdown of such communities, and where the very conditions of social life have the consequences of furthering such a breakdown? More poignantly, what is to be done when we realize how much of humanity has been systematically excluded and prevented from participating in such dialogical communities?" (Bernstein 1983, 226). In other words, how can relying on a tradition possibly mired in ideology allow us to come to a truthful (i.e., non-ideological) understanding?

Let me speak to this issue in two stages. First, I do not think Gadamer ever intended to say either that any single tradition is a source of freedom for all persons or that everything about a given tradition is worthy to be continued. Attention to the specific claims Gadamer makes about tradition will demonstrate this point. For example, his reference to the ancient Greek tradition is specifically directed at illuminating the way in which *theoria* and *praxis* were considered inseparable and is made in order to inspire a more effective attempt to remedy current social ills. Gadamer's claims cannot be read as implying that everything about "our" tradition—or in "the Greek tradition"—is beneficial and leads to freedom for everyone at all times. Neither is he saying that we should blindly submit ourselves to such a tradition. He himself offers an example of reflective engagement with one aspect of a tradition that he believes might prove fruitful for current practice. Furthermore, his appeal to common experiences are meant only as ways of showing that humans can still come together as humans; there is no claim implied here that all such "common experiences" were truly common to all. In fact, Gadamer remains sensitive to the fact that much work needs to be done to increase our solidarity, that we have not yet extended the "we" far enough. Thus a fair reading of Gadamer in this regard should see him as maintaining that while there are elements of "our" tradition that we both do and should appeal to, e.g., all humans should be treated with equal worth and dignity, we can at the same time critically challenge our tradition by changing the definition of what counts as a human.

Second, in light of the previous discussion, it becomes crucial to remind ourselves that *phronesis* is not all there is to Gadamer's esteem of the practical. For, in defining hermeneutics as practical philosophy, he believes there is important work to be done on the theoretical level as well. It is not that there is no legitimate way to appeal to *theoria* to distance ourselves in a limited sense from practice. This is precisely what Gadamer seems to have in mind when he writes: "Where can we find an orientation, a philosophical justification, for a scientific and critical effort which shares the modern ideal of method and yet which does not lose the condition of solidarity with and justification of our practical living?" (Gadamer 1975, 311). It is in response to just this question that Gadamer develops Aristotle's notion of *praktike episteme*. For, unlike practical reason, practical philosophy aims to reflect on human practice wherever it is found. It is at once a more theoretical and universalized approach to the good than practical reason. He writes, "practical philosophy needs to raise to the level of reflective awareness the distinctively human trait of having *prohairesis*" (Gadamer 1992c, 92). This point can be clarified by attending to his essay, "Hermeneutics as a Theoretical and Practical Task," where he reflects on the difference between the art of hermeneutics or "philosophical hermeneutics" (as that which is akin to practical philosophy) and the hermeneutical moment of all human understanding or "self understanding" (akin to practical reasonableness). Gadamer says that this distinction is analogous to the difference between the formal method of logic and our use of "logical" to refer to someone's manner of daily speech. When we criticize someone for being "illogical" in everyday speech, we do not mean that she or he did not conform herself to the formal laws of logic but to the "logic" that governs our everyday speech. Practical philosophy is thus to practical reasonableness as formal logic is to the logic of the everyday. That is to say, practical reasonableness concerns our everyday ability to make decisions, whereas practical philosophy reflects the more theoretical approach to the good. Thus while practical reason reflects elements of practical philosophy, the former is not reducible to the latter. For, practical philosophy offers a type of reflection on the practical good that is not available through practical reason itself, and yet, practical philosophy ultimately is born out of and returns back to practice. It is not, then, that Gadamer wants to do away with *theoria*. Rather, he desires to challenge the "critique of ideology's [overestimation of] the competence of reflection and reason" (Gadamer 1975, 315).

Another way of defending Gadamer against claims that he downplays hermeneutics' theoretical capacity is to take him as being true to his hermeneutical commitments. It is not that he belittles theoretical approaches to social issues, rather, he is sensitive to the way in which the very questions we pose betray modern assumptions. Asking how we can ensure that our social discourse is completely free from distortion assumes that an evaluatively neutral stance is possible. Instead, Gadamer calls on us to ask: "How can we learn to recover our natural reason and our moral and political prudence?" (Gadamer 1975, 314). It is not that Gadamer turns a blind eye to the diagnosis of the critique of ideology, rather, he wants us to pay attention to how certain questions betray a commitment to the bifurcation of theory and practice that got us into trouble in the first place. I read Gadamer as maintaining that once we get rid of the theory-practice dichotomy, questions of the sort "how can we get more theory?" fall flat. But this is not the same as saying that our social reason is not in trouble and that we do not need to recover the vital dialectic between *theoria* and *praxis*.

The above discussion that demonstrates how Gadamer's account of understanding embraces the dialectic of *theoria* and *praxis* has relevance for his claim that "hermeneutics is philosophy, and as philosophy it is practical philosophy" (Gadamer 1992c, 111). For, Gadamer insists that hermeneutics-as-practical-philosophy differs from the ubiquitous and universal experience of understanding that we all share (what was referred to earlier as "pre-understanding"). On one hand, there is hermeneutical philosophy that takes up a theoretical approach and "describes what always happens wherever an interpretation is convincing and successful" (Gadamer 1992c, 111), which includes texts but also "our communicatively unfolded orientations in the world" (Gadamer 1992c, 112). *Phronesis*, on the other hand, is what is demanded of every human—not only those engaged in *theoria*. In spite of their different objects and ways of proceeding, there is nonetheless a basic harmony between the "theory" of philosophical hermeneutics and the "practice" of self-understanding more broadly construed. This leads Gadamer to insist that the "heightened theoretic awareness about the experience of understanding and the practice of understanding, like philosophical hermeneutics and one's own self-understanding, are inseparable" (Gadamer 1992c, 112). "Inseparable," however, does not mean reducible to the other but rather it means requiring the other. *Dasein's* understanding (the theme of philosophical hermeneutics) requires both *theoria* and *praxis*.

Phronesis and the Universality of Hermeneutical Consciousness

The way in which the foregoing analysis emphasizes the importance of maintaining a dialectic between *theoria* and *praxis* has relevance for resolving questions concerning the meaning of the universality of hermeneutical consciousness in general and, more specifically, the extent of the scope of Gadamer's notion of truth. In other words, the above discussion can be used to clarify how Gadamer construes the relation between truth and method. Is it, as some have claimed, that Gadamer opposes truth to method?[13] That is to ask, to what extent does Gadamer believe that the theoretical tendencies of method stand opposed to truth? While the earlier discussion made clear Gadamer's interest in reviving the inextricability of *theoria* and *praxis*, in what follows I will attempt to show the implications of this discussion for questions regarding the legitimacy of a "scientific" and "methodological" theory.

That Gadamer is not against method per se is seen in the following statement in his "Afterword" to *Truth and Method*: "No productive scientist can really doubt that methodological purity is indispensable in science; but what constitutes the essence of research is much less merely applying the usual methods than discovering new ones—and underlying that, the creative imagination of the scientist" (Gadamer 1992b, 551-2). It is inaccurate to assign to Gadamer the view that there is no truth in method or that there is never any appropriate use for method. Without decrying the illegitimacy of scientific truth, Gadamer's point is that the truth experienced in art cannot be reduced to methodological terms. That his insistence on a non-methodological truth is not evidence of a rejection of scientific truth per se is made clear in a later piece, "From Word to Concept," where he writes "the scientized historical method of understanding . . . should not be the only permissible approach. I fully believe and hope that here, and everywhere, a balance between both forms of knowledge is attainable, a balance that accepts both the scientific and the artistic sides" (Gadamer 2007, 116). Discussing the way in which both require measuring, although in different senses, he tells us that "one form of measuring is not more important than the other. Rather, both forms are important" (Gadamer 2007, 116).

Without wanting to diminish the contributions of scientific method to knowledge, Gadamer draws our attention to how scientific pursuits ultimately stem out of a basic desire to make what is unfamiliar familiar, and though removed from any practical aims, maintain their origin in the life-world. That this translates into a method unique to science, where the knowledge sought is unchangeable, relies on proof, and can be learnt by anyone, does nothing to dispel its origins. I contend that the esteem Gadamer gives to *theoria* can translate into an insistence on the legitimacy of such "scientific" and "methodological" pur-

---

13. See chapter 4 p. 75 for Ricoeur's iteration of this worry.

suits: both reflect a deep need within humanity. Gadamer's criticism of method is not meant to deny its efficacy but to insist on our being aware of its limitations. It is not only scientific method, though, that cannot tell us everything we want to know: in fact, all forms of theory (philosophy included) must take into account their origin and destiny in practice that reveals their finitude. For example, the need for grasping the limits of method is demonstrated by the caveat Gadamer issues both to science and to philosophy: "Thus it is essential that philosophical ethics have the right approach, so that it does not usurp the place of moral consciousness and yet does not seek a purely theoretical and 'historical' knowledge either but, by outlining phenomena, helps moral consciousness to attain clarity concerning itself" (Gadamer 1992b, 313). This quotation elucidates how the underlying assumption for Gadamer is not that method must be jettisoned altogether, but that it must be "entirely determined by the object" (Gadamer 1992b, 313). When we seek to know the part of reality governed solely by physical laws (i.e., nature) we will have a different approach than when we seek to know the part of reality where non-natural laws are at work (namely, human interactions). Thus the use of method itself requires *phronesis*—for there are different ways of knowing and we must discern where and when each is appropriate.

That it is in the context of his account of Aristotle's moral thought (Gadamer 1992b, 312-23) that we find Gadamer distinguishing amongst at least four types of knowledge is no coincidence. Gadamer speaks about: 1) purely theoretical/scientific/objective knowledge, 2) *techne*, 3) *Geisteswissenschaften*, knowledge of the human sciences (what in English encompasses both the humanities and social sciences), and 4) moral knowledge, in order to demonstrate that knowledge of the human sciences is more similar to moral knowledge than to scientific knowledge or *techne*. For, the human sciences and moral knowledge concern themselves with the way in which human beings are actors that give shape to their own laws and are not wholly determined by the physical realm— the object of study of the "purely theoretical" sciences. However, as the argument of *Truth and Method* goes, there is a legitimacy to speaking of truth in this "other" realm. Gadamer's analysis of *phronesis*, then, serves as the cornerstone in the book's intent to make a case for how truth occurs not just in the hard sciences but also in the human sciences. Both the *Geisteswissenschaften* and *phronesis* reflect the presence of choice in the realm of existence that is marked by freedom rather than determination. But, as the preceding sections have shown, this does not mean that *theoria* is necessarily a deformed or illegitimate form of knowledge.

To further tease out Gadamer's point about the legitimacy of different types of knowledge, it might be helpful to place them on a continuum that delineates different degrees of *praxis* and *theoria*. On the far left we could put methodological or scientific knowledge[14] followed to the right by *techne*, human scien-

---

14. It should be noted that Gadamer uses *"theoria"* and *"episteme"* interchangeably.

tific understanding, practical philosophy, and finally *phronesis*, on the far right. The crux of Gadamer's innovative argument that challenges modernity's reductive model of knowledge is that no point along this continuum of knowing escapes historical and social embeddedness or the need to begin from and return to practice. What differentiates the different modes of knowledge from each other are the ways in which each is marked to a greater or lesser extent by the dictate of physical laws and, conversely, by the need for reflective choice and application. Similarly, another way of describing the legitimacy of different types of knowledge, and that thus affirms the possibility of there being truth in method, is to recall the foregoing analysis of *techne* and its relation to *theoria*, as well as his account (discussed in chapter 2) of the relation between scientific and pre-scientific knowing. These accounts demonstrated that there is a legitimate desire for knowledge for knowledge's sake, pure theory, reflecting the desire of humans to overcome their estrangement. Yet, as we have seen, as finite, mortal beings, this is never attainable absolutely. It is something towards which we strive, requiring a degree of bracketing of immediate needs, distinguishing it from pre-scientific knowledge. Gadamer's account of knowledge reveals a continuum of knowing, where all knowing is marked by a prior ethos but some knowledge makes sense extracted from this ethos and other knowledge does not. To put it in Gadamer's own terms: some knowledge is more defined by becoming than being. That moral knowledge and hermeneutical knowledge are both marked to a greater extent by the former (Gadamer 1992b, 312) does not render methodological or scientific theory effete. We could say that while even theoretical mathematics ultimately originates out from the life-world, there is a legitimacy to its goal of attempting to transcend it. And thus we could describe *Truth and Method*'s aim as showing how truth ranges along the entire continuum that comprises both theoretical and practical knowledge.

Gadamer, then, following Plato and Aristotle, affirms the productive tension between being embedded in a world and desiring to transcend it that marks human beings. When Gadamer writes: "Aristotle sees ethos as differing from physis in being a sphere in which the laws of nature do not operate, yet not a sphere of lawlessness but of human institutions and human modes of behavior which are mutable, and like rules only to a limited degree" (Gadamer 1992b, 312), we see expressed the condition of human beings: not governed solely by laws of nature but nonetheless needing laws. Yet the best laws we can give are always changing on account of our changing practices. The dialectic between moral laws and moral practices affirms the need both for transcending one's situation and for interpreting from within it.

However, it is important to note that when Gadamer writes that "hermeneutical consciousness is involved neither with technical nor moral knowledge" (Gadamer 1992b, 315) he means that hermeneutics' purpose is not to "determine and guide action" (Gadamer 1992b, 315), even though all types of knowledge are linked by "*the same task of application*" (Gadamer 1992b, 315). For, the sense in which Gadamer uses "application" is to be distinguished from modernity's impoverished understanding of this term. Here, "application" refers to the way in which understanding is always embedded in practical concerns. Gadamer tells us that Aristotle's treatment of moral knowledge "offers a kind of *model of the problems of hermeneutics*. We too determined that application is neither a subsequent nor merely an occasional part of the phenomenon of understanding, but codetermines it as a whole from the beginning. Here too application did not consist in relating some pregiven universal to the particular situation" (Gadamer 1992b, 324). It is not that we "apply" an a priori set of rules to a situation; rather application means possessing the know-how that allows one to choose properly. In other words, while Gadamer goes on to express in what way moral knowledge differs from technical and theoretical knowledge, we can understand his main point of emphasis to be that what binds all three types of knowledge together is their common origin in the life-world. That is to say, there is a moment in all three that reflects the conditionedness of knowing. But at the same time, to pursue knowledge means to possess the desire to transcend such conditionedness: hence the universality of hermeneutical consciousness.

A final way to address the question of the universality of hermeneutical consciousness that nonetheless admits of the legitimacy and uniqueness of *theoria* is to attend to his account of Aristotle's relation to natural law. Reflecting on Aristotle Gadamer notes: "Certainly he accepts the idea of an absolutely unchangeable law, but he limits it explicitly to the gods and says that among men not only statutory law but also natural law is changeable" (Gadamer 1992b, 319). In other words, Gadamer does not rule out the existence of an unchangeable law which is only accessible to the gods; nor does he denigrate the relevance of such a law for humans, for, the human condition remains marked by a desire for a purity of knowledge, characterized by *theoria*. Yet, when it comes down to it, humans in their finitude can only make sense of a changeable natural law. This would seem to accord with Gadamer's point about the importance of the difference between the divine and human for both Plato and Aristotle, and how the failure to acknowledge such a difference was one of the sources of misreadings of both ancient thinkers. Gadamer reads Aristotle as maintaining that "the idea of the natural law has only a critical function. No dogmatic use can be made of it—i.e., we cannot invest particular laws with the dignity and inviolability of natural law" (Gadamer 1992b, 320). The "critical function" Gadamer finds in Aristotle's use of natural law maps on to the way in which Gadamer interprets Plato's use of the good and its critical role in all understanding. There is legitimacy in speaking of the transcendent without requiring that it be conceptually transparent.[15] We cannot maintain: "This is the good/natural law therefore all must abide by it." For, there is no particular law that can be named as *the* natural law. To do so would be to attempt a full articulation of, and thus subject to being, what is beyond being.

---

15. This claim will be taken up in the latter half of chapter 5.

The above discussion of the role and meaning of application in knowing has further implications in terms of debates over essentialism and realism in Gadamer's thought. Appeals to essentialism and/or realism traditionally have been made in order to provide constraint on what we may believe. The appeal to "the way the world really is," for example, has been taken by the dominant part of the western philosophical tradition to serve as the criterion for truth. Yet to make this move is to assume that we can first know the way the world really is, and then "apply" this knowledge as a criterion against which to measure other beliefs. But, as the above discussion has made clear, this is decidedly not Gadamer's point, and reflects the bifurcation between theory and practice he rejects. Rather, he insists that "the nature of the thing" is not "a fixed standard that we could recognize and apply by ourselves." Nor does it refer to "guiding principles" but is "valid only as schemata. They are concretized only in the concrete situation of the person acting" (Gadamer 1992b, 320). Any standard that may ensue from our action can always and only be a posteriori and therefore can never serve as our guide. The point is that even sophisticated charges of realism, such as Wachterhauser's "perspectival realism,"[16] make no sense once we drop the fundamental requirement of realism, namely its function as an epistemic constraint. Truth, on Gadamer's hermeneutical account, cannot be defined as a criterion. Whether we refer to the true nature of things as "schemata" or as the "natural law" known only to the gods, I think the consistent way to interpret Gadamer's meaning here is metaphorically. That is to say, in the process of understanding we evoke a necessary assumption that can never be named, for Gadamer insists that the natural law cannot exist apart from our activity of trying to understand it. To want a comprehensive, a priori account of it is to forget that Gadamer is making a point about hermeneutical understanding when he writes: "There can be no anterior certainty concerning what the good life is directed towards as a whole" (Gadamer 1992, 321). Gadamer's desire to follow Plato in naming the good as that which transcends and enables understanding will be discussed more fully in chapter 5.

In the meantime, the next chapter expands the discussion of hermeneutics' dialectic to Gadamer's notion of truth. Specifically, the tension between the withdrawal inherent in *theoria* and its connectedness to the embeddedness of *praxis* will be mapped onto similar moments in the event of truth, which will be shown to comprise moments of both distance and familiarity, respectively.

---

16. See the discussion in chapter 1, pp. 3-4.

Chapter 4
Truth's Dialectic

The preceding chapter presented one way in which Gadamer's hermeneutics demonstrates a dialectic inherited from Plato and Aristotle, namely, that between *theoria* and *praxis*. This chapter furthers the argument for the dialectical nature of Gadamer's hermeneutics by extending it to his notion of truth. How does the in-betweenness characterizing hermeneutics contribute to our understanding of a Gadamerian notion of truth?

Certainly assessing exactly what Gadamer means by truth is no easy feat since Gadamer gives no explicit definition of truth in *Truth and Method*.[1] But let our inquiry begin with the stated aim of *Truth and Method*: namely, to work out "how is understanding possible" where "understanding" refers "to all human experience of the world and human living" (Gadamer 1992b, xxx). When we take this general orientation to guide us in our grasp of his conception of truth, we find that the whole book, as an explication of understanding, is an explication of truth. That is to say, when we put the question to Gadamer, "What is truth?", we can reply with a general answer: "the event of understanding." Gadamer suggests as much when he writes: "In understanding we are drawn into an event of truth" (Gadamer 1992b, 490).[2] And Rudolf Bernet affirms: "The game of understanding and the game of truth are . . . for Gadamer one and the same game" (Bernet 2005, 793). In other words, critics who charge that since there is no explicit definition of truth in *Truth and Method* there must be no

---

1. See, for example, Bernstein 1983, 151-2; Dostal 1987; and Grondin 1982 where such a claim is made.
2. Indeed, this claim would also accord with the fact that the original title of Wahrheit und Methode was to be Verstehen und Geschehen.

definition at all seem to forget the forest for the trees. For, the whole book is an attempt to define truth in terms of its basic structure as that which is indeed "common to all modes of understanding"—whether scientific, moral, or human.

In other words, reworking our expectations for what truth means can lead to increased clarity about the dialectical nature of understanding. For, defining truth in terms of understanding reveals the continual nature of both, suggesting that truth is not the trophy awarded to the clearest and most distinct idea, but is more like the ongoing nature of a game. Taking seriously Gadamer's Platonic leanings helps us see truth not as something to be predicated of ideas, but as something that humans engage in, as, for example, with dialogue.[3] "Event" thus comes to replace "method" as the defining mark of truth. (But, as discussed in the previous chapter as well as below, this is not to say that Gadamer rejects method as a form of knowledge.)

In what follows, the event-like nature of truth will be demonstrated to comprise both the movement away from the particularities of the self toward the other and the subsequent movement of the return to self—what Gadamer terms "*Heimkehr*" (Gadamer 1992b, 448). Describing the event of truth as a dialectical movement between the familiar and the distant recalls the role of the *chorismos* in Platonic dialectic; it also echoes the productive movement of the hermeneutical circle: namely, the continual movement between part and whole. Finally, Gadamer's account of truth will emerge as dialectically ethical to the extent to which it both incorporates the chorismatic tension between distance and nearness and requires attention to our comportment towards another.

If it seems surprising to talk about a hermeneutical conception of truth by relying on a concept of self, then we need only heed Gadamer's statement that "all understanding is self-understanding." In fact, recalling Gadamer's claim will also extend a bridge between his writings on Plato and Aristotle and his more explicitly hermeneutical writings. This is not to say, of course, that there was anything like a conception of self for Plato and Aristotle. Rather, when Gadamer uses "self" he is highlighting the extent to which when we understand something we always understand it anew—what the discussion in the previous chapter referred to as the practical moment of application. For example, Gadamer tells us: "For the hermeneutic process involves not only the moments of understanding and of interpretation but also the moment of application; that is to say, understanding oneself in a part of this process. . . . I mean that it is to be applied to oneself" (Gadamer 2001, 37-38). That all understanding must be taken up by the individual understander and be put in his or her "own words," so to speak, highlights the role of the self in understanding, and provides a corrective to the Cartesian commitment to "pure method" that saw the self—i.e., the socio-historical component of the I—as a liability for knowledge. On that model, truth could only be attained where the particularities of self are restricted,

---

3. The common pursuit of truth will be further explicated in terms of dialogue in the first part of chapter 5.

indeed, eradicated. The self became a stumbling block for those seeking after truth. Hermeneutics, on the other hand, reveals the necessity of the self for understanding, and thus for truth. Perhaps one could even go so far as to say that the self is the paragon prejudice: the ultimate prejudice that productively undergirds all attempts at understanding, one from which we can never escape and yet must always struggle to work out. Hermeneutics, therefore, seeks to avoid the "misautic" commitments of Cartesian rationalism.

But how does the dialectical account of truth developed in this chapter pertain to our common understanding of truth as correspondence? For example, how might such an account aid us in our quest to find out the truth of statements such as: "did Gadamer really live to be one hundred and two years old?" Given Gadamer's fundamental interest in clarifying the sort of conditions that make human understanding possible, I do not think he was speaking to our commonsense use of truth as correspondence at all. He was not interested in answering how individual sentences—either on a practical or theoretical level—could be true. He was aiming at a more fundamental level where truth reflects not criteria but a process, a process dependent upon the fact that "language has its true being only in dialogue, in *coming to an understanding*" (Gadamer 1992b, 446). Yet he goes on to warn us that we should not infer from this statement that language is a tool to be used for the sake of understanding: "This is not to be understood as if that were the purpose of language. . . . For language . . . fully realizes itself only in the process of coming to an understanding. That is why it is not a mere means in that process" (Gadamer 1992b, 446). Gadamer was interested in exposing language as the ground of our being and resituating truth in this context, as it were. Putting it another way we could say that Gadamer thought philosophy had nothing interesting to say about how our commonsense use of truth functions. For in this case, the sufficiency and adequacy of criteria is a purely practical matter. How do I assess the truth of the claim that Gadamer lived to be one hundred and two years old? I check biographies, newspapers, etc. There is nothing philosophically noteworthy here. What is of interest to Gadamer is the event of truth that underlies and makes possible our everyday experience of truth-as-correspondence. To put it in "Heideggerese, " perhaps we could say that Gadamer was concerned that our obsession with "truths" (i.e., a property of propositions) occludes our more appropriate task to understand "Truth" (i.e., defined as an event).

That Gadamer was critical of theoretical attempts to formalize such notions, e.g., theories of correspondence or coherence, is a different matter, however. Yet I do not read him as critical of such efforts per se, but only of the possible hubris entailed thereby. Below I will confront with more detail attempts to align Gadamer's account of truth with such formalized efforts. Suffice it to say here, though, that his main focus of criticism was not the formalization of such theories per se but attempts to grasp an "absolute criterion for truth" which would render us divine (Gadamer 2004, 46). A Gadamerian conception of truth thus refuses criterial status due to the fundamental nature of our being: we are not gods. Thus his criticism is aimed neither at our practical, commonsense use of correspondence nor at all efforts to formalize such a process. Rather, his target is formal accounts that deny the processes underlying them and that thereby reduce truth to an outcome. In other words, Gadamer attempts to expose what makes possible both our commonsense use of correspondence and formalized versions of the same: namely, the event-like character of understanding.

Conceiving of truth dialectically not only provides a coherence to Gadamer's evocative writings on truth and his account of understanding, but also helps us avoid the false dichotomy into which many interpretations of Gadamer's notion of truth fall. On one hand, there are those who, in defending Gadamer's account of truth, attempt to align it with realism or essentialism.[4] On the other hand, there are those who are more critical of Gadamer's account of truth and point out that his challenge to method implies a disdain for any sort of distantiation or critical reflection thus yielding an inherent conservatism.[5] I find both of these positions untenable since they obfuscate how Gadamer ultimately conceives the relation between truth and method.

The first position downplays (albeit unintentionally in some instances) the extent to which Gadamer wants to distinguish his project from a modern epistemological one that defines truth as a criterion. Linda Alcoff, for example, maintains that "Gadamer's philosophical hermeneutics is actually a theory of knowledge, . . . his epistemology is coherentist on both justification and truth . . ." (Alcoff 1996, 19). Throughout she speaks of coherence as the "criterion of justification that will be used to evaluate an interpretation . . ." (Alcoff 1996, 47). But in their laudatory attempt to both extend hermeneutical truth to method and to insist on the viability of knowledge in the realm of art and other forms of human experience, such theorists end up unwittingly defining truth too much in terms of "method" and the epistemological tradition from which it arises. By expanding truth's realm, they do not do enough to distinguish it from its modern use as a criterion for determining what we should believe. They thus attempt to read Gadamer's work too much in light of an aim with which he is not concerned: namely, defending truth as a criterion for determining what we should believe. Gadamer insists that "if we want to know what we are supposed to believe" we "arrive too late" (Gadamer 1992b, 490). Approaching truth dialectically better positions us for seeing how Gadamer not only refuses to go along with the Cartesian quest (i.e., the search for what is indubitable), he also refuses to take up its tools (i.e., the use of an objective standard to determine what counts as knowledge).[6]

4. See Alcoff 1996, Schmidt 1996, and Wachterhauser 1999.

5. See, for example, Bernstein 1983, 1986; Habermas 1986; Honneth 2003; and Ricoeur 1986, 1991. I discuss these criticisms in more detail in chapter 5.

6. This is most explicitly true for Alcoff (1996) who wants to align Gadamer's "theory of truth" with a coherentist theory like that of Davidson and implicitly so for Wachterhauser (1994, 1999). While Wachterhauser would certainly affirm Gadamer's refusal to go along with the Cartesian quest, my point is that Wachterhauser's interpretation

If the first group of commentators attempts to read Gadamer's notion of truth too much in light of what it has in common with method, the second type of criticism comes from those who read Gadamer as going too far in the other direction: namely, dispensing with any need for method at all. Accusations along these lines maintain that he has purged his hermeneutics of any and all degree of distance afforded by method. For example, Paul Ricoeur asks: "The question is to what extent the work deserves to be called *Truth AND Method*, and whether it ought not to be entitled instead *Truth OR Method*." (Ricoeur 1991, 71). Ricoeur goes on to explain: "Whence the alternative underlying the very title of Gadamer's work *Truth and Method*: either we adopt the methodological attitude and lose the ontological density of the reality we study, or we adopt the attitude of truth and must then renounce the objectivity of the human sciences" (Ricoeur 1991, 75). Gianni Vattimo puts the challenge in this way: "Every reader of *Truth and Method*, and perhaps also of Gadamer's later works, will know that it is not clear how far Gadamer intends, in that work to claim the capacity for truth *also* for the human sciences founded upon interpretation, or whether he wishes to propose this 'model' of truth as valid in general for every experience of truth, and thus for the experimental sciences, too" (Vattimo 1997, 78). Critics such as Ricoeur and Vattimo express concerns regarding the exact nature of the relationship between truth and method. Ricoeur fears that by elevating "truth" over "method" Gadamer renders critique (i.e., distance) impossible. The result of privileging the embeddedness of the life-world over a theoretical examination of the same precludes the very possibility for critique. Vattimo's related concern is whether Gadamer's hermeneutical "model" of truth remains applicable for the natural sciences or is exclusive to the human sciences. To ask about whether there is one truth or two truths underlying the human and natural sciences is to ask about truth's relation to method and the legitimacy of distantiation for understanding.

This chapter affirms the conjunctive intent of the title by arguing that those who take Gadamer to be opposing truth to method, averring either that method has no truth to it or that truth never has any method to it, neglect Gadamer's desire to uncover "what is common to all modes of understanding" (Gadamer 1992b, xxxi): namely, the event of truth that is marked by a dialectic between distantiation and embeddedness.

In what follows, I will demonstrate how Gadamer's concepts of *Bildung*, *sensus communis*, taste, experience, play, and transformation into structure reveal an inherent ongoing dialectical movement away from the particularities of the self toward the other/universal, followed by a return to self. Gadamer's interest in these notions prepares the way for thinking about a conception of truth that remains irreducible to scientific method and elucidates what is peculiar about such "non-scientific" ways of knowing. My analysis of these concepts will

---

does rely on its tools. See chapter 1 for my account of how Wachterhauser's account relies on epistemological assumptions.

focus on the way in which each conveys a dual movement of withdrawal (away from the particularities of the self to the universal/other) and return (to the self) that comprises what I am calling the dialectical movement of truth. It is an attempt to describe truth in light of the following statement by Gadamer: "The state of being completely involved in something, of seeing it, intending it and thinking it, is necessarily presupposed if there is to be any possibility of 'returning' to oneself" (Gadamer 1996a, 134).

Truth and the "Guiding Concepts of Humanism"

Beginning with the eighteenth century concept *"Bildung,"* originally signifying culture or the cultivated person, Gadamer describes how it comes to reflect a motif central to the ancient mystical tradition: *"The concept of self-formation, education, or cultivation* (Bildung) . . . evokes the ancient mystical tradition according to which man carries in his soul the image of God, after whom he is fashioned, and which man must cultivate in himself" (Gadamer 1992b, 9, 11).[7] What is the nature of such "cultivation"? Noting that the Latin for *Bildung* is *formatio*, Gadamer helps us see how "formation" does not mean an *ex nihilo* creation, but requires an image or picture (*Bild*) of something other. In and through *Bildung* the self is to be con-formed to the other (in the ancient tradition referred to here as "God"); there is no unbounded, free-form creation of the self. At the same time, it is not a mere copying of this other (where one simply represents (*darstellen*) what is there) but a recognition (*Wiedererkennung*) that yields a living and expansive form-ation. Recognition, for Gadamer, implies more than simply seeing again what one already has seen before; recognition implies an element of knowledge. Here we could think of Aristotle's concept of *techne* and the role he assigned to memory in terms of recreating. To remember does not mean to locate a static original but to produce in a new way. In the same way, *Bildung* does not entail re-presenting oneself as an exact replica of this other. Rather, keeping in mind the religious tradition invoked, to be con-formed to another means being able to be with another, and one cannot be with another if one becomes the other. Being with another suggests listening to, knowing, and encountering the other in such a way as to allow one's self to be changed but not eradicated by such an experience.

The con-formity of oneself to another that occurs through *Bildung* produces a transformation. The importance of *Bildung* for Gadamer's account is how such a transformation requires the ability to transcend the immediate and present circumstances by means of the universal. Gadamer writes: "Bildung, as a rising to the universal, is a task for man. It requires sacrificing particularity for the sake of the universal. But, negatively put, sacrificing particularity means the restraint of desire and hence freedom from the object of desire and freedom for its objec-

---

7. For an historical analysis of Gadamer's use of Bildung see Davey 2007.

tivity" (Gadamer 1992b, 12). *Bildung* thus conveys the necessity of rising above the particularity of one's own desires, needs, interests, etc., and the movement toward the universal implies the ability to "know how to limit oneself" (Gadamer 1992b, 13). (Note that the goal is not to eliminate oneself but to limit oneself.) The limitation resulting from the attempt at universality implies a rising above one's own particularity (which, as will be developed below, means that one rises above one's own standpoint in order to find what one has in common with another). The mark of *Bildung* is a "receptivity to the 'otherness'" and "keeping oneself open to what is other—to other, more universal points of view. It embraces a sense of proportion and distance in relation to itself, and hence consists in rising above itself to universality" (Gadamer 1992b, 17). It is this movement away from the particularities of the self by means of the universal that reflects the first part of the movement in the dialectic of truth. Yet it is important to note what Gadamer means by "universal" here: "This universality is by no means a universality of the concept or understanding" (Gadamer 1992b, 17). In other words, while one often does associate the term "universal" with what is abstract or conceptual, it is crucial to acknowledge how Gadamer insists that through the universal we are connected to what is other, fostering a deepened understanding. The move toward the universal, away from our parochial self, is primarily a move that unites us to others rather than drawing us away from them. Such an emphasis can be seen by Gadamer's choice of word for "universal": namely, "*allgemein*." "*Allgemein*" is more suggestive of that which is common and general than that which is transcendent, as reflected by the German "*Universalität*." Thus the movement away from ourselves is always understood in the humanistic tradition as a move outward toward others and not upwards towards a heavenly realm. Furthermore, as a cultivated sense (i.e., arising out of culture) it is not an a priori sense but one that is held in common:

> Thus the cultivated consciousness has in fact more the character of a sense. For every sense—e.g., the sense of sight—is already universal in that it embraces its sphere, remains open to a particular field, and grasps the distinctions within what is opened to it in this way. In that such distinctions are confined to one particular sphere at a time, whereas cultivated consciousness is active in all directions, such consciousness surpasses all of the natural sciences. It is a *universal sense*. (Gadamer 1992b, 17)[8]

But the movement toward the universal is only the first part of the movement. We must also make the return. Gadamer writes: "To recognize one's own in the alien, to become at home in it, is the basic movement of spirit, whose being consists only in returning to itself from what is other. . . . Thus what constitutes the essence of Bildung is clearly not alienation as such, but the return to

---

8. The German is more direct here: "Das gebildete Bewusstein übertrifft nur jeden der natürlichen Sinne, als dies je auf eine bestimmte Sphäre eingeschränkt sind. Es selbst betätigt sich in allen Richtungen. Es is ein allgemeiner Sinn" (Gadamer 1990, 23).

oneself—which presupposes alienation, to be sure" (Gadamer 1992b, 14). The significance of what is meant by "return" is further made clear in Gadamer's claim that "in Bildung . . . that by which and through which one is formed becomes completely one's own" (Gadamer 1992b, 11). The point of *Bildung* is not to remain alienated or distanced from oneself but to cultivate what one has gained in the maneuver of withdrawing so that one can subsequently make the return. Gadamer also describes this process of return as one of preservation, safe keeping, *Aufbewahrung*. *Bildung* thus elucidates the dual movement of both withdrawal, which draws one away from oneself, and return, marked by immanence that is a preservation, thus reflecting the dialectic of truth.

Gadamer's discussion of Vico's notion of *sensus communis* also contributes to our understanding of the dialectic of truth. For it not only provides further insight into the way in which "universal" is meant, but it also aids us in making sense of the role of the self. For, *sensus communis* refers to the sense upon which community or shared existence is built: "The main thing for our purposes is that here sensus communis obviously does not mean only that general faculty in all men but the sense that founds community" (Gadamer 1992b, 21). *Sensus communis*, as that which develops or founds the community, and as such develops and grows along with the community, is more than merely a completed or innate sense that is there in each individual qua individual. *Sensus communis* implies a "concrete universality represented by the community of a group, a people, a nation, or the whole human race" (Gadamer 1992b, 21). Gadamer notes how for the humanist tradition the appeal to *sensus communis* contributed to their practice of education, where education reflects not facts and method but the ability to integrate the universality of community with individual responsibility. The appeal to *sensus communis*, then, is made not only to foster an individual's movement away from herself toward the concrete universal, it also requires a return to the particulars of one's situation in which one must discern what is true and right. This way of integrating the universal with particular, Gadamer tells us, ties the eighteenth century German notion of *sensus communis* to the notion of judgment, which, as an ability to subsume a particular under a universal, cannot be taught, but is more like a sense. My interest in rehearsing these details is to note how the individual's ability to make a decision based on the "sense of the common" (Gadamer 1992b, 32) reflects the dialectical tension between universal and particular to the extent that knowledge implies the ability both to transcend one's immediate proclivities and to exercise practical choice. Judgment is not something that can be taught in a theoretical or abstract way, rather, it is more like a sense: "It is something that cannot be learned, because no demonstration from concepts can guide the application of rules" (Gadamer 1992b, 31). And he goes on to note how both German terms "*Gesunder Menshenverstand*" (good sense) and "*gemeiner Verstand*" (common understanding) are connected to judgment. Judgment does not consist in the mimicking of another but in the ability to balance the far and near, other and self, universal and particular. Although judgment reflects what is held in common, Gadamer comments that "the universality (Allgemenheit) that is ascribed to the faculty of judgment is by no means as common (gemein) as Kant thinks. Judgment is not so much a faculty as a demand that has to be made of all" (Gadamer 1992b, 32). Kant, however, strips judgment of all its moral sense, severing its connection to *sensus communis*. As a result, *sensus communis* gets narrowed to taste, which, as Gadamer tells us that Balthasar Gracian pointed out, was not only the most immediate and primal of senses but it also had a spiritual sense that balanced the sensory and intellectual. Taste not only connoted the immediacy of a sense ("Taste is therefore something like a sense. In its operation it has no knowledge of reasons" (Gadamer 1992b, 36)), it also refers to that which can be cultivated in order to allow one to gain the distance necessary to make a good judgment. Gracian's "ideal of the cultivated man (the discreto) is that, as an '*hombre en su punto*,' he achieves the proper freedom of distance from all the things of life and society, so that he is able to make distinctions and choices consciously and reflectively" (Gadamer 1992b, 35). Taste requires looking beyond the influences of one's immediate community and society; the person of taste is one who can distance herself from her own, immediate, private preferences. Taste echoes the communal concerns—for there is no such thing as one's own "private taste"— and in this way shifts the focus away from our particular and situated judgment toward the whole of society. Gadamer's account of taste, then, helps us see that the significance of the universal is not to escape to a transcendent realm; the appeal to the common, the reliance on taste, unites the individual with the common.

My point has been to show how in all of these concepts central to Gadamer's account of a knowledge that is peculiar to the human sciences there is an emphasis on the movement away from the self towards the universal, followed by a return. Gadamer's interest in these concepts of the humanist tradition is meant to show how there is a legitimacy to speaking of truth in the realm of human experience that can never be adequately captured by method, i.e., the attempt to objectify and quantify such experience. Refusing to define truth solely in terms of objectivity is not to deprive the realm of human experience of truth. Rather, what the humanistic tradition teaches us is that there is a validity to affirming both the importance of starting with the individual's embedded experience in the life-world and the attempt to transcend the limitations of the self. To say that we can never get away from the prejudicial and socio-historical nature of the self is not to belittle the need to look beyond ourselves to what is other, universal. It is Gadamer's acknowledgment of the legitimacy of both these tendencies that I take as undergirding his notion of truth. My claim is that all of these examples help us see what is common to all modes of understanding: namely, the dialectic of truth. Yet, since Gadamer himself says nothing explicitly about truth in these contexts, I now turn to consider Gadamer's more explicit claims about truth in order to show how they correlate with his conception of understanding.

Experience: From *Erlebnis* to *Erfahrung*

According to Gadamer, the culprit who narrowed down truth to the realm of the conceptual, where truth ultimately becomes only the result of scientific method, was Kant.[9] Aesthetic taste thus became purely subjective and knowledge was restricted to the sphere of the conceptual. Gadamer writes, "The radical subjectivization involved in Kant's new way of grounding aesthetics was truly epoch-making. In discrediting any kind of theoretical knowledge except that of natural science, it compelled the human sciences to rely on the methodology of the natural sciences in conceptualizing themselves" (Gadamer 1992b, 41). Gadamer challenges the assumption that truth pertains only to conceptual knowledge and attempts to recover the possibility of truth in non-conceptual realms. His more specific move is then to re-introduce the possibility of truth for art, which he does by tracing the history of the word "experience" from "*Erlebnis*" to "*Erfahrung*." He aims to show the possibility of a knowledge that is not conceptual. I will not rehearse his account of the history of these terms; instead I will focus on Gadamer's claim about one type of experience in particular, namely, aesthetic experience, which serves as the paradigm of experience in general. For, if we can recover truth for aesthetic experience, Gadamer assumed, we will be closer to recovering it for human experience in general. As Gadamer tells us: "at the end of our conceptual analysis of experience we can see the affinity between the structure of Erlebnis as such and the mode of being of the aesthetic. Aesthetic experience is not just one kind of experience among others, but represents the essence of experience per se" (Gadamer 1992b, 70). The reason why aesthetic experience "represents the essence of experience per se" is that it requires both a withdrawal from the ordinary context of one's life and a return to the particularities of one's life. Commenting on how it is that the movements of both withdrawal and return are reflected in *aesthetic* experience, Gadamer writes: "The power of the work of art suddenly tears the person experiencing it out of the context of his life, and yet relates him back to the whole of his existence" (Gadamer 1992b, 70). Note the dialectical movement required by *Erlebniskunst*: the removing of oneself from the immediacy of experience and the subsequent return to a fuller conception of the "whole of [one's] existence." The flight from the immediacy of one's life, which at the same time requires a relating back of that withdrawal to one's own life, suggests the dialectic of truth.

Understanding the nature of truth in terms of its dialectical movement also helps provide an account of what happens when truth does not occur, which any conception of truth needs. Where truth is conceived as the ongoing movement between distance and embeddedness, failure can take place in either one of two ways. The first way corresponds to what Gadamer calls the "aesthetic stance" or "aesthetic consciousness," and occurs when there is too much emphasis placed

---

9. For a reading of Gadamer's complicated relation to Kant see Gjesdal 2007.

on the first part of the movement, the withdrawal. The result is an "excess of distance" thwarting any subsequent return. We could say, then, that when this excess of distance occludes the second part of the movement, i.e., the return to self, understanding, and thus, truth, fails. Gadamer describes the dangers of the excesses of aesthetic consciousness that pays heed only to the transcendent move:

> Here the actual process of cultivation—i.e., the elevation to the universal—is, as it were, disintegrated in itself. "The readiness of intellectual reflection to move in generalities, to consider anything at all from whatever point of view it adopts, and thus to clothe it with ideas" is, according to Hegel, the way not to get involved with the real content of ideas. Immermann calls this free self-overflowing of the spirit within itself "extravagantly self-indulgent." (Gadamer 1992b, 88)

As an example of aesthetic consciousness, Gadamer points to Schiller's attempt to abstract the work of art from its religious, moral, or practical context, thus eliminating any access to its function, content or matter. The concept of a work of art sundered from the life-world that gave it birth also feeds into the idea of the free artist, the one whose essence demands her to forsake claims of commissions, themes, occasions, etc., indeed any response[ibility] to others.

In a similar vein, Gadamer details how striving after such a free-floating experience leads to "hermeneutic nihilism," where any interpretation is deemed as good as any other and there is "no criterion of appropriate reaction" (Gadamer 1992b, 94). In other words, against those like Paul Valery who insisted that there are no standards for assessing a work of art and that all interpretations are legitimate, Gadamer maintains that it is precisely our ability to see the work "as" something that infuses it with meaning by delimiting interpretation. Viewing a work of art in such a way that sees it "as" something provides grounds for distinguishing legitimate from illegitimate interpretations. For, seeing a work as one thing means we do not see it as another and enables us to rule out certain interpretations. But the criteria for determining legitimate interpretations cannot be accessed prior to the experience itself; it is not accessible in advance and therefore refuses epistemological demands. Furthermore, standing at a distance from the interpretive context will never allow us to see the work "as" something. As Heidegger demonstrated, the as-structure is dependent upon a world; Gadamer's point is that legitimate interpretations will always be based on our embeddedness within a world, a tradition. We are not isolated monads floating above history and community, but persons influenced by our tradition and connected to other persons via our very questioning. In order to avoid aesthetic consciousness and its excesses as found in "hermeneutic nihilism," then, we must acknowledge the rootedness of the self in its socio-historical tradition.

Yet to emphasize rootedness to the exclusion of all else suggests a second way that truth can fail, namely, when it focuses too much on the return to self without having successfully completed the withdrawal. For example, those who attach a degree of conservatism to Gadamer maintain that Gadamer endorses tradition as a normative force.[10] But what such positions have failed to see, and what conceiving truth dialectically reveals, is that embeddedness is only one part of understanding: there also must be a movement of distancing from self and an opening to the other. When we focus only on our embeddedness, without being open to what lies beyond the immediacy of our experience, we do not experience truth. The importance of the move away from self to other can also be seen in Gadamer's account of self-understanding. Gadamer has said that all understanding is self-understanding and that "[s]elf-understanding always occurs through understanding something other than the self, and includes the unity and integrity of the other" (Gadamer 1992b, 97). Self-understanding thus means not a uni-directional act of understanding that has as its sole object the self. Self-understanding is not adequately characterized in terms of focusing only on oneself but requires an openness to encountering "the unity and integrity of the other." Understanding that has as its sole focus the self would be senseless in Gadamer's account, for all understanding requires a claim made on us that initiates a move away from self toward what is other.[11]

The dialectical tension also is evident in Gadamer's discussion of *Erfahrung der Kunst*, the "true" experience of art, which Gadamer appeals to in order to oppose the shortcomings of aesthetic consciousness. Whereas the excess of aesthetic consciousness was made possible by a distortion of *Erlebniskunst*, Gadamer shows how in *Erfahrung der Kunst* truth implies a change for the one who encounters it. That is to say, "*Erfahrung*," as the richer sense of experience, occurs when we open ourselves to a claim, allowing ourselves to "be claimed." "Being claimed" by a work of art contrasts with the ability to reduce the meaning of an artwork to a conceptual "claim." For only the former never "leave[s] him who has it unchanged" (Gadamer 1992b, 100). In being claimed we are drawn beyond and out of ourselves but also must return to ourselves and understand for ourselves (i.e., engage in application). Without such a return to self, one might say that the claim enacts an abduction (taking us away from ourselves, de-contextualizing us) not a production, where only the latter defines the creative application necessary for true understanding. For, production requires that we put something in our own words and in so doing we neither merely paraphrase nor subvert a given meaning but create a new one.

The culmination of Gadamer's account of true experience occurs in his discussion of transformation into structure: i.e., the transformation of play into a work of art, which Gadamer refers to as "transformation into the true. " Let me draw attention to the two components required by Gadamer's notion of transformation into the true that suggest the dialectic of truth. First, there is the loss of intentionality, as illustrated by play, which corresponds to the withdrawal

10. See, for example, Caputo 1987, 2000; Lafont 1999 (whom I discuss below); and (albeit to a lesser degree) Warnke 1987.

11. For more on Gadamer's discussion of the "claim" see the section, "Truth's Dialectic between the Other and the Familiar," below.

from the self to the universal that leads to the encounter with the other. Second, there is the moment of self-recognition, requiring the creative act of application, which corresponds to the return to self. The following section provides a closer look at each of these moments.

Transformation into Truth

Gadamer uses his analysis of play to lead into a discussion of how truth can be conceived in art. Given the adequacy of the literature, I will not rehearse in detail Gadamer's account of play.[12] What is important for our purposes is the general sense of play that expresses (following Heidegger[13]) how we are caught up in the world in a way that surpasses our own intentional willing and knowing, and that draws us away, out of ourselves, so to speak. To the extent to which play draws us out of and away from ourselves, it expresses the first part of the movement. As Gadamer is fond of saying: play plays us and in so doing takes us out of ourselves: "Play draws [the player] into its dominion and fills him with its spirit. The player experiences the game as a reality that surpasses him" (Gadamer 1992b, 109). However, two caveats are necessary at this juncture. First, as will be argued below, this does not make play equivalent with truth, for it is not yet transformed into structure, which reflects the second part of the movement, the return. Second, it is important to emphasize here that the experience of being drawn out of ourselves does not mean that we transcend our historical conditionedness altogether. In order to avoid a one-sided reading of Gadamer, a distinction must be made between the fecund necessity of our historical conditionedness—which can never be transcended—and the particular limitations of oneself—which we can aim to transcend. Thus the importance of play for a model of truth is its ability to draw us out of ourselves, meaning away from the local perspective, i.e., away from ourselves, but not out of our historical situatedness. Play is marked by the ability to lose oneself, to relinquish control, and to get caught up in something bigger than oneself. That this is not all there is to truth is seen in Gadamer's insistence that truth occurs in the transformation of play into structure.

The importance of the connection between play and art in Gadamer's narrative, then, is the way in which the former comes to be transformed into the latter. Gadamer describes how the movement of play, characterized by the lack of subjective intentions, is transformed into art once appearance takes over and this playful structure stands on its own apart from the players. "I call this change, in which human play comes to its true consummation in being art, *transformation into structure*" (Gadamer 1992b, 110). The key to such transformation lies in the

---

12. See, for example, Weinsheimer 1985.

13. For a reading of Heidegger's notion of truth as dialectical in nature and thus as important for Gadamer's own see Barthold 2005a.

possibility of playfulness (marked by a loss of intentionality on the part of the players) to culminate in a permanent structure. Yet in contrast to a traditional sense of permanence, the permanence occurring from the transformation is not defined by its atemporality but by relationality. That is to say, permanence results from its becoming a representation for someone else, not from its ability to stand alone through time. This transformation means that what becomes concretized in play speaks to others and makes a claim on them—which Gadamer identifies as truth. Watching a game or someone play does not make a truth claim on us; presumably a game's only function for the observer is as entertainment, which could be said to indeed draw one out of oneself but not return one to oneself. Where there is only play nothing makes a claim and there is not yet truth. It is thus the ability of art, as play transformed into structure, to keep on speaking to others that leads Gadamer to surmise that such a transformation, signified by appearance, is more true, more lasting (Gadamer 1992b, 111). That this is not a statement endorsing realism or essentialism can be attested to if we note that a comparison is being made here. More true, more lasting than what? Than was found in "mere" play, for now we have the "play of art," the play of structure (Gadamer 1992b, 111). Thus far from being evidence of Gadamer's essentialism or realism, the lastingness and truthfulness of such a structure suggests both its self-containedness and its ability to speak to others. Regarding the first, which is just the opposite of a realism that takes truth as a standard for what is "really there," Gadamer's point is that the truth claim of art refuses reference to anything outside of the claim itself. In fact, for Gadamer, demanding a reference to an original means one has not really understood. Gadamer illustrates his point with an example of a play:

> Thus the action of the drama . . . exists as something that rests absolutely within itself. It no longer permits of any comparison with reality as the secret measure of all verisimilitude. It is raised above all such comparisons—and hence also above the question of whether it is all real—because a superior truth speaks from it. . . . In being presented in play, what is emerges. It produces and brings to light what is otherwise constantly hidden and withdrawn. Someone who can perceive the comedy and tragedy of life can resist the temptation to think in terms of purposes, which conceals the game that is played with us. (Gadamer 1992b, 112)

In order to be engaged with truth, one must forego purposive thinking that ultimately stymies the play and leads to aesthetic consciousness. Only one who lets herself get absorbed into the whole, relinquishing the tendency to control in order to experience "what is" (which Gadamer describes, as we shall see below, as recognition), experiences reality being "raised up" (*Aufhebung*) and experiences truth (Gadamer 1992b, 113). What remains untransformed is not yet truth. And what specifically is the nature of the truth that here appears as transformed? Gadamer tells us: "what we experience in a work of art and what invites our attention is how true it is—i.e., to what extent one knows and recognizes something and oneself" (Gadamer 1992b, 114). In other words, in the play of art we are not only drawn out of ourselves, caught up in a whirl (as indicative of play), but we also find ourselves in the still small voice that lies at the heart of the whirl. As Gadamer reminds us: "One must lose oneself in order to find oneself" (Gadamer 1989, 57). When Gadamer speaks about recognition here, he is suggesting that what is recognized is not something that has been reproduced but that which suggests the very possibility for reproduction, that which can be "brought forth" (Gadamer 1992b, 114).

One way to understand what is meant by "bringing forth" is to take it as reflecting the negative character of experience that, as Gadamer tells us, stands over and against a scientific account of experience. Where a scientific approach regards experience only in terms of its result and ignores its process, the negativity of true experience suggests an openness to more experience and hence leads to more knowledge. It is not the result of an experience per se that counts so much as how that experience changes us and changes our way of seeing. Gadamer's Hegelian reflections on experience suggest that experience is not something that fills us up and completes us (something we passively take in) but is something that opens us to what is new or other in a way that relates this other to us: "The dialectic of experience has its proper fulfillment not in definitive knowledge but in the openness to experience that is made possible by experience itself" (Gadamer 1992b, 355).[14]

And what is the purpose of such openness? Is openness an end in itself? This may be the case where openness is seen to lead to a knowledge defined only in terms of an accumulation of new facts. But Gadamer's point, like Socrates' to Agathon in the *Symposium*, shows us that the process of acquiring knowledge is not like filling up a jug, but refers more broadly to "the vocation of man—i.e., to be discerning and insightful" (Gadamer 1992b, 356). What characterizes such "insight," then, is not the accrual of isolated facts but its ability to "[teach] us to acknowledge the real . . . to know what is. But 'what is,' here is not this or that thing, but 'what cannot be destroyed' (Ranke)" (Gadamer 1992b, 357). That this statement does not reflect a realism or essentialism can be seen in Gadamer's emphasis that seeing "what is" fundamentally means seeing one's situatedness in history and acknowledging one's finiteness. The importance of one's historical situatedness challenges not only the atemporal assumptions of Descartes' quest for certainty, but also its excessive individualism. For the acknowledgment of our historicity and finitude implies our fundamental connectedness with another, as seen in the primordial nature of the I-Thou relation.

14. While Hegel's account of the dialectic of consciousness figures prominently into Gadamer's own account of experience, note that Gadamer rejects the completeness and finality that lead to a self-certainty that is defined by its ability to convert what is other to what is oneself. For this reason, Gadamer rejects Hegel's move to apply such a "science" of experience to history: "We can now understand why applying Hegel's dialectic to history, insofar as he regarded it as part of the absolute self-consciousness of philosophy, does not do justice to hermeneutical consciousness" (Gadamer 1992b, 355).

Gadamer insists that not only does the appearing of the true mean issuing forth a new creation, but this bringing forth also implies a spectator, which returns us to the second of the above points regarding the underlying relationality implied by the structure. In fact, while Gadamer indeed speaks of "essence," he specifically clarifies the meaning of essence in terms of the "essential relation" to a spectator: "Imitation and representation are not merely a repetition, a copy, but knowledge of the essence. Because they are not merely repetition, but a 'bringing forth,' they imply a spectator as well. They contain in themselves an essential relation to everyone for whom the representation exists" (Gadamer 1992b, 114-115).

The emphasis on the integrity between essence and spectator prevents taking Gadamer's point here to be an epistemological or a metaphysical one. When Gadamer speaks of the structure he insists that "[i]t does not exist in itself, nor is it encountered in a mediation (Vermittlung) accidental to it; rather, it acquires its proper being in being mediated" (Gadamer 1992b, 117). Gadamer emphasizes how there is no original, per se, to which the work of art refers. In the same way, we must refuse to attribute to Gadamer a view that speaks of truth as what reflects an original, static essence. Based on the foregoing discussion, there is no room for essentialism in Gadamer. What Gadamer is trying to get at is the importance of the full involvement of a spectator. The "essence" spoken of here implies an "essential relation" not an "essence" hearkening back to an original. Furthermore, the role of the spectator suggests that to be present is not just to "be there" in any old way, but to participate, to be involved and "fully" present.

Truth happens when an "essence" is revealed, where "essence" refers to the new possibility for someone. Thus transformation into structure speaks to, indeed requires, a spectator, to whom it is revealed. We could say, then, that truth entails not only an "as-structure" (i.e., seeing something as something) but also a "for-structure" (i.e., seeing something as for oneself). This explains why aesthetic consciousness fails: it precludes both "as-ness" and "for-ness." In its striving for universality it speaks to no one.

In light of the above discussion, we can appreciate the importance of being aware of our finitude and of being open to the possibility for change—both of which imply a fundamental connection with another. This tension recalls Gadamer's account of the origin of the Greek "*theoria*," which means to be a delegate and to be there fully participating—not just doing one's own thing—but being swept away by and caught up in what one sees. Gadamer writes:

> Considered as a subjective accomplishment in human conduct, being present has the character of being outside oneself. . . . In fact, being outside oneself is the positive possibility of being wholly with something else. This kind of being present is a self-forgetfulness, and to be a spectator consists in giving oneself in self-forgetfulness to what one is watching. Here self-forgetfulness is anything but a privative condition, for it arises from devoting one's full attention to the matter at hand, and this is the spectator's own positive accomplishment. (Gadamer 1992b, 125-126)

Thus the appearing of the true in the structure reflects the way in which the spectator is involved with what is presented. "Essence" does not mean a stable original, but that which flows forth engulfing the spectator. It is not a term reflecting what was (nor what will be) but the presence that engages a spectator. Gadamer goes on to mention how the nature of the spectator's involvement, then, is one marked by self-forgetting that leads, ultimately, to self-understanding. What draws one out of oneself, eliciting self-forgetting and thus self-understanding, is *der Anspruch*, the "claim," that comes out of this "essential encounter." The claim of the work of art, in and through which we experience truth, means that there is something soliciting us to which we respond and is the condition for our movement beyond ourselves. One does not just go outside of oneself, becoming "beside oneself" in a mad or drug-induced frenzy, but is drawn outside of oneself to something else. It is a true experience that confronts us with something new, but not just any new thing, e.g., that which strikes one's fancy, curiosity, etc. (which entails only a passive response), but to that which is lasting and permanent, to that which shows us who and how we are. Gadamer's point is that the movement that draws us outside of ourselves, in order to qualify as truth, entails an active, creative, relation with the claim. It is the reproductive engagement with the structure's claim that reflects what is lasting and permanent.

That Gadamer's emphasis on seeing what is suggests more than an essentialism can be further demonstrated by his appeal to the tragic as "exemplifying" the fundamental structure of truth found in the aesthetic work's claim (Gadamer 1992b, 129). For the tragic, Gadamer relates, in its ability to at once draw us outside of and return us to ourselves, allows us to become one with what is (Gadamer 1992b, 131). When Gadamer speaks of tragedy's ability to "dissolve this disjunction from what is," and the ensuing "return to ourselves" (Gadamer 1992b, 131), he is trying to capture the claim of truth in which "[t]he spectator recognizes himself and his own finiteness in the face of the power of fate" (Gadamer 1992b, 132). Gadamer goes on to explain:

> Tragic pensiveness does not affirm the tragic course of events as such, or the justice of the fate that overtakes the hero but rather a metaphysical order of being that is true for all. To see that "this is how it is" is a kind of self-knowledge for the spectator, who emerges with new insight from the illusions in which he, like everyone else, lives. The tragic affirmation is an insight that the spectator has by virtue of the continuity of meaning in which he places himself. (Gadamer 1992b, 132)

The power of a tragedy is to provoke an *ekstasis* that affords knowledge, a self-knowledge that reveals our fundamental connectedness to others. For this reason, tragedy comes to exemplify the claim of truth found at the heart of aesthetic experience.

In light of the preceding discussion, it is not accurate to maintain that Gadamer's notion of play in and of itself is adequate to capture the movement of truth. For Gadamer, play serves only to illustrate the first part of his account of truth. Truth is achieved only after play is transformed into structure, allowing a claim to issue forth to the spectator. This suggests that it is not quite accurate to take Gadamer as saying that we are always already in truth. The tendency by some scholars to claim that the fore-structure of understanding, i.e., the way in which we are already thrown into a world, means we are already in truth, is exemplified by James Risser who writes, "We are, by virtue of our beginning, already in the truth. . . . " (Risser 1997, 152). Similarly, Brice Wachterhauser, describing what he calls a "hermeneutics of trust," writes: "What this understanding of truth entails for Gadamer is a new openness to our experiences of truth in the human sciences that assumes that such experiences are true (or have their truth) until proven false (or until the limits of such truths are shown)" (Wachterhauser 1999, 13). The problem with this position is that it appears to conflate "truth" with Heidegger's notion of thrownness and Gadamer's notions of fore-meaning and prejudice. To be sure, Heidegger's notion of thrownness certainly reveals how much we must accept, rely on, presuppose, and assume in order for us to acquire knowledge. And while Wachterhauser's Davidsonian description that Gadamer's hermeneutics is one of trust proves helpful, it is a category mistake to apply "true" to the pre-givenness of the world. Davidson's principle of charity, for example, does not reflect a theory of truth. What is pre-given must be mapped onto Gadamer's notion of prejudice—not onto his view of truth, for prejudices are things we have without justification. I will connect up truth with justification in chapter 5 where my Gadamerian account of dialogue harkens back to Socratic dialogue's esteem of *logos* and *arete*. Suffice it to say here, however, that discussions that emphasize the role of *einleuchtend* for truth tend to overlook the importance of justification (see Risser 1997, Schmidt 1996, and Wachterhauser 1999). Relinquishing the need for absolute certainty does not require us to label our background assumptions about the world as "true." For, if we start applying "true" to all those prejudices and beliefs that we simply hold until proven "false" then I think we have relinquished an essential dimension to truth, not to mention to Gadamer's notion of prejudice. Prejudices are, as it were, pre-truths; in their unexamined state they are neither true nor false but come to be labeled as true or false as the result of dialogue-based justification. When Gadamer says, "prejudices are biases of our openness to the world. They are simply conditions whereby we experience something—whereby what we encounter says something to us" (Gadamer 1977, 9), he is describing the necessary conditions for truth to occur, but the sufficient conditions must yet be delineated. Prejudices indeed make truth possible but truth is not reducible to prejudices. Nowhere does Gadamer insist that prejudices are true, which it seems we would have to if we maintain that we are "already in truth." Prejudices, like the pre-given unity of the "I and Thou," count as neither true nor false: they precede both descriptions. To claim that whatever we hold in its pre-given state is true until proven false is a category mistake. Truth, for Gadamer, cannot be aligned with prejudices, fore-meaning, or play.

Without entering into a detailed defense against charges of conservatism and traditionalism aimed at Gadamer, let me briefly note how the foregoing account can provide a response to such charges. For, I believe that if we follow some of Risser's and Wachterhauser's assumptions through to their logical conclusion, then we open ourselves to charges of conservatism.[15] Cristina Lafont, for example, locates in Gadamer's emphasis of our embeddedness in a world a normative claim that (in order to right the wrongs of the Enlightenment) we must listen to tradition. While her account of the way in which Gadamer develops this linguistic embeddedness from Heidegger is perspicuous, she makes the mistake common to those commentators mentioned above, namely, the identification of our tradition-embedded-language with truth. She writes:

> The "constitution of meaning" inherent in the linguistic world-disclosure determines the "essence" of beings, *what* they are. In this sense, it is the final court of appeal for our knowledge about them. It is thus the originary truth, which nothing within the world can contradict, for it is the very condition of possibility of the intraworldly. To precisely this extent, it is a "happening of truth." (Lafont 1999, 109)

Identifying "prior embeddedness" with both "language" and "tradition," she argues that Gadamer's "rehabilitation of the authority of tradition" is a normative move (Lafont 1999, 108-9). But this claim seems to yield the following contradiction. On one hand, she provides a helpful account of the inescapability of tradition and of how there is no understanding without it. But when she supplements this claim with her insistence that tradition is normative she would require us not only to be able to say precisely just what our tradition is in order to follow it (and this would not seem to fit with her emphasis on the unconscious or tacit nature of our linguistically constituted tradition (Lafont 1999, 83)), it would also mean that as normative we could refuse it (since there is no point in having a standard if we cannot but adhere to it). But if tradition is that which encompasses the very possibility of the constitution of meaning, how could we ever refuse it? For if we could, would that not require us to escape from the limits of tradition? Thus she seems to insist on what Gadamer denies, namely, the ability to critique our tradition from outside of that tradition. When we recognize that Gadamer's emphasis on the potential for reason and truth in tradition is made in order to correct both the Enlightenment's and Romanticism's skewed views of tradition, then we are less inclined to procure a normative assessment of tradition. What both held in common was tradition's opposition to reason and this is what Gadamer's account of tradition opposes. Gadamer's main point, then, is not to have us follow tradition, much less to conceptualize it in order to provide a "final court of appeal" (as if we have only one, clearly definable tradition). And if tradition functions more as a tacit rather than as a methodologically explicit form of knowledge, how does normativity get its grip?

15. A result neither Risser nor Wachterhauser would welcome.

To reiterate: Gadamer is not saying that we must follow tradition due to tradition's a priori status as a receptacle of truth. Rather, he is saying that the fact that tradition emerges as that which is preserved *yields* elements of universality and thus reason within it. But note that this does not imply anything a priori about tradition. It is the active production of tradition that produces truth, universality, reason—not the other way around. Whereas Lafont would say that world-disclosure produces understanding and that truth pertains to world-disclosure, I want to argue truth occurs in the process of understanding itself—not prior to it. Of course this is not to argue that tradition is not a *source* of truth. However, tradition only becomes true to the extent to which we make it so. Ingrid Scheibler captures this point when she emphasizes that the "educative function" of our engagement with tradition "must be made explicit, and in doing so we strengthen the critical force of Gadamer's conception of a reflective return to tradition" (Scheibler 2000b, 880). To this extent, as the previous chapter argued, it bears a relation to *phronesis*. To make an analogy with the foregoing discussion of play: not everything in our past is true. What emerges as true, and what thus counts as tradition, is what we ourselves have re-created—there is no tradition that stands apart from, much less prior to, our interpretation of it. As such, far from being defined in terms of either an essential, pre-given tradition or our prior embeddedness in the world, truth can be more fruitfully understood as the dialectic of withdrawal and return, as demonstrated in Gadamer's discussion of the truth of the work of art. These points come together in the following quotation describing both the distance and nearness involved in experiencing truth in a work of art:

> The spectator is set at an absolute distance, a distance that precludes practical or goal-oriented participation. But this distance is aesthetic distance in a true sense, for it signifies the distance necessary for seeing, and thus makes possible a genuine and comprehensive participation in what is presented before us. A spectator's ecstatic self-forgetfulness corresponds to his continuity with himself. Precisely that in which one loses oneself as a spectator demands that one grasp the continuity of meaning. For it is the truth of our own world—the religious and moral world in which we live—that is presented before us and in which we recognize ourselves. Just as the ontological mode of aesthetic being is marked by parousia, absolute presence, and just as an artwork is nevertheless self-identical in every moment where it achieves such a presence, so also the absolute moment in which a spectator stands is both one of self-forgetfulness and of mediation with himself. What rends him from himself at the same time gives him back the whole of his being. (Gadamer 1992b, 128)

The heart of this quotation reveals my motivation for speaking of the dialectical movement between distantiation and *Heimkehr*. The foregoing phenomenological account of truth as structurally akin to understanding has nothing to do with guaranteeing certainty and accuracy. Rather, truth comprises the activity of understanding in which the self is drawn outside of itself and then returns to itself.

Truth's Dialectic Between the Other and the Familiar

Part of the reason for the puzzlement over Gadamer's conception of truth is that he has no clear-cut "concept" or "theory," per se.[16] Rather, his writings about truth are evocative, summoning images, even metaphors, to make his point. With this in mind, I now turn to examine three other essays by Gadamer on the subject of truth that further my argument about the dialectical movement of truth. First, we will see the way in which Gadamer's emphasis on the "call" proceeding from an "encounter" with another (whether another person, history, tradition, etc.) maps onto the first part of the movement of truth: away from the self. In order to heed the call, to respond to the encounter, one must be open, which suggests the movement away from oneself. Second, we will attend to how Gadamer uses poetry as an example of how truth brings the distant near, making the unfamiliar familiar, thus suggesting the return to self, the *Heimkehr,* the second part of the movement. In the end, I will show that the key to taking his writings on truth as a coherent unity reflecting what goes on in understanding in general is the dialectical nature of truth.

Against those who impute to hermeneutics a penchant for preserving what is familiar and avoiding what is other, Gadamer explicitly affirms we must heed the call of the other. And even though, as we shall see, this eventually entails making what is other familiar, this is not the same as attempting to preserve what is already familiar. Understanding means making familiar that which is other, foreign, unknown. Understanding is not a reiteration of the same. Mindless mimicking has nothing to do with what goes on in understanding. For, Gadamer insists that we cannot experience truth unless we are open to "the provocation" [*Anstoss*] (Gadamer 1994a). Where we are simply looking for what fulfills our expectations, we do not experience truth: "It is important to recognize—against ourselves—where new provocations [Anstösse] will be given" (Gadamer 1994a, 29). In other words, while all understanding certainly begins from ourselves, that is to say, our prejudices and rootedness in tradition, truth occurs only when we experience a call, a claim, that takes us out of ourselves, away from the familiar. This move recalls his emphasis on the negativity of experience: true experience is not about confirming what we already know but about being pulled-up short in regards to what we do not know. And this is not an easy or comfortable endeavor, in fact, Gadamer speaks of it as a "barely fulfillable task." Such a task, Gadamer goes on to tell us, is to "recognize the new and fruitful, which we ourselves do not see because we have our own ways before our eyes" (Gadamer 1994a, 29). The event of truth, then, should be entered into with trepidation; it entails a struggle to forsake our propensity to hold onto old ways in order to experience the breaking in of a claim that will permanently change us.

16. See, for example, Grondin 1982 for a defense of this claim.

If truth does not entail simply preserving what has always been, neither does it mean embracing whatever is new. It is not newness that is a criterion of truth but, to borrow Hannah Arendt's term, "natality."[17] That is to say, truth is experienced when a new creation is given birth. Whereas the merely new can reflect what is (re)produced by the imitation and repetition of technology, truth concerns the actual power to create—and for humans, as Gadamer stresses, this is seen primarily in language (discussed in chapter 3), and more specifically (as will be seen in chapter 5) in dialogue. Gadamer follows Heidegger in emphasizing how it is language that transforms the earth into a world. But he goes further by suggesting that the power of a dialogic encounter with another lies in the fact that we cannot predict the outcome. Gadamer writes:

> Most astonishing about the essence of language and conversation is that I myself am not restricted by what I believe when I speak with others about something, that no one of us embraces the whole truth within his beliefs but that the whole truth can, however, embrace us both in our individual beliefs. A hermeneutics that was adequate to our historical existence would take as its task the development of this meaningful relation between language and conversation that carries us away in its play. (Gadamer 1994b, 46)

That truth, then, is marked more by natality than newness means that when encountering what is other, one can be freed from one's own limited view allowing a new vista to be born. The above account of the nature of true experience illustrates the way in which the truth born of experience reveals to us not only our historical situatedness but also our fundamental connection with another and thus can be taken as an endorsement of the viability of dialogue. For, by encountering another in dialogue one has the ability to go beyond oneself and what one believes. And thus we gain another glimpse into the sense in which ethical dialectic remains at the core of Gadamer's work: the dialectic that emerges from our in-between status is one that enjoins us with another. In other words, that truth transcends what any single individual can possess means that truth is created in the play of dialogue. Where one individual tries to manufacture, or make claim to, truth, there ideology holds sway. Truth, we could say, is begotten (through the process of dialogue) not made (by the will of an individual). This means that truth emerges above and beyond the intentions of the individual. Truth, like language, is historically rooted, and yet when we engage in dialogue, we have the chance to create anew. Inasmuch as truth is "begotten not made" we can never predict or control its effect. We could also say that the begottenness of truth suggests a future rather than past orientation, further defending the claim that tradition cannot be equated with truth. That truth, then, is marked by a looking ahead to what could be, in a hopeful rather than purposive way, also reminds us of Gadamer's insistence on the importance of the "negativity" of experience: "To acknowledge what is does not just mean to recognize what is at this mo-

---

17. See Arendt 1989.

ment, but to have insight into the limited degree to which the future is still open to expectation and planning or, even more fundamentally, to have the insight that all the expectation and planning of finite beings is finite and limited" (Gadamer 1992b, 357). To see what is, then, requires a confrontation with our limitations—but in a hopeful and not despairing way since it joins us with others and allows us to create a world.

Another way of grasping what it means to say that in truth something is created is to note Gadamer's interest in poetry. For, Gadamer refers to the poetic word as "more saying" or "more telling, " as bringing into presence that which previously had not existed. To make his point, he holds up poetry as the paragon of truth and there are several reasons why this is so. First, a true poem speaks not on behalf of the poet but for itself. It rises above all the contingencies that brought it to life, and as such, is transformed into structure. For example, a poem that only can be understood by grasping the author's intentions (Gadamer has in mind a teenage love poem) is not an example of true poetry. He writes: "What is truly unique to it is the fact that a literary text raises its voice from itself, so to speak, and speaks in nobody's name, not in the name of a god or a law but from itself!" (Gadamer 2007, 145). By holding up a poem that speaks only for itself as illustrative of truth, Gadamer means to emphasize the completeness and universality of truth. What makes a poem true is not the fact that it refers to something in an accurate way or that it successfully communicates specific content but that it has a binding force for the reader (Gadamer 1996b, 106).

The fact that a poem is not trying to refer to anything, nor communicate content, leads to his second point: namely, that the truth of a poem is an *Aussage*, literally, an "out-saying" (Gadamer 1996b, 110). It is a word that presences itself, that makes and takes a stand. Gadamer explains: "What is it that is there in everything that is said and comes to stand before us, when the *Aussage* [assertion, declaration, statement] takes place or happens? I think it is self-presence, the being of the 'there' [*Sein des 'Da'*], and not what is expressed as its objective content" (Gadamer 2007, 148). He goes on to explain what he means by this in terms of how in poetry the idealized reveals "what is"—not in terms of the objective essences of "beings" but our connectedness to the whole of "being:" "When a word resonates, a whole language and everything it is able to say is called forth—and it knows how to say everything. So what comes out in the word that 'speaks' more is not so much a single sensory element of the world but rather the presence of the whole built through language" (Gadamer 2007, 152). This statement is illustrative of the natality resulting from our linguistic relations with others and evokes the dialectical nature of truth. Thus when Gadamer speaks of presencing he is not referring to the presencing of particular propositional content. Rather, like Heidegger, Gadamer appeals to *aletheia* to describe truth, which suggests truth's proclivity to foster "openness" and "unconcealedness," where unconcealedness means more than this or that specific content and instead refers to the possibility of making what is unfamiliar

familiar. The power of the presencing brought about by poetry is described by Gadamer:

> It is nearness or presentness not of this or that but of the possibility of everything. This is what distinguishes the poetic word. It fulfills itself within itself because it is a "holding of the near" and it becomes an empty word when it is reduced to its signifying function, for then it stands in need of communicatively mediated fulfillment. (Gadamer 2007, 153)

It is not, then, that "true truth" gives an adequate representation of something, rather it brings what is distant near. According to Gadamer, the significance of the word is that "it is capable of capturing and holding within itself this nearness, that is, it is able to call a halt to what is fleeting" (Gadamer 2007, 155). And this, after all, recalling our earlier discussion of *theoria*, is what humans desire: to find permanence in a world of flux. Gadamer describes how, if the poetic word is a statement (*Aussage*) and all statements are answers to a question, then we must figure out what is the question that the poetic word of truth answers. As seen above, this takes the form of the search for nearness: "The truth of poetry consists in creating a 'hold upon nearness'" (Gadamer 1996b, 113). Is his point that, in our questioning and searching for how to find permanence, poetry provides us with an answer? The following quotation suggests as much: "Whenever we have to hold something, it is because it is transient and threatens to escape our grasp" (Gadamer 1996b, 114). That is to say, poetry reflects our desire to make things stable so we feel at home. Bringing to presence means making the unknown, the strange, and the transient familiar and permanent—or at least stable for a time. In other words, truth allows for a presencing, a presencing that is also a creating of something that shelters us from the flux. While this way of putting things may be reminiscent of Heidegger's statement that language is the house of being, Gadamer problematizes the nature of such "home-making":

> The word of the poet does not simply contrive this process of *Einhausung*, or "making ourselves at home." Instead it stands over and against this process like a mirror held up to it. But what appears in the mirror is not the world, nor this or that thing in the world, but rather this nearness or familiarity itself in which we stand for a while. This standing and this nearness find permanence in the language of literature and, most perfectly, in the poem. (Gadamer 1996b, 115)

In other words, the making of poets is not the construction of an edifice, but a revealing that shows us our nearness. To clarify Gadamer's above point: the actual process of *Einhausung* is not so much issued forth by poetry but reflected in it. If we are to accuse Gadamer's hermeneutics of being "domesticating" (as Habermas and Caputo do in different ways), this cannot be taken in a bourgeois sense. For, if poetry itself functions as a mirror rather than a roof, the intended result is discomfort rather than ease. The intimacy resulting from our gaze into the mirror is a disquiet one.

Yet does not Gadamer's insistence on the completeness of the poetic word to capture what is, such that nothing more needs to be added to it, place it in opposition to the continual nature of Socratic dialogue Gadamer has esteemed? Furthermore, might it not suggest that the self-sufficiency of truth opposes my claim about the synonymy of truth and understanding, where understanding is considered an ongoing process? If the poetic word symbolizes truth to the extent to which "[i]t is a saying that says so completely what it is that we do not need to add anything beyond what is said in order to accept it in its reality as language" (Gadamer 1996b, 110), then how can truth be accounted for in terms of an ongoing dialectic? Gadamer's insistence on the completeness of the poetic word emphasizes the fact that it does not refer to something outside of itself but remains complete in itself. At the same time, the self-sufficiency of the poetic word does not rule out the need for it to be continually understood and interpreted anew. In fact, we would not be able to see within it our own longing for nearness unless we kept understanding afresh the meaning of the poem for us. E.g., recall how Gadamer defines a "classic" as that which keeps speaking through, and in spite of, time. Thus on one hand the poetic word is self-sufficient, but at the same time it incites an ongoing dialogue about it. It never leads to stale conjectures or idle talk. The way in which self-sufficiency serves to foster ongoing understanding is analogous to Gadamer's remarks on friendship where he points out that being a friend with oneself, i.e., achieving a degree of completeness and unity in oneself, is the condition for, not the opposite of, being a friend with another.[18] Self-sufficiency and unity do not signify impenetrability, stasis, or isolation, but are precisely the conditions for openness to another that fosters listening and dialogue. For, self-sufficiency connotes fullness, that which overflows. It is thus interesting to note how Gadamer changes our images for truth: the poetic word cannot be false (in the traditional sense of false, since it does not refer) but it can be empty (Gadamer 1996b, 139). That the opposite of truth is emptiness, suggests that self-sufficiency (like the ability to be a friend with oneself) is a form of fullness. Thus the truth of the poetic word invites us to keep listening to it and speaking about it; its fullness invites a plethora of interpretations. And, as the final chapter will make clear, the fullness that yields on-going interpretations best finds its expression in the ongoing nature of dialogue.

The foregoing account has attempted to make sense of a Gadamerian notion of truth in light of the dialectical tension marking understanding, a tension characterized by the in-betweenness of self and other, particular and universal, and distance and familiarity. The advantage of highlighting the dialectical nature of truth is to provide support for Gadamer's rejection of truth as a set of criteria or constraints that tells us which propositions we should believe and that finds us

---

18. For a more detailed analysis about the relation between understanding and the Aristotelian notion of friendship in Gadamer see Barthold 2010.

arriving after the event, so to speak (Gadamer 1992b, 490). The upshot is that truth, rather than a tool for alleviating anxiety, is an event that requires risk, both in terms of being open to what is other, and in terms of the subsequent perilous homecoming that finds us changed.

Postscript: Oedipus' "Dialectically Ethical" Truth

The happening of truth that requires risk can be illustrated by Oedipus' quest for truth (which also affirms the centrality of the tragic for a Gadamerian account of understanding). I read this myth as symbolizing the hermeneutical refusal to define truth solely in terms of a relationship of correspondence. It thus gives meaning to the movement of truth in which one is constantly drawn out of oneself toward another, as well as called to return. Consider: Oedipus is seeking the truth of who murdered his father. From an epistemological perspective, we could characterize Oedipus' initial understanding of truth as the attempt to fill in the predicate: "the murderer of King Laius of Thebes is 'x'." His goal is to find out what name can be inserted into the variable in order to attain a positive truth value. But a hermeneutical reading insists that to state that "the murderer of King Laius of Thebes is Oedipus," although a true proposition, would remain, finally, incomprehensible to Oedipus. A correspondence theory of truth is inadequate here since it fails to elucidate all that is required for understanding. Why? For although the proposition, "the murderer of King Laius of Thebes is Oedipus" is true on one level, it remains limited and incomplete and does not capture what Gadamer means by "self-knowledge." The ability to replace the variable with the correct name is not sufficient for Oedipus to develop the richer experience of the self-understanding necessary to hermeneutical truth.[19] For as incomprehensible it would fail to make a claim on him.

The aim of this chapter's dialectical account of truth has been to underscore the event-ial component of truth. Truth is an event into which we must enter, losing ourselves, being drawn toward another, and making the applicative move back toward ourselves. Hinted at in this chapter, and to be more fully developed in the one that follows, is the role language plays in such a movement, specifically in terms of our dialogue with another. For Oedipus, in the end, did not encounter the truth by himself: the knowledge gained from his exile depended upon the accompaniment of Antigone. His exile was not a move beyond language or one that keeps him alien to himself. Although he stops being able to see, he never stops being able to hear (although earlier he had expressed his wish for this) and engage with others. He thus remains in need of others and it is only this recognition that allows him to continue on his journey for authentic self-knowledge. Oedipus never gets beyond the reach of language nor does he

---

19. For a slightly different take on the relevance of Oedipus for Gadamer's hermeneutics see Bruns 1992.

ever end up completely alone. He needs accompaniment, and it is this accompaniment that ultimately returns him to himself, and only then can he enter fully into the event of truth.

I believe this tragedy suggests that in order to work our way out from under the Cartesian influence in thinking about a truth characterized by epistemological reductionism, we need to grasp truth as the experience of both being called away from and returning to ourselves. That is to say, Oedipus must first be bloodied and blinded, expelled from what is known and familiar, jettisoned to the land of the other, before he is able to experience truth, before he is able to achieve self-understanding, before he is able to return to himself, before he is able to hear that the murderer, conceivable initially only as "another," is, in fact, he himself. Similarly, Gadamer's hermeneutics teaches us that the search for truth is not about seeing what is "really there," but is a process of encountering alienation that makes the *Heimkehr*, while far from easy, rewarding and fecund. And that this is not a journey to be undertaken alone returns us to the meaning of the dialectical ethics. For, as we have seen, Gadamer insists that in seeking shelter, in our experience of holding near, we also find connection linguistically with others. Such a bond, Gadamer tells us, occurs when we "enter into genuine dialogue with another" (Gadamer 1996b, 106). Thus the conditions of truth imply dialogue: a genuine listening and speaking to one another that does not leave us unchanged but connects us to another. It is to this we now turn.

Chapter 5
Hermeneutics' Dialectical Ethics: Dialogue and the Good

> Philosophical dialogue and textual hermeneutics are essentially ethical, Gadamer argued from the beginning until the end of his career, because they entail respect for the integrity and independence of the other, not only in the initial attempt to understand but also in the peaceful nonviolent character of the accord or agreement at which dialogue aims.[1]

> Gadamerian ethics is wholly an affirmation of the value of dialogue.[2]

The aim throughout this work has been to elucidate the dialectical nature of understanding as expounded by Gadamer. This chapter explores in more detail how hermeneutics' dialectic, with its origin in Gadamer's interpretation of Plato, manifests itself in both dialogue and the role of the good in understanding. The result will be to more fully come to terms with the meaning and centrality of the dialectical ethics at the heart of his hermeneutics. Recall that one way of getting at the meaning of dialectical ethics was to align it with practical philosophy, particularly as Gadamer avows the theory-practice tension within hermeneutics, the subject of chapter 3. This chapter examines another way of conceiving of dialectical ethics, namely, in terms of hermeneutics' requirement of a dual role for the good: as both "for us" and "beyond being." As the first section of this chapter will maintain (developing the argument of chapter 1), there is warrant

1. Zuckert 2004, 234-5.
2. Vattimo 1997, 37.

for understanding the good-for-us in terms of inter-personal dialogue. That is to say, the practical sense we can give to the good is in terms of our ability to engage in justification with another.[3] But Gadamer's Platonism demands that we account not only for a good-for-us but also a good-beyond-being. The second and third parts of this chapter, then, take up the role of the good-as-transcendent, whose purpose is to effect understanding. Building on Gadamer's reading of Plato's notion of the good, we will think through what it means that understanding requires us to assume a transcendent good.

Dialogue

In the Introduction I emphasized that it is not wholly satisfactory to take Gadamer as equating dialectic with dialogue. Nonetheless, an important relation remains between the two, as demonstrated in the first chapter (based on Gadamer's early work), which offered an initial assertion that dialogue is indeed one manifestation of the productive and constant chorismatic tension. That the chorismatic tension necessary to dialectic can concretely be exemplified in dialogue is subsequently confirmed by Gadamer's 1960 statement that "dialectic is nothing but the art of conducting a conversation and especially of revealing the mistakes in one's opinions through the process of questioning and yet further questioning" (Gadamer 1992b, 464). And forty years later he remained committed to the idea that the dialectical nature of understanding is reflected in dialogue:

> "[C]oming to an understanding" of our practical situations and what we must do in them is not monological; rather, it has the character of a conversation. We are dealing with each other. Our human form of life has an "I and thou" character and an "I and we" character, and also a "we and we" character. In our practical affairs we depend on our ability to arrive at an understanding. And reaching an understanding happens in conversation, in a dialogue. (Gadamer 2001, 79)

Yet in spite of the centrality of dialogue for Gadamer's project, he has no protracted discussion of it. And as Richard Bernstein points out, this is not just of theoretical but also practical concern:

> If the quintessence of what we are is to be dialogical—and if this is not just the privilege of the *few*—then whatever the limitations of the practical realization of this ideal, it nevertheless can and should give practical orientation to our lives. We must ask what it is that blocks and prevents such dialogue, and what is to be done, "what is feasible, what is possible, what is correct, here and now"

---

3. Note that my concern here is with inter-personal dialogue as opposed to person-text/tradition dialogue. Elsewhere I have referred to the hermeneutical requirements for dialogue of the latter sort as "ethical-like" (Barthold 2010).

[TM xxv/WM xxv] to make such genuine dialogue a concrete reality. (Bernstein 1983, 163)

This first section attempts a more comprehensive reflection on dialogue in order to clarify to what extent understanding is both dialectical and, given that understanding requires another, is also ethical. As Gianni Vattimo affirms, "Hermeneutics, born out of Heidegger's polemic against metaphysics, remains to this day a thinking motivated primarily by ethical considerations" (Vattimo 1997, 30). Situating hermeneutics' ethical impulse in dialogue challenges those who hesitate to impute any sort of ethics to Gadamer. For example, P. Christopher Smith insists that for Gadamer "ethical reasoning is *interpretation*" and not the other way around (Smith 1988, 86). And Rudolf Bernet (2005) essentially asks that if our bond with another is one marked by a relinquishing of will, of what happens above and beyond our willing and intending, then what is the exact meaning of "ethics" here? I would reply, however, that rather than severing the relation between understanding and ethics, truth and good, a new way of thinking about the very origin of ethics emerges. While one main tradition in western ethics has always looked to ethical norms to constrain the actions of individuals (and in this sense Smith is correct to say that Gadamer's hermeneutics is not "ethical"), could not Gadamer's Platonic rendering of dialogue suggest it is the nature of our dialogical interactions with others that serves as the motivation and guide for philosophical ethics? That is to say, given the dialogical nature of understanding, true understanding already reflects and presupposes an ethical orientation. Thus any attempt to conceptualize ethical norms must begin with an investigation of the practice of true dialogue that remains always and already ethical. It is my hope that the claims of this chapter will suggest the relevance of hermeneutics for contemporary ethical discussions. And while I cannot develop this trajectory here, let me say that I see a connection between hermeneutics' dialectical ethics and a feminist ethics of care, which has been a challenge to the foundationalist and individualist approach of much of traditional western ethics. Gadamer's dialectical ethics affirms that any ethics must start from where we already are, i.e., as implicated in our commitment to understand another, and not from an objective stance. To the extent that understanding demands listening and responding to another, Gadamer's account of understanding could possibly add to the discussion in the literature about what it means to "care" for another.[4] It would also widen the meaning of the ethical for Gadamer's hermeneutics and thus challenge claims like the following by Honneth: "Gadamer allocates the moral quality of an intersubjective relation only on the basis of whether it is able to preserve the surprise-value of any particular Other" (Honneth 2003, 10).

In other words, if the dialogue between the I and Thou, as Gadamer tells us in *Truth and Method*, is to serve as a model for understanding, then the following should be read as a deepening of this descriptive endeavor that nevertheless

---

4. For a sample of the vast work on the philosophical importance of care see Noddings 1986 and Held 1995.

speaks to our ethical, i.e., inter-subjective, interactions. As Gadamer remarks: "The ability to understand, then, is a fundamental endowment of man, one that sustains his communal life with others and that, above all, takes place by way of language and partnership in conversation" (Gadamer 2007, 158). Thus attending more closely to the meaning of dialogue helps us appreciate the dialectically ethical component of understanding.

At the same time, focusing more closely on the role and meaning of dialogue for understanding yields insight about hermeneutical truth. The first part of this chapter adds to the earlier discussion of truth (in chapter 4) by defending a hermeneutical conception of truth against accusations of ideology, relativism, newness, and/or conservatism. A succinct way to summarize such charges is to say that Gadamer's conception of openness allows no critical component since there is no room for reflective distance in either the "I-Thou" relation or in our relation to history and tradition.[5] What the following phenomenology of dialogue reveals is that openness, while an important component, is not the only one. Acknowledging the connectedness between dialogue and dialectic leads us to consider the importance of our practical relation with another, specifically in terms of the type of justification required by dialogue. For the point is not that we are blindly open to another or to anything new, but that openness is always shaped by our need to justify our position to another. To be open means not just to allow a question to be raised, but to heed its demand for a response.

In getting clear about the key components of dialogue it is first necessary to make a distinction between "conversation" and "dialogue."[6] While neither Plato nor Gadamer relies on such a distinction, I find it helpful in order to provide a unity to what Gadamer wants to get across when he speaks of "genuine conversation," "true dialogue" or "authentic dialogue" (Gadamer 1992b, 363). Not all "conversations" have the same hermeneutical worth. Therefore, I will define "conversation" as any meaningful oral exchange between two or more conversants, and "dialogue" as the specific form of conversation that has as its focus *die Sache*. Again, while Gadamer does not put the distinction in exactly these terms—for he uses "*Gespräch*" and "*Dialog*" interchangeably—the spirit of such a distinction presents itself in several places. For example, he distinguishes between the "most extreme and deepest meaning of conversation" and other various forms of conversation (Gadamer 2005) and differentiates between "authentic and inauthentic dialogue" (Gadamer 1992b, 363). That is to say, and as Gadamer often makes clear, there are many ways of conversing that do not entail that we really hearken unto what the other is saying; in such instances there is only an appearance of a concern with *die Sache* (Gadamer 1992b, 363).

5. See Bernstein 1983, 1986; Decker 2000, Honneth 2003; Hoy 1978; Kögler 1999; and Rasmussen 2003.
6. My emphasis on and attempt to get clear about dialogue productively re-orients the question raised by the Derrida-Gadamer encounter regarding the difference between speech and writing. For example, as Robert Dostal notes, for Gadamer "[t]his is not so much a priority of speaking over writing but a priority of dialogue" (Dostal 1987, 418).

The first component crucial for a Gadamerian conception of dialogue, then, is the Platonic emphasis on *"die Sache,"* the subject matter.[7] Gadamer tells us: "To conduct a [dialogue] means to allow oneself to be conducted by the subject matter to which the partners in the dialogue are oriented" (Gadamer 1992b, 367).[8] Just as Plato relied on *die Sache* as a correction to the relativism and ideology of the Eleatics and sophists, so too we can understand Gadamer's hermeneutics as esteeming *die Sache* in order to help us distinguish between ideological forms of speech and true dialogue. In other words, dialogue possesses a degree of constraint not found in all modes of conversation. The following are examples of just such non-dialogical conversation: when our interest is to obtain a psychological or empathetic understanding of another, when we chat about the weather or our health, whenever we do not really care about the topic at hand but are using conversation to break the ice, put the other at ease, provide distraction, charm, deceive, manipulate, etc. The same can be said for conversations in which one or more of the conversants primarily wants to be heard rather than to understand or where one exercises undue subjective influences. Here we see that one of the benefits of the constraint provided by a focus on *die Sache* is to curtail the possible detrimental subjective influences that could devolve into ideology. For example, agreeing with another due to the other's power, fame, success, popularity, etc., does not yield true understanding as brought about by dialogue. In order to obtain understanding there must be an explicit attempt to reach agreement over the subject matter.

The focus provided by *die Sache*, however, does not mean that agreement will be achieved easily, quickly, or at the expense of the otherness of the other. This is crucial to emphasize, for it protects Gadamer from criticisms that his view of understanding is one that maximizes agreement by expunging difference. Far from advocating an easy or ideological agreement, Gadamer stresses that we must guard against a form of self-deception in which we too quickly and too easily claim to have understood another, and where the dialogue would be inappropriately silenced. The smiling and closed-lip nod of agreement is not the aim of Gadamerian dialogue. In fact, this is just what Gadamer terms "false understanding." In order to avoid this sort of false understanding, when one seeks agreement regarding *die Sache*, one must refrain from making claims of "understanding the other"—for the focus is not on the other but on the subject matter. And if the object of understanding is not the other, per se, but *die Sache*, then, while openness to the other is required (and more will be said about this below), the aim of dialogue is not to assimilate the other's position to one's own but to enable both interlocutors to come to agreement over the subject matter. In other words, the otherness of the other is left intact since the goal is not to make

7. Gadamer 1991, 17-29; Gadamer 1987, 15-23; and Gadamer 1992b, 362-369.
8. "Ein Gespräch führen heisst, sich unter die Führung der Sache stellen, auf die die Gesprächspartner gerichtet sind" (Gadamer 1990, 373). I modified the Weinsheimer and Marshall translation of "Gespräch" as "conversation" to read "dialogue" in order to be consistent with my philosophical point.

words, the otherness of the other is left intact since the goal is not to make the other think just like oneself. This emphasis disarms accusations that Gadamer's concept of understanding privileges "agreement at any cost" over true understanding and/or that it precludes acknowledging the otherness of the other.[9] Instead, we learn that we must remain focused on "purely substantive shared understanding" (*sachlicher Verständigung*).

Another form of degenerative speech can be illustrated by the ancient Greek notion of "*phthonos*." Gadamer instructs us that *phthonos*, as the "concern about being ahead of others or not being left behind by others" (Gadamer 1991b, 44-45), means we are more concerned with what others think than with truth, per se. This form of speech becomes degenerative to the extent to which the aim is to allow the speaker to be revealed in a certain light, with no, or little, regard for the subject matter. The focus of the conversation is the speaker and specifically what drives the dialogue is the speaker's desire to be right and/or to win—not *die Sache*. The speaker presents himself as already possessing a determined answer and thus emerges as one who cannot be refuted. Where the answer is predetermined, one cannot enter into genuine dialogue. Gadamer describes how a rhetoric aimed only at persuading others through the beauty and power of one's speech falls short to the extent to which it "convince[s] the others of something by means of this deception and . . . talk[s] them into something that concerns the speaker" (Gadamer 1991b, 49).

Emphasizing the importance of the subject matter for dialogue also helps us see how it is not hopeless to bring together those who come from opposing positions. For example, if we take the subject matter as the clear launching point, we do not need first to pinpoint any explicitly agreed upon assumptions in order to get the dialogue off the ground. Getting the subject in view is the necessary (although by no means sufficient) requirement for dialogue. We could say that the common focus on *die Sache*—i.e., that both parties are concerned about the same issue—provides the point of overlap between the two horizons allowing them to fuse. This also means that there is always at least a possible point of contact between two positions. (This is not to say, however, that it is easy for both sides to agree on what it is they actually disagree about.) For, as long as there is disagreement, there is disagreement over *something*. Gadamer suggests as much when he writes: "There can be no communication and no reflection at all without a prior basis of common agreement . . . insofar as speech and communication are possible at all, agreement would seem to be possible as well" (Gadamer 1975, 315). We need only posit a common meeting point of the subject matter—whether we share more or fewer assumptions is of little importance.[10]

A second component of dialogue, then, is that there be a shared commitment on the part of each interlocutor to coming to an understanding. What does

---

9. See, for example, Kögler 1999 and Caputo 1987.
10. See the discussion in chapter 3 on the importance of solidarity for understanding.

this "good will" to understand entail?[11] Gadamer describes the basis for understanding as the desire to create a "we," to foster solidarity that comes about through dialogue: "there must be a readiness to allow something to be said to us. It is only in this way that the word becomes binding, as it were: it binds one human being with another. This occurs whenever we speak to one another and really enter into genuine dialogue with another" (Gadamer 1996b, 106). This "good will" to understand functions to help us be open to the other and to forsake a will to power that precludes truth. The distance of someone's position from ours is not what erects a barrier to dialogue; the barrier is established by a lack of willingness on the part of one or more of the interlocutors. Consider the following example. Liberal-minded university professor, "Rachel," clashes with fundamentalist Christian freshman, "Rod," over the topic of whether homosexuality should be regarded as a legitimate practice in society. It would be easy to jump to the conclusion that since there appears to be no overlap between their belief communities, it is useless to think that Rachel and Rod can enter into a rational encounter. But the Gadamerian conception of dialogue I am presenting here does not require symmetry, only openness. Furthermore, it does not depend on there being specific beliefs held (or even taken to be held) in common. That neither can pick out shared beliefs ahead of time is not what is at issue. Even if neither Rod nor Rachel considers the other a member of his or her own belief community (i.e., someone to whom beliefs must be justified), this is not reason enough to prevent them from entering into a dialogue.[12] It is not the difference of beliefs per se that prevents dialogue, but the unwillingness on the part of the interlocutors. In other words, what prevents us from engaging dialogically with another is not the distance of her position from ours or the lack of shared assumptions, but the lack of a good will to dialogue. Gadamer tells us that the incapacity for conversation occurs when

> one says "there is nothing to say to you" and through the Other then it is the feeling or even the experience of not being understood. This allows one to grow silent for a while or even to press one's lips together bitterly. In so far as the "incapacity for conversation" is in the final analysis always the diagnosis that one makes of the Others, it is when the one has not placed himself in the conversation or is not successful at entering into conversation with the Other. The incapacity of the Other is also always at the same time the incapacity of the One. . . . The "incapacity for conversation" looks to me more like the accusation that one makes against another who does not want to follow one's thoughts, rather than a deficiency actually possessed by the other. (Gadamer 2005, 10, 12)

---

11. See the Gadamer-Derrida "encounter" over the "good will" in Michelfelder and Palmer 1989.

12. See Barthold 2005b for a discussion of how this point disputes with claims made by Rorty.

Willingness, however, does not mean a false sense of openness to another. Nowhere does Gadamer insist on the virtues of empathy, that one must imagine what it might be like to be, or empathize with the position of, a member of al-Qaida, for example. But this is not due to the fact that we "know ahead of time" that the other side is wrong. Neither does it mean that to enter into a dialogue with a member of al-Qaida one need relinquish one's abhorrence to acts of terror or the death of innocents, etc. It is not that one must somehow muster a dose of empathy, unjustifiably according to one's own belief structure, and strain to forsake one's own commitments. The reason we do not try to put ourselves in another's shoes, however, is not due to the limitations of empathy (nor to the limitations of Schleiermacher's excessively psychological account of interpretation). Rather, what is at stake is the extent to which one can suspend or remove certain beliefs without this having an effect on other beliefs. In other words, by rejecting a view of knowledge-as-piecemeal or of beliefs as free-floating, independent entities we also deny the possibility that we can consciously and intentionally pick out and discard beliefs at will. Exercising the intention to listen to another in which one is prepared to learn something from the other and to be changed does not require one to reject or even suspend, for example, one's belief in the repulsiveness of terrorism. Not only does putting one's beliefs in abeyance smack of the Enlightenment's "prejudice against prejudice" Gadamer rejects, but it also would remove all grounds upon which to justify one's own position. One cannot enter into a dialogue if one has no deeply held commitments from which to argue. Dialogue invites us to enter into a reasonable encounter in which it is not known ahead of time which beliefs/prejudices will be revealed to be worthy and which unworthy. To this extent, then, dialogue is certainly risky—for we cannot know where we will end up—but not irrational.

But might a commitment to openness preclude the very possibility of a "critical perspective" as David Rasmussen and Axel Honneth have maintained? For example, Rasmussen writes: "The very attempt to reach a critical perspective would go against the authenticity of the experience of openness as Gadamer has described it" (Rasmussen 2002, 509). This question introduces a third component of dialogue: justification. I believe that those who find fault with Gadamer's espousal of openness do so because they fail to note the way in which dialogue, as the paragon of understanding, requires a focus on *die Sache* and a willingness to justify oneself to another. In other words, having a good will to understand means not just being committed to listening to another but also being committed to justifying oneself. This prevents dialogue from turning into a noncritical encounter in which we unrealistically suspend our own beliefs or in which anything new is deemed worthy. When Gadamer insists that in order to enter into true dialogue one must be committed to the truth of either one's own or the other's claim, we can read him as emphasizing the need for justification. When he describes this presupposition of truth as the "basic presupposition of the dialogue" (Gadamer 2004, 49) and also as the "anticipation of completeness/perfect coherence" (Gadamer 1992b, 134),[13] we can read him as describing truth as the idealized event of understanding. And when he maintains that truth is the goal of all understanding (although of course there is never any guarantee we will achieve it) and that we cannot understand unless we expect to understand, he is drawing our attention to the importance of being willing to justify oneself. This hearkens back to the discussion in chapter 4 on the way in which being open does not mean accepting whatever is new, but pertains to the ability to create anew. It is our willingness to seriously sustain a dialogic justification that fosters natality and creates a new world.

But even though Gadamer censures our longing for a criterion for truth (as chapter 4 made clear) the result is not relativism. For, what we learn from Gadamer's account is that our commitment to truth prevents us from devolving into relativism to the extent to which such a commitment entails a willingness to justify ourselves. Thus when Bernstein argues that Gadamer has not been thorough enough in providing "a form of argumentation that seeks to warrant what is valid in this tradition" (Bernstein 1983, 155) I believe he fails to see the extent to which this is precisely the task assigned to Gadamerian dialogue itself. Again, we may be tempted to ask, what is the point of justification if there are no external criteria against which to judge/measure? Hermeneutics rejects a hidden assumption of epistemological accounts of truth: namely, that truth is atemporal, unchanging, clear, and distinct. Hermeneutics shows us otherwise: truth as the event of understanding is not something we can possess, reify, or finalize. This means that neither certainty nor terminability are the defining traits of understanding.[14] Gadamer insists, in fact, that when one is engaged in true dialogue one will always want to say more: dialogue catches us up in its movement just like play does. We want to keep going. The ideal of terminability is not one that hermeneutics endorses; it is one that belongs to the decrepit objectivism-relativism paradigm—which Richard Bernstein has shown to be dubious.[15] Rejecting the ideal of terminability has important ramifications not only for a conception of truth but also for political debate, as Georgia Warnke notes: "We need not agree with each other in the end, but we can all come to recognize the partial and one-sided character of our initial positions and incorporate into our

---

13. See also the following discussions in Truth and Method: "Heidegger's disclosure of the fore-structure of understanding" and "The Problem of Historical Consciousness."

14. Alasdair MacIntyre, for example, seems to require terminability as a condition for rationality: "The most striking feature of contemporary moral utterance is that so much of it is used to express disagreements; and the most striking feature of the debates in which these disagreements are expressed is their interminable character. I do not mean by this just that such debates go on and on and on—although they do—but also that they apparently can find no terminus. There seems to be no rational way of securing moral agreement in our culture" (MacIntyre 1984, 6).

15. See Bernstein 1983, esp. 1-10. For his discussion of Gadamer's role in overcoming the relativism-objectivism dualism see part three, "From Hermeneutics to Praxis," 109-165.

more considered views the insights we have come to learn by trying to understand other interpretations" (Warnke 1993, 132). She refers to this as the "interpretive turn in political philosophy." Indeed, linking truth to dialogue shows there is truth that extends beyond simple agreement, that truth is a matter of continually coming to an understanding of both one's own and another's interpretations. Again, Warnke expresses it well: "In our dialogue with one another over our interpretations and evaluations we need not seek consensus. The point from both sides is to make sure their own interpretations are as compelling and inclusive as they can be" (Warnke 1993, 133).

Yet in spite of her endorsement of the importance of hermeneutics for political theory, Warnke goes on to ask: "How do we differentiate, within hermeneutic conversation, between the potentially educational insights of others and systematic distortions in understanding and communication?" (Warnke 1993, 141). Warnke, however, had effectively already answered this question in an earlier essay where she attempted to defend Gadamer against Habermas's criticism that we need more than dialogue: that we also need a critique that uncovers the distortions inherent within the dialogue itself. She writes that Gadamer

> assumes conversation can ultimately disclose the same ideological factors that constrain it. . . . [In fact,] the only means that we have for reaching clarity about our situation . . . lies in continued dialogue about it. Certainly such dialogue can be systematically distorted; but, for Gadamer . . . it is to see through such distortions and to develop our insights that we must continue to talk. If conversation is reason's only hope, in other words, reason is also conversation's point. (Warnke 1990, 157)

Thus while reason is not a guarantor of truth, in pursuing truth we become more reasonable. The aim of dialogic understanding is to enter into truthfulness, i.e., a genuine understanding with another, rather than to come away with a finalized and reified truth.

A slightly different way of voicing a concern with Gadamer's conception of dialogue comes from Richard Bernstein who worries that Gadamer does not do enough to spell out how, if understanding is *phronesis*- and *praxis*-oriented, one may achieve understanding where the conditions that make *phronesis* and *praxis* possible are corrupt or altogether absent. Gadamer's point, as I believe Warnke expresses it in the above quotation, is that dialogue born of solidarity is enough, since for Gadamer "the displacement of human reality never goes so far that no forms of solidarity exist any longer" (Bernstein 1983, 264).[16] I take Gadamer to be making a Davidsonian point here: just as Davidson maintained that it would be senseless to worry that most of our beliefs are false, so Gadamer is implying that it makes no sense to worry that the entire basis for our solidarity is corrupt. To understand why this is so we need to realize that Gadamer insists that truth is not only reflected in speech but in the way we live our lives. In other words,

---

16. See also pp. 63-4.

Gadamer brings truth "down" to the practical level; truth is not just about the "truth of speech" (Gadamer 2004, 47). In making his point, Gadamer insists that one cannot distinguish the sophist from the philosopher by speech alone; one must also take into account how one lives: "In truth, the question of what we *do* right or what we *do* wrong is what genuinely concerns us" (Gadamer 2004, 48, emphasis added). Our anxiety about truth is misplaced if we are worried about locating external criteria. For even if we were able to articulate such criteria, this would not help us distinguish the philosopher from the sophist. Gadamer shows us how truth is related to our very existence in the world, which is ultimately reflected in our ability to justify ourselves to another. The point is that since there is no guarantee of ever knowing fully or immediately the truth then it is our ability to successfully justify ourselves to another that counts. Thus the "constraints" on a dialogue that is "too open" come not from a theoretical critique but from the lived practice of justification.

I have been trying to demonstrate just what counts as "successful justification": openness per se is not enough; one must be willing not only to listen to the claims the other raises but also to respond in justification. The dialogic procedure characterized by the back and forth of justification precludes relativism and summons reflective and critical interaction. The Socratic component of asking for reasons means that it is not the case, as Axel Honneth has claimed, that "any intrusion by reflection would therefore be only disruptive [to the immediacy of the 'I-Thou' experience], since it would take the ground from the prior bond (between subject and history), on the presupposition of which the necessary trust can first be advanced" (Honneth 2003, 12-13). It is not the case that openness means a blind trust in another. Every perspective is not as valid as every other one; one must work to defend his or her position. Gadamer's Platonic leanings mean that dialogic interaction is not any sort of back and forth; nor does it mean asserting one's own opinion in a way that precludes the interaction on the part of the other. True dialogic interaction occurs where each of the partners raises a question or claim and demands an answer or justification from the other. On this model of dialogue, by asserting a position one assumes that the other will respond to it by giving further justification for it or raising problems against it. As should be clear by now, neither nodding in appeasement to the claim of another nor threatening the other with force if one does not agree qualifies as dialogue. Gadamer maintains that where we "understand" too quickly we have not really understood. The justification of oneself in light of one's *arete* that we saw Socrates demand of his interlocutors adds a necessary, if frequently overlooked, component to a Gadamerian conception of dialogue. Furthermore, that such an appeal to one's *arete* can only be done in light of the good should make us dubious about charges that Gadamer "seems always only to recognize in reflexive acts the negative side of distanciation or externalization . . ." (Honneth 2003, 16). In other words, it is important to specify that, for Gadamer, openness signifies being open to hear *and* to interact with the claims of the other; it does not simply signify immediate acceptance or a naive intimacy.

The above requirements for justification entail that such a demanding back and forth cannot happen in any setting, amongst any number of people, however. Gadamer instructs his readers that "a conversation is never possible with many at the same time or even only in the presence of many. Our so-called panel discussions, these conversations around a semicircular table, are always half dead discussions" (Gadamer 2005, 8). Dialogic justification must be aimed at a specific concrete other human being and must take place on the level of the particular other. (Of course this does not deny the trans-subjective influences that go on in dialogue, that dialogue is akin to play to the extent that it transcends the subjective willing of the participants.)[17] One cannot have dialogue between communities, ideologies, etc. And I would also tend to agree with Dieter Misgeld's observation that Gadamer would rule out the possibility for dialogue to occur electronically: "Communication provided by the electronic media . . . can never convey or institute this sense of solidarity. . . . Gadamer wants to protect forms of intimate and deeply engaging conversation from the technologically reinforced invasion of culturally and intellectually still viable institutional spheres, capable, in his view, of maintaining the mentioned forms of communication" (Misgeld 1990, 161, 162). For, as Gadamer writes: "Only the individual human being has a thou [*ein du*]" (Gadamer 2001, 58). This means that we must approach the other in terms of her individuality, not as a representative of certain beliefs. That the pro-life movement shares no important common assumptions with the pro-choice movement is not ultimately what is at issue when it comes to the possibility of dialogue. When encountering an individual from an opposing position, it is important to listen and respond to the specific claims she is making without reacting to the whole host of beliefs that can be attributed to the other position in general. By keeping in mind that we are speaking with an individual and not a general position, we are able to effect a dialogue that unravels, and not reinforces, prejudices. In other words, dialogue is about avoiding generalizations and stereotypes and addressing the specific claims put before one. Even though one is unlikely to be able to address a whole perspective in one dialogue, one may nevertheless learn something from the encounter with an individual. Furthermore, the focus on the particular other in dialogue reveals that the ideal of inclusiveness can only be achieved on the individual level. For example, when Warnke justifiably expresses the concern that factors external to our conversations like "social and economic conditions and relations of power . . . mean that there may always be voices and interpretations that have been systematically left out of a society's interpretive conversations from the start" (Warnke 1993, 149), we can take her as referring to conversations that take place only on a societal (as opposed to individual) level. It is important, as I have insisted, to distinguish between conversation and dialogue, for dialogue, as an intimate form, is less likely to succumb to hidden

17. I wish to thank Hans-Herbert Koegler for pointing out the possibility for a misreading here.

likely to succumb to hidden power since it is constrained by *die Sache*, which is not the case for all conversations.

Fourth, as Socrates modeled it, one of the pre-conditions for dialogue is an underlying belief on both sides that one "knows that one doesn't know." This means forsaking the position that one "knows in advance." However, to the extent that "knowing that one doesn't know" is also a form of knowledge, this does not mean that one suspends all of one's beliefs or assumptions (something not even possible, according to Gadamer). Rather, one chooses to seek out the truth of the subject matter by asking: why is it that the other holds to a position that seems counter to mine? What is it that she knows that I do not? What Gadamer calls "radical negativity," as demonstrated in Socratic dialogue of question and answer, refers to the culmination of true experience in which we recognize our finitude. Question asking in its true form, i.e., when it is not slanted or rhetorical, is motivated by this admission of ignorance. Stressing the connection between dialogue and dialectic, Gadamer tells us: "The art of questioning is the art of questioning even further—i.e., the art of thinking. It is called dialectic because it is the art of conducting a real dialogue" (Gadamer 1992b, 367). The degree to which we are moved to question requires an admission of our ignorance, that we, like Socrates, know that we don't know. But such an assumption does not mean attempting the impossible: a suspension of all our prior beliefs. Openness does not mean we come to the table with nothing to offer. Rather, it arises from an encounter with the specific claim of another. After all, Socrates' declaration of ignorance was a result of trying to figure out an answer to a specific question: namely, what can it mean that he is the most knowledgeable person alive? Thus there is a degree of reciprocity between our openness to others and our assumption of ignorance that makes it difficult to state precisely which comes first. But does it matter that we cannot? For, while Gadamer insists that one of the "crucial conditions" of dialogue is "that one knows to recognize the other as other" (Gadamer 2005, 9), could we not also say that such a recognition comes as the result of genuine dialogue? Might it help to draw an analogy between dialogue and play to the extent to which while we intentionally enter into both play and dialogue our intentions become relinquished when we get caught up in something bigger than ourselves? Indeed, that the "play" of dialogue reminds us of what Gadamer told us about the claim of truth experienced in art finds defense in the following statement:

> What is conversation? Naturally we think of a transaction between humans, who for all the broadening and potential endlessness nevertheless posses a oneness and a closeness of their own. Something is a conversation for us if it leaves something behind in us. It is not that we have found out something new which makes a conversation a conversation, but that we encounter something in the other that we have not encountered in the same way in our own experiences of the world. . . . Conversation has a transformative power. Where a conversation is successful, something remains for us and something remains in us that

has transformed us. Thus a conversation is in the particular neighborhood of friendship. (Gadamer 2005, 6-7)

Here we see intimations of Gadamer's discussion of truth in *Truth and Method*. A "conversation," i.e., here a genuine "dialogue" in the terms I am using, is not an accumulation of new data. Rather, it is something that changes us, recalling Gadamer's insistence that truth is that which does not leave the one who encounters it unchanged. So, too, does genuine dialogue change us. It is something in which we get caught up and of which we are unable to determine the outcome. Dialogue, like truth, requires a relinquishing of self that yields a new creation.

Furthermore, just as in a game we want to keep playing, so in genuine dialogue we want to keep conversing. Gadamer writes: "In a conversation one does not know beforehand what will come out of it, and one usually does not break it off unless forced to do so, because there is always something more you want to say. That is the measure of a real conversation" (Gadamer 2001, 59). What keeps a dialogue going, then, is openness to the genuine otherness one has yet to encounter. To the extent that the ideal dialogue is continuous, claims to have fully or exhaustively understood the other are never a legitimate outcome of dialogue. The dialectic of dialogue is never completed.

Recalling the discussion of truth in chapter 4, what remains clear is that genuine recognition of the other requires a relinquishing of our will that yields a recognition of our own finitude—something not easy to achieve. Certainly, it is much easier and less painful to see the other only as a "mirror image" of oneself, a move that would presumably contribute to a delusion of infinitude. Furthermore, as Gadamer tells us, a genuine encounter with another both reminds us of our finitude and offers a promise of moving beyond it: "Precisely in our ethical relation to the other, it becomes clear to us how difficult it is to do justice to the demands of the other or even simply to be aware of them. The only way not to succumb to our finitude is to open ourselves to the other, to listen to the 'thou' who stands before us" (Gadamer 2004, 29). Dialogue is always risky to the extent that we must be prepared for it to change us in ways not anticipated. Dialogue is an antidote against a conservatism that fears what is new and strange, for it bids us take seriously the claims of the other. There can be no understanding where we seek to preserve what is and what is already known. To understand is always to understand anew. As such, it possesses transformative powers that we can neither anticipate nor control: we are drawn in and cannot help ourselves.

It should be evident, then, that the hermeneutical point about dialogue is not that it is merely a poor substitute for a critique that is untenable—but that the spontaneity and natality[18] of dialogue actually offer us the best hope for break-

18. See the discussion of natality in chapter 4 and the one on spontaneity below. Gadamer's proximity to Arendt on these points can be seen in his writings on practice (1992c, 1996a, 1999), specifically where he writes, "The spontaneity of the user of tech-

ing out of distortive communicative practices. Cornel West is one of the few thinkers to have picked up on the social and critical relevance of hermeneutics. West, unlike other critical theorists, refuses to see Gadamer's thought as imbued with conservatism: "Tradition per se is never a problem, but rather those traditions that have been hegemonic over other traditions" (West 1989, 230). I would stress the similarity between Gadamer's thought and West's own brand of prophetic pragmatism that "conceives of philosophy as a historically circumscribed quest for wisdom that puts forward new interpretations of the world based on past traditions in order to promote existential sustenance and political relevance" (West 1989, 230). Furthermore, West takes truth and good as inherently connected to the extent to which both are needed to "enhance the flourishing of human progress" (West 1989, 230).

Taking seriously the ethical implications of dialogue means that morality proceeds not from an "ought," a divine command from on high, but from the desire to listen to, hear, and understand the other. Understanding another is thus always an ethical act—but not just because we are called to have a good will to listen and be open. There is another sense in which Gadamer's hermeneutics can also be taken as ethical: it can be read as showing that Marx assumed a false dichotomy between understanding and change. For, Gadamer helps us see that understanding always necessitates a change in being. Hermeneutics, as we have seen, is practical philosophy. Only if we buy the *theoria-praxis* split will we accuse interpretation of being effete. But this is not the worst that will happen. We will also assume that our interpretations, our theories, our philosophies are socially, politically, and ethically neutral. I believe, although Gadamer never articulated as much, that hermeneutics provides the incentive to cultural critique to the extent that it is an attempt to dispel the myth of neutral theory, neutral and thus apolitical philosophizing. Once we take seriously hermeneutics' claim about the embeddedness of understanding in history, then we must become astute listeners to the historically effected/effective society we call our own. While we will never be able to predict or control the outcomes of any given thought, it is incumbent upon us to think through as far as possible the prejudices giving rise to our own theories. If we never can operate prejudice-free, then we must live and work in a state of constant openness to the voices of the oppressed around us. Hermeneutics is not a worldless philosophy, but emerges from a world in which we find ourselves thrown together. Far from connotating homogeneity, this thrownness only illuminates our differences and the struggles necessary for survival. Consequently, interpretation becomes paramount, not as a guarantee against violence (for interpretation can also be violent) but as a possibility that the differences will be subject to mutual interpretations, creating new worlds, new meanings. Hence, there is a life-giving force to dialogue.

---

nology is in fact more and more eliminated precisely by this technology" (Gadamer 1996a, 18).

Put in the above terms, it should be clear that dialogue, far from being a means to impose our world-view on another and thereby eradicate difference, works best when difference drives the very play of dialogue itself. We could even go so far to say that dialogue presupposes difference/otherness. Dialogue's possibility for generating an organic, spontaneous agreement is due to the free play that takes place therein, where "every concrete determination by the individual contributes to socially meaningful norms" (Gadamer 1992a, 173). In other words, the ubiquity of hermeneutical experience implies that we all have a responsibility to understand and thus exercise practical judgment for ourselves, and this does not occur where we simply follow a prescription for what to do, say, or think. Of course, Gadamer is not saying that there is no legitimacy to ideology critique or that it may not help us see ourselves and our situations in a new way. Remember: he is not against method, per se, only its abuses. His point is that all critique emerges out of a socio-historical situatedness and, as a form of understanding, must be made our own. This is the case even where ideology is already at work. As Dieter Misgeld warns: "[T]here can be no political ideal, no public conception of justice or morality, which could be equally attractive to thoughtful human beings as the dialogue they freely and openly engage in, uncoerced by the need for compromise or the weighing of momentous economic, military, and ideological situations" (Misgeld 1990, 174). Misgeld presents a picture of dialogue that is less idealistic than many political solutions, for, dialogue does not require consensus. We do not have to agree with—either at the start or finish—our interlocutor; what is required is an openness to enter into the process of truth. Furthermore, dialogue does not impose a similarity on another, but finds it through playful interchange that changes those involved. The solidarity wrought by understanding is not inimical to difference. Rather, it affirms that the acknowledgment of difference is the starting point of all genuine dialogue.[19]

Although the four components of dialogue offered above do nothing to guarantee that such an encounter will be entered into (since they rule out ahead of time so many difficult situations, e.g., where neither party is willing to be truly open), they move us toward grasping what understanding looks like and how it is best achieved. In addition, they expose the way in which understanding is, at its core, dialectically ethical by highlighting the ethical-like nature of understanding. As Gadamer ends part two of *Truth and Method*: "To reach an understanding in a dialogue is not merely a matter of putting oneself forward and successfully asserting one's own point of view, but being transformed into a communion in which we do not remain what we were" (Gadamer 1992b, 379).

19. This point is endorsed by feminist theorists like Linda Alcoff who argue that the acknowledgment of difference—as opposed to its denial—is ultimately more likely to lead to productively unified communities. Alcoff writes that "the acknowledgment of the importance of differences in social identity does not lead inexorably to political relativism or fragmentation, but that, quite the reverse, it is the refusal to acknowledge the importance of the differences in our identities that has led to distrust, miscommunication, and thus disunity" (Alcoff 2006, 6).

For Gadamer, as we have seen, dialogue is ethical and dialectical: ethical to the extent that we must take seriously the demands of the other, dialectical to the extent to which it is an ongoing and back-and-forth movement. In the following section I turn to examine a further consequence of the dialectical ethics of understanding, namely its requirement of the good-beyond-being.

The Good of Understanding

The main focus of this section is to show how the good-as-transcendent functions as a structural component of understanding. As such, I hope to provide an answer to the challenge posed by Zuckert that "[a]lthough Gadamer admits that the *eide* are purely noetic, it is difficult to see how he could admit the existence of any eternal truths or ideas" (Zuckert 2002, 220). But must taking seriously his debt to Plato mean attributing to him the belief in "eternal truths" per se? This study shows how we can make sense of a good-beyond-being without making the standard move of defining it as an "eternal truth." As transcendent, the good is that at which we necessarily aim but never achieve, providing a reference beyond ourselves, without which meaning and understanding elude us. For, without a reference beyond ourselves, as Plato insisted against the sophists, we are left with only instinct and whim. This section demonstrates the legitimacy of the transcendent good for Gadamer's hermeneutics without aligning it either with a metaphysical realism[20] or with a formal ethics that articulates a concrete content.

The significance Gadamer attaches to the good cannot be minimized; he describes the good as "a final end" and insists that "[i]t's an expression for this thing that is never quite attainable. I think it is precisely what justifies hermeneutics. Actually, one always sees it as a transcending of what one already thinks one knows" (Gadamer 2004, 36). As Gadamer construes it, the good justifies hermeneutics, and yet remains something we can never grasp. The good stands as that which transcends the known and as that which is thus beyond being. Gadamer is one of the few who takes Plato seriously at this point: to maintain that the good is beyond being means that it is beyond any fully specifiable definition; it is not, therefore, able to be rendered into a formal ethics or prescription for moral behavior. The problem then becomes to admit as much while deflecting criticisms, as diverse as those made by Aristotle, Karl Popper, and Richard Rorty, that such a notion of the good is merely an "empty form" irrelevant for human practice and thus useless.[21]

To avoid reducing the meaning of "beyond being" to a banality it is worth recalling the quotation from chapter 1 wherein Gadamer describes the good as a structural component of understanding and as ultimately connected to truth:

20. See Wachterhauser 1999, p. 59 and passim.
21. See also Santos 1989 who argues, in a slightly different vein, that although the good is indeed formal, it is not useless.

> The idea of the good is not an entity any longer, at all, but an ultimate ontological principle. It is not a substantive determination of entities but the thing that makes everything that exists understandable in its being. It is only in this universal ontological function that the idea of the good is in fact the ultimate basis of *all* processes of coming to an understanding—not as a highest-level, universal eidos but as the formal character of everything that can really be called "understood," which means, however, as the angle of vision to which the claim to understanding itself submits itself. In this respect, the idea of the good is nothing but the ideal of complete cognizability and cognition. (Gadamer 1991b, 76-7)

I take Gadamer to be making an anti-metaphysical-realist point here by rejecting the good as an *eidos*. It is more like an ideal, something at which we aim yet is never fully achievable, than an "idea" that exists in and of itself. Here the words of William James prove illustrative: the good functions as an "ideal standard" that is regulatory in nature (James 1996, 308-9). Wachterhauser offers a similar insight by describing the good as "a regulative ideal for the exercise of practical intelligence . . . that can lead to substantive bases for human action" (Wachterhauser 1999, 44, 45). It is what makes understanding possible in so far as it describes the desired, yet ultimately unattainable, goal of "complete cognizability and cognition." That the good takes on the "formal character of everything that can really be called 'understood'" means that the good is present to the extent that understanding occurs; it functions as a tacit assumption necessary for understanding. As transcendent it is not an entity of being but allows being to be comprehended. It is a regulative principle that orients our efforts to understand,[22] as it did for Socrates who, Gadamer tells us, sought "the Good with an attitude of not-knowing" (Gadamer 2007, 112). Gadamer's Platonic point, then, seems to be that there is a way to approach the good other than by trying to conceptualize it. The good-as-transcendent does not play a normative role; it is not defined by its propensity to dictate what we should do. It does not reflect a given code or law; its orienting role is to foster, indeed, permit, understanding. Here we could make an analogy between the role of the good in understanding and Plato's use of utopia (discussed in chapter 3), which serves as "not a guide for action but a guide for reflection" (Gadamer 1992c, 82). Again Wachterhauser offers a helpful insight: "It is concern for the Good and the question of how to live or what Heidegger called 'care' that forms, for Gadamer, the foundation of our attempts to know. . . . Such a concern does not culminate in a clear and distinct idea but it is an ideal which forms the constant and final framework for our thought" (Wachterhauser 1999, 50).

---

22. Along similar lines, Jens Zimmerman concludes that for Gadamer, "transcendence is the absolute limit of our knowledge and allows true conversation to begin" (Zimmerman 2002, 209).

Where humans fail to gesture to the good-beyond-being, there remains no defense against relativism—understood primarily as a moral as opposed to epistemological threat. To further grasp this point, let us recall the first chapter's discussion regarding how Plato's esteem of the good was intended to avoid the relativism of the sophists, which was premised on their esteem for the "useful." Gadamer, too, looks to the good to prevent us from accepting too readily the "useful" as the measure of all things. He writes:

> I think Plato essentially wants to say that there can't be any knowledge of the better without a knowledge of the good or without us keeping our eyes open for the good. The polemic against the Sophists has only one meaning—to show that they couldn't have any real knowledge of the better because they established their foothold on the knowledge of the useful, which seemed precisely to be the immediate utility of the city. But that happened only because they didn't have a correct understanding of the good, which, on the contrary, constitutes the *basis* for what is genuinely useful, the general advantage of the state. (Gadamer 2004, 42)

Gadamer insists that a search for the better is only possible in searching and "keeping our eyes open" for the good. There is no sense of better except "in relation to a final end" (Gadamer 2004, 42). In order to clarify the sense in which "final end" is meant here it helps to recall the point made in chapter 1 that our fundamental relation to the good is an assumptive one: one must assume the good-beyond-being in order to criticize or evaluate practices that "seem good" in the moment. Also in that chapter we discussed how the good functioned to unify knowledge by serving as the final, indivisible *eidos*. Thus final end—and perhaps "highest end" is a better term—does not refer to that which we will eventually and finally achieve, but that which transcends all other ends and will never be achieved. As such, we could say it lies just beyond our horizon and moves constantly as does our horizon. Its necessity for understanding allows us to escape the ethically detrimental effects of judging everything in terms of immediate utility. In order to develop further Gadamer's meaning here, I will draw on Hannah Arendt's critique of *homo faber*, which helps elucidate the hermeneutical connection between meaning and transcendence.[23]

Arendt maintains that meaning cannot occur in a world of only means and directs her criticisms against philosophies that espouse the importance of usefulness as a criterion to determine worth.[24] She describes how where usefulness is the criterion, there is no final end since every end subsequently becomes another means. This tendency reflects the situation of what she calls "*homo faber*": to be caught up in an endless process of re-making the world via instruments. For example, the chair-as-end justifies the violence accorded to nature in order to get

---

23. See Arendt 1989, chapter 4.
24. Gadamer has a similar criticism aimed at Richard Rorty's pragmatism. See Gadamer 2004, chapter 3.

the wood. However, the chair does not remain as an end, rather it becomes a means for a new use: comfort for a person. If nothing remains as an end for very long and the endlessness of the means-end chain continues, then, according to Arendt, the distinction between meaning and use gets blurred.

She explains how this is due to the fact that philosophies that leave no space for an ultimate end are unable to distinguish between "in order to" and "for the sake of," and reduce the latter to the former. "In order to" reflects a motivation of means: I perform A in order to achieve B. "For the sake of" reflects that which lies beyond the mere calculation of means to an end in itself. Thus she uses "for the sake of" to designate that which is done for an end in itself, and "in order to" to designate that which is done for a means (or what ultimately becomes a means). For example, an attitude toward nature other than a utilitarian one is to view nature as a force in its own right. Here we could call on her distinction between *homo faber* and *animal laborans*. Where the former uses things in order to separate for humans a world, the latter works with the natural process of life itself, getting caught up in it. In labouring, according to Arendt, the process is not determined by human intention and will, but by the very process of nature itself into which humans are drawn. Thus she contrasts the life process, which has no clear beginning or end, with the process of fabrication which has a "definite beginning and a definite, predictable end" (Arendt 1989, 143). Thus I think we can understand the sense in which "for the sake of" is meant here as coinciding more with *animal laborans* who, unlike *homo faber*, is not "master of himself and his doings" (Arendt 1989, 144). And while Arendt is certainly no Platonist, she does make a "Platonic" point here that without a final end all we can do is appeal to the immediacy of usefulness. Arendt argues that *homo faber* runs into a problem when trying, in pursuit of meaning, to align utility with "for the sake of." She explains:

> The ideal of usefulness permeating a society of craftsmen—like the ideal of comfort in a society of laborers or the ideal of acquisition ruling commercial societies—is actually no longer a matter of utility but of meaning. It is "for the sake of" usefulness in general that *homo faber* judges and does everything in terms of "in order to." The ideal of usefulness itself, like the ideals of other societies, can no longer be conceived as something needed in order to have something else; it simply defies questioning about its own use. Obviously there is no answer to the question which Lessing once put to the utilitarian philosophers of his time: "And what is the use of use?" The perplexity of utilitarianism is that it gets caught in the unending chain of means and ends without ever arriving at some principle which could justify the category of means and end, that is, of utility itself. The "in order to" has become the content of the "for sake of which"; in other words, utility established as meaning generates meaninglessness. (Arendt 1989, 154)

Arendt maintains there is something incoherent about utility posing as a final end, placing itself in the role of "for the sake of," for, there is no ultimate justification of the means-end relation. Arendt's point, however, is not that without a first principle one is left with circular arguments and thus meaninglessness. Her point is an ethical not epistemological one: she maintains that meaninglessness derives from the way in which *homo faber* degrades everything to a means, and thus all of life becomes instrumentalized. For once an end is achieved, she writes, it "ceases to be an end and loses its capacity to guide and justify the choice of means, to organize and produce them" (Arendt 1989, 154-55). Without a final end—i.e., an end that can never be finally achieved—there is no permanence or stability. Once an end is achieved it no longer remains an end and becomes converted to a means. Meaning, however, "must be permanent and lose nothing of its character, whether it is achieved or, rather, found by man or fails man and is missed by him" (Arendt 1989, 155). Meaning is not subject to the manipulation of humans. She continues:

> The only way out of the dilemma of meaninglessness in all strictly utilitarian philosophy is to turn away from the objective world of use things and fall back upon the subjectivity of use itself. Only in a strictly anthropocentric world, where the user, that is, man himself, becomes the ultimate end which puts a stop to the unending chain of ends and means, can utility as such acquire the dignity of meaningfulness. (Arendt 1989, 155)

However, although the only way for *homo faber* to recover meaning in a world of means (where usefulness is the ultimate criterion) is to take humans-as-makers as the end, Arendt does not see the move to make humans the final end as a viable solution either. For, where humans declare themselves as the end, we are back to reducing everything in the world to a means: everything is for the use of humans.

Both Arendt and Gadamer note how for the ancient Greeks the appeal to efficiency and usefulness diminished the highest calling of humans: namely, *theoria*. What is made, what is a matter of craft, remains deficient compared to the life of *theoria*. Arendt comments, "It is quite obvious that the Greeks dreaded this devaluation of world and nature with its inherent anthropocentrism—the 'absurd' opinion that man is the highest being and that everything else is subject to the exigencies of human life (Aristotle)—no less than they despised the sheer vulgarity of all consistent utilitarianism" (Arendt 1989, 157). Arendt's account of the futility of a life lived in a world of means parallels Gadamer's caution regarding the ubiquity of scientific method and concern over the dogmatism implicit in science, which he describes as: "the inherent tendency of scientific doctrine . . . to make superfluous the scrutiny of ends by successfully providing and 'controlling' the means at one and the same time" (Gadamer 1992a, 169). Gadamer's stance toward science is not a derogatory one, but is based on a desire to reinvigorate the ancient Greek conception of theory and to thus make science more humane by showing its origin in the life-world.

But what is really so wrong with humans positing themselves as the end? Arendt's answer returns us to the importance Gadamer attaches to dialogue. Arendt says:

> The point of the matter is that Plato saw immediately that if one makes man the measure of all things for use, it is man the user and instrumentalizer, and not man the speaker and doer or man the thinker, to whom the world is being related . . . . [T]o follow Plato's own example, the wind will no longer be understood in its own right as a natural force but will be considered exclusively in accordance with human needs for warmth or refreshment—which of course, means that the wind as something objectively given has been eliminated from human experience. (Arendt 1989, 158)

As soon as humanity positions itself as the end in a world of means, any possibility of acting as a thinker, as a speaker, or as a political being evaporates. In Arendt's terms, we lose the possibility for "spontaneity" in a world in which everything is instrumentalized. And for Arendt true action is impossible without spontaneity; where there is no possibility to act anew, there is no possibility for action, period. Thus a final end is necessary to restore meaning to human (inter)action.

Arendt's argument that meaning requires a final end is analogous to Gadamer's conception of understanding that requires the good, which I am defining as a tacit assumption necessary for all understanding and thus truth. All understanding requires that we proceed "as if" there were a final end—though what that final end is can never be, finally, fully specified and nor can it be achieved. What unifies both thinkers at this point is their common interest in illuminating the conditions of meaning for inter-subjective interaction that summons the notion of a final or transcendent end. Thus just as Arendt sees transcendence as required for spontaneity and political activity, so we could say that Gadamer defends the role of the good as making possible true understanding by serving as a thing's "for the sake of which," which always requires dialogical justification.[25] As explained earlier in this chapter, the understanding that goes on in true dialogue is something that takes one beyond what one individual can predict, control, or manipulate. The goal of dialogue is that which transcends individual intending and requires the openness of a continual pursuit—i.e., that which refuses instrumentalization. Such openness required by true dialogue means that the end of understanding cannot be articulated, much less determined, in advance. We cannot bring our own immediate desires to bear on our encounter with another—to do so would be manipulative (indeed, "strategic") to the extent that we already have an end in mind that we are seeking at all costs to get the other to agree to. Hidden agendas cannot be tolerated.

Thus we could contrast the power plays and ideology that are so counterproductive to true dialogue with "natality."[26] In a true dialogic encounter both parties remain open to being changed in ways that cannot be predicted. This is

---

25. See chapter 1, pp. 8 ff.

26. See my discussion of the relationship between natality and our linguisticality in chapter 4, pp. 92-95.

the risk of "keeping eyes open for the good." Indeed, the openness to the "transcendence of the beyond" is exactly what Gadamer names as the good (Gadamer 2004, 36). Gadamer's Arendtian point is that the dialogue form itself cannot be evaluated in terms of its usefulness, nor can it be instrumentalized; to attempt as much is to deprive it of its truth. Where humans come together to act and speak, there is not only lively risk, but the power of true creativity. Gadamer tells us that "in genuine dialogue, something emerges that is contained in neither of the partners by himself" (Gadamer 1992a, 462). This is due to the creative power of language, which for Gadamer is most fully realized in dialogue. In dialogue, we could say, language is most itself. Gadamer makes an Arendtian point when he writes:

> But there is another dialectic of the word, which accords to every word an inner dimension of multiplication: every word breaks forth as if from a center and is related to a whole, through which alone it is a word. Every word causes the whole of the language to which it belongs to resonate and the whole worldview that underlies it to appear. Thus every word, as the event of a moment, carries with it the unsaid, to which it is related by responding and summoning. The occasionality of human speech is not a casual imperfection of its expressive power; it is, rather, the logical expression of the living virtuality of speech that brings a totality of meaning into play, without being able to express it totally. (Gadamer 1992b, 458)

That we can never say everything, far from being a stain on our humanity, is what incites the erotic drive to keep saying more and leads to reproduction in speech of new worlds. To say, as both Arendt and Gadamer do, that understanding is, ultimately, made possible by the good-beyond-being returns us to an appreciation for the importance of dialogue. Both thinkers fear that should the instrumentalization with which we imbue the world eventually take over, we will be unable to create, to get beyond the demands of the immediacy of usefulness, indeed engage in dialogue at all. Dieter Misgeld also recognizes in dialogue an antidote against the urge to instrumentalize or technologize human interaction:

> Dialogue as a form of communication, therefore, is the opposite of the imposition of categories on one's understanding, which are not derived from the process of understanding itself. Nor is it a process for which beginning and end are easily identified in advance . . . [T]he very play of identity and difference gives dialogue the power to convey something to our understanding, while also making participants more present to themselves and each other as capable of understanding. On all these grounds, the dialogical principle can be suitably regarded as the opposite of technical, technological making or of instrumental action. Engaging in dialogue also entails the absence of strategic thinking or of the strategic placement of words in conversation. (Misgeld 1990, 168)

The anti-instrumental conception of dialogue reveals why Gadamer has never been drawn to adapting elements of critical theory to his hermeneutics. For such a critique stems out of a form of scientism that propounds the possibility of a purely neutral stance. For example, Gadamer speaks of "Max Weber's exaggerated differentiation between value-free science and ideological decisions" (Gadamer 1992a, 174). Although the arguments of Habermas are more subtle, he makes the same appeal to and claim about the social sciences.[27] Thus ultimately dialogue is not, to use Arendt's terminology, "in order to" achieve a political consensus; rather it is "for the sake of" our humanity that we dialogue. The same sentiment is captured by Gadamer's statement: "To become capable of conversation again and again—that is, to listen to the Other—appears to me to be an authentic raising of human beings to their humanity" (Gadamer 2005, 11). We can only approach such dialogical understanding with an assumption of the good whose transcendence reminds us not to approach the other as a means for our use but as an end in herself.

I believe that the unpopularity of speaking of "the" good-as-transcendent is often due to the fact that it is taken to refer to, in the words of Richard Rorty, "unconditional and categorical obligations" (Rorty 1999, 73). What I have tried to show, however, is that if we take Gadamer's reading of Plato seriously, we see that Plato, far from maintaining the good as a categorical standard, insists that the good can never be known. This move prevents a methodological approach to the good that attempts to fully and finally articulate it. Instead, Gadamer insists that "the Socratic thinking . . . constantly questions things, seeking the Good with an attitude of not knowing . . ." (Gadamer 2007, 112). Plato's talk of the good was not to hand us a blueprint for the moral life but to challenge the easy appeal to what we take to be the good in the immediate moment, and to show that it deserves more thoughtful analysis based on something that transcends our immediate desires and aims. Such a transcendence, far from being a-human, reflects the way in which human reason, human meaning, transcends what any one individual can attain or possess. And because no one individual can ever attain it, transcendence demands not a withdrawal from the solidarity of humanity, but a deeper commitment to it through dialogue. What hermeneutics helps us see about the good, then, is that the good is not a set of obligations that we must conform ourselves to; to say as much would be to contradict Plato's espousal of the good as that which lies beyond being. Gadamer's Platonic intuitions reveal the crucial role the good plays in our understanding: namely, as a reference point that lies beyond the finitude of the moment and yet bids us join with others in its pursuit.

---

27. See especially Habermas 1988 and 1995. Although he has modified his position over the years with regard to the role the social sciences can play in grounding his critique, there still persists an element of his earlier emphasis.

The Relevance of the Good-Beyond-Being

Let me close by offering one more defense of an anticipated criticism, one that takes a deflationary or reductionistic view of the good and that challenges the benefit of speaking of the hermeneutical role of the good. We could put the objection this way: does it make sense to speak of aiming at something (like the good) that we do not know in advance what it is? Richard Rorty, for example, maintains that you cannot aim at a generalized conception like "moral perfection" because you would not know when you have achieved it.[28] He suggests that it is futile to claim that one wants to be a better person, without immediately knowing what that may mean. Such a view assumes that one's final end, one's good, is fully articulable. But I want to take a closer look at the legitimacy of this claim. Now, while it is true that you cannot aim at a tangible target unless you can see it, e.g., in archery, the preceding section argued that the human condition cannot be accurately accounted for solely in instrumental terms. This means that making an analogy between a practice defined by tangible ends and human life is illegitimate. The human condition remains more complicated and thus diffuse and unknowable than the practice of taking up arms and aiming at a target. Gadamer, via Plato, has shown that it is *theoria* rather than *techne* that accords with the nature of humanity. We are neither machines nor automatons. We do not operate according to algorithms or pre-established ends. As humans, caught up in a web of understanding, played by the game of language, we *can* aim at general and diffuse goals which are constantly changing. If we knew exactly what we were aiming at, we would be less than human. (On the other hand, if we had no need to aim at anything, we would be gods.) A Platonic hermeneutics, such as Gadamer's, esteems the importance of aiming in general at the good-beyond-being, where specifics become clearer only in the actual striving. In fact, Rorty himself actually seems to come close to saying as much when he writes: "It is what the Founding Fathers of my country attempted when they asked people to think of themselves not so much as Pennsylvanian Quakers or Catholic Marylanders but as citizens of a tolerant, pluralistic, federal republic" (Rorty 1999, 88). In other words, here Rorty seems to assume that there is something to be said for striving for what cannot be fully articulated in advance and that transcends the particulars of one's life, namely a "tolerant, pluralistic, federal republic." For while it is true that there is ultimately no such thing as a citizen of a "tolerant, pluralistic, federal republic" who is not also a Pennsylvanian Quaker or Catholic Marylander or Episcopalian Virginian, etc., this is not to say that there is no benefit to be derived from thinking beyond one's parochial existence or aiming at, hoping for, what cannot be fully conceived. Rorty esteems in the ideals of the Founding Fathers precisely the fact that progress can be made only when we are able to think beyond our parochial goals to something bigger than ourselves and which is not yet fully conceivable. As he himself admits, it is

---

28. See Rorty 1999, 82.

an intentionally vague ideal meant to spur people on to new ways of thinking and living. It is this notion, then, of a vague ideal that helps us makes sense of a good-beyond-being. In fact, Plato's exultation of the good sounds an awful lot like the "fuzziness" Rorty extols in another essay, where he emphasizes how pragmatists prefer the more general and loose language of striving for a "better future."[29] Rorty explains there that "better" means

> better in the sense of containing more of what we consider good and less of what we consider bad. When asked, "And what exactly do you consider good?", pragmatists can only say with Whitman, "variety and freedom," or with Dewey, "growth." "Growth itself," Dewey said, "is the only moral end." They are limited to such fuzzy and unhelpful answers because what they hope is not that the future will conform to a plan, will fulfill an immanent teleology, but rather that the future will astonish and exhilarate. (Rorty 1999, 28)

But, why is aiming at a fuzzy goal like growth any more acceptable than aiming at a vague notion of what is good? Is not esteeming "fuzziness" over a blueprint meant to eliminate the very possibility of knowing what your target looks like in advance? I find the following point of concurrence between Plato and Rorty: both acknowledge that we want something more, something that we cannot fully articulate and that emerges out of a dissatisfaction with the present. Rorty, then, appears to be caught in a contradiction: on the one hand, he lauds a general, "fuzzy" ideal; on the other, he implies that generality is ultimately fruitless since we have to know exactly at what we aim.

Gadamer's dialectical hermeneutics, too, acknowledges that humans function best when aiming at diffuse goals, for this encourages us to transcend the limits of the moment. If we have only a specific goal, there is no room for creativity, risk, change, etc.—not to mention understanding. And this is especially true when it comes to dialogue: we must have only a general sense of what understanding would look like. If we already "know" in advance what the outcome of the dialogue will be, it will be impossible to approach the dialogue with the openness necessary for true understanding. Putting it in Gadamer's terms: if we think we know the outcome of the event of understanding in advance we will always arrive too late to experience truth. We join linguistically with others in pursuit of a general, vague goal—one neither fully expressible nor achievable but that nonetheless makes possible natality. The moral emerging from Gadamer's dialectical hermeneutics is that humans have a peculiar task, namely, to live in-between the transcendent and immanent, between the universal and particular, between the diffuse and the concrete, and that to privilege one side over the other is to either elevate humans to the status of gods or to reduce humans to the status of automatons. Hermeneutics esteems the value of living in light of the

---

29. See his "Truth without Correspondence to Reality" (Rorty 1999, especially 27-28).

transcendent, which, rather than being a hindrance to movement provides us with a call, the details of which it is our lifelong task to fill in.

In order to illustrate further the way in which the good functions as a tacit assumption never fully reachable yet necessary for knowledge, let us consider the situation of Lambert Strether in Henry James' *The Ambassadors*. On one level, the novel suggests, in good Aristotelian fashion, that the key to morality is in the details, in being able to see the particulars, which can only occur as a result of an engaged seeing.[30] As Martha Nussbaum argues, morality is marked more by our sensitivity to the particulars of a given situation than by direct knowledge of a transcendent good. Consequently, Nussbaum reasons that it is the richness of details that makes literature so crucial for discussions about morality. However, without wanting to dispute Nussbaum's point about the value of being "finely aware and richly responsible,"[31] I want to suggest that James' novel also shows us the importance of the transcendent good for gaining (self) understanding.

Strether's ability to perceive with increasing moral sensitivity and rigor what is really the best for him to do certainly requires an awareness of the details of the concrete situation in which he finds himself embedded. But he also requires an awareness of something that transcends his situation. For, as the discussion about *arete* in chapter 1 demonstrated, if we are to speak of rational judgment then we must be able to make sense of the way in which such judgment refers to something beyond itself; otherwise, we have only Sartrian brute choice. In making decisions about one's life one cannot simply rely on the details of the particulars.[32] One needs a framework that makes sense of the way in which these details constitute a moral struggle. Why do we feel a pull between two (or more) options? Why could Strether not just be happy to remain in Paris with Maria? What helps us think beyond the immediacy of our situation and to actually wrestle with the various options that present themselves to us is our tacit assumption that it is worthwhile to struggle with these problems. If our choices feel weighty to us, then it must be due to our belief in something external to our situation that signifies that our choice has a larger significance. The very practice of reflective judgment betrays that we indeed do believe that one decision, choice, way of living, is ultimately better than another—if we did not assume this from the outset then we would at best be left with brute choice, and at worst left to starve along with Buridan's ass. What Strether's experience as an (failed) ambassador suggests is that in making a decision about what is the best way to live, our assumption about the good is not simply one about maximizing the benefits based on the exigencies of the immediate situation. If this were the case, Strether would have likely stayed in Paris and pursued a relationship with

---

30. Martha Nussbaum makes this point; see in particular her essay "Perceptive Equilibrium: Literary Theory and Ethical Theory" (Nussbaum 1990).

31. Nussbaum 1990, 168-194.

32. This recalls Gadamer's point about the requirement of a good beyond the immediacy of pleasure. See the discussion in chapter 1, pp. 10 ff.

Maria. At the same time, the novel also shows that far from experiencing a relativistic conversion to another point of view (where no particulars were taken into account), Strether worked hard to insure that he knew the particular facts so he could make the right decision. He was not blindly seduced by Paris. Yet all the while he maintained that there was a greater good—albeit not one that served as an instruction manual for his ambassadorship—and it was this very belief that allowed his transition from one position to another to be a meaningful one. Talk of his "conversion" from the parochial values of Woollett to the cosmopolitan ones of Paris would not have made sense without him assuming that there was a good transcending his own desires. Without a commitment to an overarching good that transcends the values of Woollett and of Paris, there would be no moral tension. We would be left with moral incommensurability. Yet, this "good" was not concrete in nature; it was not one he could fully articulate. What this novel shows is the way in which he is constantly gesturing towards the good that lies just beyond being, protecting him from moral incommensurability. He assumes the good to be there but he can never grasp it sufficiently to make it fully accessible either to others or to himself. For if the good were able to be fully apprehended there would be no moral dilemma; we would know with clarity and distinctness what is right to do from the outset. It is this tacit sense of the good-as-transcendent that I believe captures the meaning of the hermeneutical good, without which not just choice, but also understanding, would be impossible.

In closing, let me now relate the role of the good back to the dialectically ethical implications of Gadamer's hermeneutics. The ethical bent of Gadamer's hermeneutics becomes clearer when we acknowledge that understanding's task is one that finds us together, not alone, and that we are all faced with working through the "angst . . . that threatens everyone" (Gadamer 2004, 142). And in doing so, as we gesture toward the transcendent, we face "a task that unites us all in our mutual understanding. This ultimate ethical task cannot be separated from the one task of questioning and understanding our own existence" (Gadamer 2004, 143). Hence, we perceive not only the dialectical aspect of the ethics marking Gadamer's hermeneutics but also the way this focus contributes to a further clarification of the scope of hermeneutics: understanding directed at human existence itself is ethical. The dialectical component of such an ethics can be seen not only in terms of the fundamental role dialogue plays in understanding but in the way in which as humans we struggle to understand our own existence all the while caught in-between transcendence and immanence. On one hand, as we have seen, understanding aims at the good, taking us beyond our instrumental concerns that deprive the event of understanding of a *telos*. Understanding, teleologically thus construed, requires openness and risk to enter into the precarious movement of the in-between. But while understanding requires a moment of transcendence, hermeneutics also reminds us that understanding is marked by immanence. And for Gadamer, this means that all understanding is dialogical, revealing the importance of solidarity to understanding. Gadamer's

Hermeneutics' Dialectical Ethics: Dialogue and the Good   127

dialectical hermeneutics is thus indeed practical philosophy to the extent that it shows us what we are up against, what our task is, and what is required to face it: a view to the good that summons us to solidarity through the genuine understanding evinced by dialogue. To understand implies another: both an "immanent" other with whom we struggle to hold hands and a "transcendent" other for whom we reach but never grasp. The good's transcendence, then, is at once the starting point of all understanding as well as a reminder of the exigency of dialogue that draws us into solidarity. That the ability to be taken away by the transcendent also bespeaks the need for solidarity recalls the statement by Gadamer (quoted above): "We have the ability to become so absorbed in something that we totally forget ourselves in it; this is one of the great blessings of the experience of art, as well as one of the great promises of religion. Indeed, this is ultimately one of the basic conditions that will allow us human beings to live together in a human way" (Gadamer 2007, 120).[33] That hermeneutics' dialectic between transcendence and solidarity is nonetheless difficult and fraught with uncertainty is attested to by the fact that Hermes was known as a trickster god. And this cunningness is true not only of the ancient Greek divinity. Even the Hebrew God comes incognito, for example, when engaging Jacob in a wrestling match.[34] This means that we, who remain open to an encounter with another, like Jacob wrestling with God, may not always be able to tell with whom we are dealing nor what the outcome will be. But to wish away such uncertainty is to deny the very situation into which we are thrown. Understanding is ethical, then, to the extent to which it requires dialogical engagement with another; it is dialectical to the extent that we are caught in-between our own finitude and our longing to transcend it. Gadamer's dialectical hermeneutics helps us acknowledge our long forgotten kinship as the very offspring of Hermes.

33. Chapter 3, p. 48.
34. The theme of the Rilke poem quoted in the epigraph to this book and based on Genesis 32.

Bibliography

Alcoff, Linda Martin. 1996. *Real Knowing: New Versions of the Coherence Theory*. Ithaca: Cornell University Press.
———. 2006. *Visible Identities: Race, Gender and the Self.* New York: Oxford University Press.
Ambrosio, Francis J. 1987. Gadamer, Plato, and the Discipline of Dialogue. *International Philosophical Quarterly* 27 (1): 17-32.
Arendt, Hannah. 1989. *The Human Condition*. Chicago: University of Chicago Press.
Baracchi, Claudia. 2002. The Nature of Reason and the Sublimity of First Philosophy: Toward a Reconfiguration of an Aristotelian First Philosophy. *Epoche* Spring 7 (2): 223-249.
Barthold, Lauren Swayne. 2005a. The Sheltering Sky: *Aletheia's* Region. In *Between Description and Interpretation: The Hermeneutic Turn in Phenomenology*, ed. Andrzej Wiercinski. Toronto: The Hermeneutic Press.
———. 2005b. How Hermeneutical is He? A Gadamerian Analysis of Richard Rorty. *Philosophy Today* 49 (3): 236-244.
———. 2010. Friendship and the Ethics of Understanding. *Epoche*. Forthcoming.
Beauvoir, Simone de. 1989. *The Second Sex*. Trans. and ed. H.M. Parshley. New York: Random House Books.
Beiner, Ronald, and William James Booth, eds. 1993. *Kant and Political Philosophy*. New Haven: Yale University Press.
Bernasconi, Robert. 1986. Bridging the Abyss: Heidegger and Gadamer. *Research in Phenomenology* 16: 1-24.
Bernet, Rudolf. 2005. Gadamer on the Subject's Participation in the Game of Truth. *Review of Metaphysics* 58: 785-814.

Bernstein, Richard J. 1983. *Beyond Objectivism and Relativism*. Philadelphia: University of Pennsylvania Press.
———. 1986. From Hermeneutics to Praxis. In *Hermeneutics and Modern Philosophy*, ed. Brice R. Wachterhauser. Albany: SUNY Press.
———. 1997. Pragmatism, Pluralism, and the Healing of Wounds. In *Pragmatism: A Reader*, ed. Louis Menand. New York: Vintage Books.
Berti, Enrico. 2004. The Reception of Aristotle's Intellectual Virtues in Gadamer and the Hermeneutic Philosophy. In *The Impact of Aristotelianism on Modern Philosophy*, ed. Riccardo Pozzo. Washington, D.C.: Catholic University of America Press.
Brandom, Robert B., ed. 2000. *Rorty and His Critics*. Malden, Mass.: Blackwell Publishers.
Brogan, Walter A. 2002. Gadamer's Praise of Theory: Aristotle's Friend and the Reciprocity between Theory and Practice, pre-published manuscript, later published in *Research and Phenomenology* 32 (1): 141-155.
Bruns, Gerald L.1992. *Hermeneutics Ancient and Modern*. New Haven: Yale University Press.
———. 1999. *Tragic Thoughts at the End of Philosophy*. Evanston, Ill.: Northwestern University Press.
Caputo, John D. 1987. *Radical Hermeneutics*. Indianapolis: Indiana University Press.
———. 2000. *More Radical Hermeneutics*. Indianapolis: Indiana University Press.
———. 2002. Good Will and the Hermeneutics of Friendship: Gadamer and Derrida. *Philosophy and Social Criticism* 28 (5): 512-522.
Coltman, Rod. 1998. *The Language of Hermeneutics*. Albany: SUNY Press.
Davey, Nicholas. 2007. *Unquiet Understanding. Gadamer's Philosophical Hermeneutics*. Albany: SUNY Press.
Decker, Kevin. 2000. The Limits of Radical Openness: Gadamer on Socratic Dialectic and Plato's Idea of the Good. *Symposium* 4 (1): 5-32.
Dewey, John. 1965. *Reconstruction in Philosophy*. Boston: Beacon Press.
Dobrosavlejev, Duska. 2002. Gadamer's Hermeneutics as Practical Philosophy. *Facta, Universitatis* 2 (9): 605-618.
Dostal, Robert J. 1987. The World Never Lost: The Hermeneutics of Trust. *Philosophy and Phenomenological Research* 42 (3): 413-434.
———, ed. 2002. *The Cambridge Companion to Gadamer*. New York: Cambridge University Press.
Dottori, Riccardo. 2004. *A Century of Philosophy: Hans-Georg Gadamer in Conversation with Riccardo Dottori*. Trans. Rod Coltman with Sigrid Koepke. New York: Continuum.
Eberhard, Philippe. 2004. *The Middle Voice in Gadamer's Hermeneutics*. Tübingen: Mohr Siebeck.
Fairfield, Paul. 2000. Hermeneutical Ethical Theory. In *The Ethics of Postmodernity*, ed. Gary B. Madison and Marty Fairbairn. Evanston, Ill.: Northwestern University Press.

Faulconer, James E. 1998. Whose Voice do I Hear? Risser on Gadamer on the Other. *Research in Phenomenology* 28: 292-298.

Figal, Gunter. 1995. Phronesis as Understanding: Situating Philosophical Hermeneutics. In *The Specter of Relativism: Truth, Dialogue, and Phronesis in Philosophical Hermeneutics*, ed. Lawrence Schmidt. Evanston, Ill.: Northwestern University Press.

Foster, Matthew. 1991. *Gadamer and Practical Philosophy*. Atlanta: Scholars Press.

Friedländer, Paul. 1958. *Plato*. Vols. 1-3. New York: Pantheon Books.

———. 1964. *Platon*. Bd. I. Berlin: Walter de Gruyte & Co.

Gadamer, Hans-Georg. *Gesammelte Werke*. Tübigen: J.C.B. Mohr (Paul Siebeck).

———. 1970. The Power of Reason. *Man and World* 3 (1): 5-15.

———. 1975. Hermeneutics and Social Science. *Cultural Hermeneutics* 2: 307-316.

———. 1976. *Hegel's Dialectic: Five Hermeneutical Studies*. Trans. P. Christopher Smith. New Haven: Yale University Press.

———. 1977. *Philosophical Hermeneutics*. Trans. and ed. David E. Linge. Berkeley: University of California Press.

———. 1979. Practical Philosophy as a Model of the Human Sciences. In *Research in Phenomenology* 9: 74-85.

———. 1980. *Dialogue and Dialectic*. Trans. P. Christopher Smith. New Haven: Yale University Press.

———. 1983. A Letter by Professor Hans-Georg Gadamer. In *Beyond Objectivism and Relativism*. Richard J. Bernstein. Philadelphia: University of Pennsylvania Press.

———. 1985. *Gesammelte Werke 5: Griechische Philosophie I*. Tübingen: J.C.B. Mohr (Paul Siebeck).

———. 1986. *The Idea of the Good in Platonic-Aristotelian Philosophy*. Trans. and with an introduction and annotation by P. Christopher Smith. New Haven: Yale University Press.

———. 1987. The Problem of Historical Consciousness. In *Interpretive Social Science*, ed. Paul Rabinow and William M. Sullivan. Berkeley: University of California Press.

———. 1988. Reply to Nicholas P. White. In *Platonic Readings/Platonic Writings*, ed. Charles L. Griswold. University Park: Pennsylvania State University Press.

———. 1989. *Dialogue and Deconstruction*. Ed. Diane P. Michelfelder and Richard E. Palmer. Albany: SUNY Press.

———. 1990. *Gesammelte Werke I: Hermeneutik I*. Tübingen: J.C.B. Mohr (Paul Siebeck).

———. 1991a. Gadamer on Gadamer. In *Gadamer and Hermeneutics*, ed. Hugh Silverman. New York: Routledge Press.

———. 1991b. *Plato's Dialectical Ethics*. Trans. Robert M. Wallace. New Haven: Yale University Press.

———. 1992a. *Hans-Georg Gadamer on Education, Poetry, and History*. Ed. Dieter Misgeld and Graeme Nicholson. Trans. Lawrence Schmidt and Monica Reuss. Albany: SUNY Press.

———. 1992b. *Truth and Method*. 2nd ed. Trans. Joel Weinsheimer and Donald G. Marshall. New York: Crossroad.

———. 1992c. *Reason in the Age of Science*. Trans. Frederick G. Lawrence. Cambridge: MIT Press.

———. 1993a. *Gesammelte Werke II, Hermeneutik II*. Tübingen: J.C.B. Mohr (Paul Siebeck).

———. 1993b. On the Possibility of a Philosophical Ethics. In *Kant and Political Philosophy*, ed. Ronald Beiner and William James Booth. New Haven: Yale University Press.

———. 1994a. Truth in the Human Sciences. In *Hermeneutics and Truth*, ed. Brice Wachterhauser. Evanston, Ill.: Northwestern University Press.

———. 1994b. What is Truth? In *Hermeneutics and Truth*, ed. Brice Wachterhauser. Evanston, Ill.: Northwestern University Press.

———. 1994c. *Heidegger's Ways*. Trans. John W. Stanley. Albany: SUNY Press.

———. 1995. On the Truth of the Word. In *The Specter of Relativism: Truth, Dialogue, and* Phronesis *in Philosophical Hermeneutics*, ed. Lawrence Schmidt. Evanston, Ill.: Northwestern University Press.

———. 1996a. *The Enigma of Health*. Trans. Jason Gaiger and Nicholas Walker. Stanford: Stanford University Press.

———. 1996b. *The Relevance of the Beautiful*. Ed. Robert Bernasconi. Trans. Nicholas Walker. New York: Cambridge University Press.

———. 1997. Reply to Thomas Alexander. In *The Philosophy of Hans-Georg Gadamer*, ed. Lewis Edwin Hahn. Chicago: Open Court.

———. 1998a. *The Beginning of Philosophy*. Trans. Rod Coltman. New York: Continuum.

———. 1998b. *Praise of Theory*. Trans. Chris Dawson. New Haven: Yale University Press.

———. 1999. *Hermeneutics, Religion, and Ethics*. Trans. Joel Weinsheimer. New Haven: Yale University Press.

———. 2001. *Gadamer in Conversation*. Ed. and trans. Richard E. Palmer. New Haven: Yale University Press.

———. 2002a. *The Beginning of Knowledge*. Trans. Rod Coltman. New York: Continuum.

———. 2002b. On the Truth of the Word. *Symposium* 6 (2): 115-134.

———. 2004. *A Century of Philosophy*. Trans. Rod Coltman with Sigrid Koepke. New York: Continuum.

———. 2005. The Incapacity for Conversation. Pre-published translation, later published and revised in *Continental Philosophy Review*. Trans. David Vessey and Chris Blaukamp. Vol. 39, no. 4: 351-359.

———. 2007. *The Gadamer Reader: A Bouquet of the Later Writings*. Ed. Richard E. Palmer. Evanston, Ill.: Northwestern University Press.

Gallagher, Shawn. 1992. *Hermeneutics and Education*. Albany: SUNY Press.
Gjesdal, Kristin. 2007. Reading Kant Hermeneutically: Gadamer and the Critique of Judgment. *Kant-Studien* 98 (3): 351-371.
Gonzalez, Francisco J. 1998. *Dialectic and Dialogue*. Evanston, Ill.: Northwestern University Press.
———. 2006. Dialectic and Dialogue in the Hermeneutics of Paul Ricoeur and H.G. Gadamer. *Continental Philosophy Review* 39 (3): 313-345.
Griswold, Charles. 1981. Gadamer and the Interpretation of Plato. *Ancient Philosophy* Spring 1: 171-178.
———. 1982. Reflections on "Dialectic" in Plato and Hegel. *International Philosophical Quarterly* 22: 115-130.
———, ed. 1988. *Platonic Writings, Platonic Readings*. University Park: Pennsylvania State University Press.
Grondin, Jean. 1982. *Hermeneutische Wahrheit? Zum Wahrheitsbegriff Hans-Georg Gadamers*. Königstein: Forum Academicum.
———. 2003. *The Philosophy of Hans-Georg Gadamer*. Montreal: McGill Queen's University Press.
Guignon, Charles. 2002. Truth in Interpretation: A Hermeneutic Approach. In *Is There a Single Right Interpretation*, ed. Michael Krausz. University Park: Pennsylvania State University Press.
Habermas, Jürgen. 1986. A Review of Gadamer's "Truth and Method." In *Hermeneutics and Modern Philosophy*, ed. Brice Wachterhauser. Albany: SUNY Press.
———. 1988. *On the Logic of the Social Sciences*. Trans. Shierry Weber Nicholsen and Jerry A. Stark. Cambridge: MIT Press.
———. 1995. *Moral Consciousness and Communicative Action*. Trans. Christian Lenhardt and Shierry Weber Nicholsen. Cambridge, Mass.: MIT Press.
Hahn, Lewis Edwin, ed. 1997. *The Philosophy of Hans-Georg Gadamer*. Chicago: Open Court Publishing Company.
Held, Virginia, ed. 1995. *Justice and Care*. Boulder, Colo.: Westview Press.
———. 2006. *The Ethics of Care*. New York: Oxford University Press.
Honneth, Axel. 2003. On the Destructive Power of the Third. *Philosophy and Social Criticism* 29 (1): 5-21.
Hoy, David. 1978. *The Critical Circle: Literature, History and Philosophical Hermeneutics*. Berkeley: University of California Press.
Irwin, William. 2001. A Critique of Hermeneutic Truth as Disclosure. *International Studies in Philosophy* 33 (4): 63-75.
James, Henry. 1986. *The Ambassadors*. New York: Penguin Books.
James, William. 1996. *Pragmatism and The Meaning of Truth*. Cambridge, Mass.: Harvard University Press.
Kidder, Paulette. 1995. Gadamer and the Platonic *Eidos*. *Philosophy Today* 35 (1): 83-92.
Kögler, Hans Herbert. 1999. *The Power of Dialogue*. Cambridge: MIT Press.

Krajewski, Bruce, ed. 2004. *Gadamer's Repercussions*. Berkeley: University of California Press.
Lafont, Cristina. 1999. *The Linguistic Turn in Hermeneutic Philosophy*. Trans. Jose Medina. Cambridge: MIT Press.
Langsdorf, Lenore, and Stephen H. Watson with E. Marya Bower, eds. 1996. *Phenomenology, Interpretation, and Community*. Albany: SUNY Press.
Lawn, Christopher. 2003. Wittgenstein, History and Hermeneutics. *Philosophy and Social Criticism* 29 (3): 281-295.
Long, Christopher. 2002. The Ontological Reappropriation of Phronesis. *Continental Philosophy Review* 35 (1): 35-60.
———. 2003. The Ethical Culmination of Aristotle's Metaphysics. *Epoche* 8 (1): 121-140.
MacIntyre, Alasdair. 1984. *After Virtue*. 2nd ed. Notre Dame, Ind.: University of Notre Dame Press.
Madison, G.B. 1990. *The Hermeneutics of Postmodernity*. Indianapolis: Indiana University Press.
——— and Marty Fairbairn, eds. 2000. *The Ethics of Postmodernity*. Evanston, Ill.: Northwestern University Press.
———. 2002. Gadamer's Legacy. *Symposium* 6 (2): 135-147.
Malpas, Jeff, Ulrich Arnswald, and Jens Kertscher, eds. 2002. *Gadamer's Century*. Cambridge: MIT Press.
Michelfelder, Diane P., and Richard E. Palmer, eds. 1989. *Dialogue and Deconstruction: The Gadamer-Derrida Encounter*. Albany: SUNY Press.
Misgeld, Dieter. 1990. Poetry, Dialogue, and Negotiation: Liberal Culture and Conservative Politics in Hans-Georg Gadamer's Thought. In *Festivals of Interpretation*, ed. Kathleen Wright. Albany: SUNY Press.
Nicholson, Graeme. 1997. Truth in Metaphysics and in Hermeneutics. In *The Philosophy of Hans-Georg Gadamer*. Vol. XXIV of The Library of Living Philosophers, ed. Lewis Edwin Hahn. Chicago: Open Court Publishing Company.
———. 2002. Know Thyself. *Philosophy and Social Criticism* 28 (5): 494-503.
Nietzsche, Friedrich. 1974. *The Gay Science*. Trans. Walter Kaufmann. New York: Vintage Books.
———. 2006. *On Dialogue*. Lanham, Md.: Lexington Books.
Noddings, Nel. 1986. *Caring*. Berkeley: University of California Press.
Nussbaum, Martha C. 1990. *Love's Knowledge*. New York: Oxford University Press.
———. 1995. *The Fragility of Goodness*. New York: Cambridge University Press.
———. 1996. *The Therapy of Desire*. Princeton, N.J.: Princeton University Press.
Poole, Gordon. 1995. Gadamer and Ricoeur on the Hermeneutics of *Praxis*. *Philosophy and Social Criticism* 21 (5-6): 63-79.
Rabinow, Paul, and William M. Sullivan, eds. 1987. *Interpretive Social Science: A Second Look*. Berkeley: University of California Press.

Rasmussen, David M. 2002. Hermeneutics and Public Deliberation. *Philosophy and Social Criticism* 28 (5): 504-511.
Renaud, Francois. 1999. *Die Resokratisierung Platons: die platonische Hermeneutik Hans-Georg Gadamers.* Heidelberg, Germany: Academia.
Ricoeur, Paul. 1986. Hermeneutics and the Critique of Ideology. In *Hermeneutics and Modern Philosophy*, ed. Brice Wachterhauser. Albany: SUNY Press.
———. 1991. *From Text to Action.* Trans. Kathleen Blamey and John B. Thompson. Evanston, Ill.: Northwestern University Press.
Risser, James. 1984. Practical Reason, Hermeneutics and Social Life. *Proceedings of the American Catholic Philosophical Association* 58: 84-92.
———. 1997. *Hermeneutics and the Voice of the Other.* Albany: SUNY Press.
———. 2002a. In the Shadow of Hegel: Infinite Dialogue in Gadamer's Hermeneutics. *Research in Phenomenology* 32: 86-102.
———. 2002b. *Phronesis* as Kairological Event. *Epoche* Fall 7 (1): 107-119.
Robinson, Richard. 1953. *Plato's Earlier Dialectic.* 2nd ed. Oxford: Clarendon Press.
Rorty, Richard. 1998. *Truth and Progress.* Cambridge, U.K.: Cambridge University Press.
———. 1999. *Philosophy and Social Hope.* New York: Penguin Books.
———. 2000. *Rorty and His Critics.* Ed. Robert Brandom. Malden, Mass.: Blackwell Publishers.
Rosen, Stanley. 1987. *Plato's Symposium.* 2nd ed. New Haven: Yale University Press.
Santas, Gerasimos. 1989. Aristotle's Criticism of Plato's Form of the Good: Ethics without Metaphysics? *Philosophical Papers* 28 (2): 137-160.
Scheibler, Ingrid. 2000a. *Gadamer: Between Heidegger and Habermas.* Lanham, Md.: Rowman & Littlefield Publishers.
———. 2000b. Gadamer, Heidegger, and the Social Dimension of Language: Reflection on the Critical Potential of Hermeneutical Philosophy. *Chicago-Kent Law Review* 76 (2): 853-892.
Schmidt, Lawrence, ed. 1995. *The Specter of Relativism: Truth, Dialogue, and Phronesis in Philosophical Hermeneutics.* Evanston, Ill.: Northwestern University Press.
———. 1996. Das Einleuchtende. In *Phenomenology, Interpretation, and Community*, ed. Lenore Langsdorf and Stephen H. Watson with E. Marya Bower. Albany: SUNY Press.
———. 2003. Adjudicating Ethical Prejudgments. *Journal of the British Society of Phenomenology* 34 (3): 281-296.
Shuchman, Paul. 1979. Aristotle's *Phronesis* and Gadamer's Hermeneutics. *Philosophy Today* Spring 23: 41-50.
Silverman, Hugh J., ed. 1991. *Gadamer and Hermeneutics.* New York: Routledge.
Smith, P. Christopher. 1981. H.-G. Gadamer's Heideggerian Interpretation of Plato. *Journal of the British Society for Phenomenology* 12 (3): 211-230.

———. 1988. The Ethical Dimension of Gadamer's Hermeneutical Theory. *Research in Phenomenology* 18: 75-91.
———. 1991. *Hermeneutics and Human Finitude*. New York: Fordham University Press.
———. 1998. *The Hermeneutics of Original Argument*. Evanston, Ill.: Northwestern University Press.
Stenzel, Julius. 1964. *Plato's Method of Dialectic*. Trans. and ed. D.J. Allen. New York: Russell and Russell.
Sullivan, Robert R. 1989. *Political Hermeneutics*. University Park: Pennsylvania State University Press.
Taylor, Charles. 1996. *Human Agency and Language*. New York: Cambridge University Press.
Vattimo, Gianni. 1993. *The Adventure of Difference: Philosophy After Nietzsche and Heidegger*. Trans. Cyprian Blamires with the assistance of Thomas Harrison. Baltimore: The Johns Hopkins University Press.
———. 1997. *Beyond Interpretation: The Meaning of Hermeneutics for Philosophy*. Stanford: Stanford University Press.
Vessey, David. 2006. Introduction to Hans-Georg Gadamer's "Die Unfähigkeit zum Gespräch." *Continental Philosophy Review* 39 (4): 347-350.
Wachterhauser, Brice R., ed. 1986. *Hermeneutics and Modern Philosophy*. Albany: SUNY Press.
———. 1994. Gadamer's Realism: The "Belongingness" of Word and Reality. In *Hermeneutics and Truth*, ed. Brice Wachterhauser. Evanston, Ill.: Northwestern University Press.
———. 1999. *Beyond Being*. Evanston, Ill.: Northwestern University Press.
Walsh, Robert D. 1986. When Love of Knowing Becomes Actual Knowing: Heidegger and Gadamer on Hegel's *die Sache Selbst*. *The Owl of Minerva* 17 (2): 153-164.
Warnke, Georgia. 1987. *Gadamer: Hermeneutics, Tradition and Reason*. Stanford: Stanford University Press.
———. 1990. Walzer, Rawls, and Gadamer: Hermeneutics and Political Theory. In *Festivals of Interpretation*, ed. Kathleen Wright. Albany: SUNY Press.
———. 1993. *Justice and Interpretation*. Cambridge: MIT Press.
———. 1999. *Legitimate Differences*. Berkeley: University of California Press.
Weinsheimer, Joel C. 1985. *Gadamer's Hermeneutics*. New Haven: Yale University Press.
West, Cornel. 1989. *The American Evasion of Philosophy*. Madison: The University of Wisconsin Press.
Witt, Charlotte. 1999. *Ways of Being: Potentiality and Actuality in Aristotle's Metaphysics*. New York: Cornell University Press.
Wright, Kathleen. 1986. Gadamer: The Speculative Structure of Language. In *Hermeneutics and Modern Philosophy*, ed. Brice R. Wachterhauser, 193-218. Albany: SUNY Press.
———. 1990. *Festivals of Interpretation*. Albany: SUNY Press.

Zimmerman, Jens. 2002. *Ignoramus*: Gadamer's "Religious Turn." *Symposium* 6 (2): 203-217.

Zuckert, Catherine H. 1996. *Postmodern Platos*. Chicago: University of Chicago Press.

———. 2002. Hermeneutics in Practice: Gadamer on Ancient Philosophy. In *The Cambridge Companion to Gadamer*, ed. Robert Dostal. New York: Cambridge University Press.

Index

allgemein, 77
application, xviii, xx, 4, 23, 43-44, 58, 59, 60, 68, 69, 72, 78, 82, 83
Arendt, Hannah, 92, 112, 117-22
arete, xviii, xxi, 8-16, 19, 31, 42-43, 88, 109, 125

Bernstein, Richard J., 3, 63, 100, 101, 107-108
Bildung, xx, 48, 56, 75-78

Cartesian, 4, 36, 56, 72-74, 97
chorismatic, xv, xviii-xx, 2, 18, 23, 26-27, 36-37, 46, 72, 100
chorismos, xiv, xvi, xviii, xix, xxii, 10, 18-19, 22, 42, 72
conversation, 5, 10, 12, 16, 26, 27, 35, 92, 100, 102-5, 110-12, 116, 121, 122
criterion/a, 3-4, 70, 73-74, 81, 92, 95, 107, 109, 117, 119

Descartes, 85
dialectic, xiv-xxi, 1-3, 6-7, 9, 17-23, 25-27, 29, 31, 35-36, 42, 45, 60-61, 63, 65-66, 68, 70-72, 75, 77-80, 82, 85, 90, 92, 95, 99, 100, 102, 111-12, 121, 127
dialectical: ethics, xv-xvi, xix-xx, xxii, 1, 22, 47, 72, 97, 99, 101, 102, 114-15, 126; hermeneutics, xiv-xv, xvii, xix-xx, 1, 12, 14, 21, 22, 25, 27, 45-47, 71-73, 75-76, 80, 82, 90-91, 93, 95, 96, 99, 100, 124, 126-127
dialogue, xiv-xviii, xix, xx-xxi, 1-10, 14-18, 22-23, 27, 31, 34, 35-36, 46, 63, 72, 73, 88, 92, 95-97, 99-115, 119-22, 124, 126-27
dihairesis, xvii, 19-20
distance, xiii, xvii, 22, 25-32, 36, 44, 57, 64, 70, 72, 75, 77-81, 90, 95, 102, 105

eidos, 14, 19-21, 29, 39-40, 45, 116, 117
Einhausung, 94
Eleatic, xvii-xviii, 2-3, 6, 19, 35, 103
episteme, 39, 64, 67
epistemological, 4-5, 7, 39, 54, 74-75, 81, 86, 96, 107, 117, 119

Erfahrung, 28, 80, 82. *See also* experience
Erlebnis, 29, 80, 82. *See also* experience
essentialism, 5, 20, 31, 51, 70, 74, 84-86
ethics. *See* dialectical ethics and philosophical ethics
event: of truth, xix, 23, 70-72, 75, 91, 97; of understanding, xviii, xx, 71, 74, 107, 124, 126
experience, xiii, xviii-xx, 1, 11, 13, 26, 28-29, 44, 47-48, 51-52, 54, 58, 59, 60, 64-65, 66, 71, 73-76, 79, 80-85, 87-88, 91-92, 96-97, 105-06, 109, 111, 114, 120, 124, 125, 127. *See also Erfahrung* and *Erlebnis*

fallibilism, 4
familiarity, xiii, 27, 70, 94-95
final end, 9, 115, 117-20, 123
for the sake of, 8-13, 22, 29-32, 35, 41-42, 45, 50, 73, 76, 118, 120, 122
form, 13-14, 18, 29

the good: as transcendent, xvi, xix, xxi, 13-15, 22, 27, 38, 100, 115-116, 120, 122, 125-126; beyond-being, xv-xvi, xviii-xxii, 2, 10-12, 14, 18, 22-23, 27, 37, 43, 61, 100, 115, 117, 121, 122-24; beyond-us, xvi; for-us, xv-xvi, xviii, xix-xx, xxii, 2, 10, 18, 22, 23, 27, 37, 42, 44, 99, 100; idea of, xv, xxi, 11, 14, 20, 22, 37, 38, 39, 40, 42, 46, 116; will, 5, 35, 105, 113

Hegel, xiv, xvi-xix, 7, 45, 81, 85n14
Heidegger, 27, 30-32, 50, 73, 81, 83, 88-89, 92-94, 101, 107, 116
Heimkehr, 72, 90-91, 97
hermeneutical: circle, xiii, xiv, 72; consciousness, 66, 68-69, 85n14
hermeneutics, xiii-xxii, 1-2, 5, 11-12, 17, 21, 23, 25, 27, 47, 48-49, 51, 54, 56, 57-58, 60, 64-65, 68-71, 74-75, 88, 91, 92, 94, 96-97, 99, 101, 103, 107, 108, 113, 115, 121-24, 126-27
Hermes, xiii-xiv, xxii, 21, 127
homo faber, 117-19

Honneth, Axel, 101, 106, 109
horizon, 7, 21, 28, 52, 54, 104, 117
horizonal, 20-21, 48-49, 52, 54
human sciences, 67, 75, 79, 88

idea, xv, xxi, 5, 7, 11, 14, 17, 20, 22, 37, 38, 39, 40, 44, 46, 115, 116
ideology, 5, 7, 8, 16, 60, 62-63, 65, 92, 102-03, 114, 120
immanence, 18, 22, 46, 78, 126
in order to, 118, 122
in-between, xiii-xiv, xviii, xx, xxii, 18, 22, 49, 71, 92, 95, 124, 126, 127

judgment, 13, 59, 78, 114, 125
justification, 10-11, 13, 15-16, 19, 29, 31, 49, 50, 64, 74, 88, 100, 102, 106-107, 109-110, 118, 120

knowledge. *See* moral knowledge

Lafont, Cristina, 89-90
language, xvii-xviii, 4-5, 14-15, 33, 55, 73, 89, 92-96, 102, 121, 123
logos, xvii, xviii, 3, 6, 7-8, 10, 15, 16, 19, 20-22, 31, 33, 35-36, 40, 88

method. *See* scientific method
methodological, 66-68, 75, 89, 122
Misgeld, Dieter, 110, 114, 121
modern science, xviii, 51-52, 58, 60
moral: consciousness, 18, 67; knowledge, 67-69, 72

natality, 92-93, 107, 112, 120, 124
natural sciences, 75, 77, 80
normative, xvi, 62-63, 82, 89, 116

objective, xiii, 35, 51, 52, 67, 74, 93, 101, 119, 120
objectivism, 107
Oedipus, 96-97
openness, 17, 82, 85, 88, 93, 95, 102-103, 105-106, 109, 111-14, 120, 121, 124, 126
the other, xx, 3, 5-6, 15-16, 34, 55, 56, 63, 65, 72, 75-79, 82-83, 85, 91-92, 95-97, 99, 101, 103-06, 109-15, 120, 122, 127

Philebus, 12-13, 42
philosophical ethics, xxi, 67, 101
phronesis, xix, 9, 25, 26-27, 44-45, 48, 56-58, 60, 63-65, 67-68, 90, 108
play, xx, 32-33, 49, 75, 82-84, 87, 88, 90, 92, 107, 110-11, 114
practical: philosophy, xv-xvi, xix, xxii, 1, 37, 42-45, 47, 48, 57-58, 60, 64-65, 68, 99, 113, 126; reasoning, 45, 56, 57, 60-61, 64
practice, xxi, 37, 40, 43-44, 47, 55-65, 67-68, 70, 99, 115. See also *praxis*
praxis, xv-xvi, xviii-xix, xxi, 23, 25, 27-28, 36-37, 43-48, 56-59, 61, 63, 65-67, 70-71, 113. See also practice
prejudice(s), 5, 34, 73, 88, 91, 106, 110, 113

realism, 3-4, 16, 51, 70, 74, 84-85, 115
relativism, 1, 3, 4, 10, 16, 102-03, 107, 109, 114, 117
relativistic, 10, 125
Ricoeur, Paul, xivn4, 66n13, 75
Risser, James, xvii, 25n1, 88-89
Rorty, Richard, 3, 105, 115, 117, 122-124

Sache, die, xviii, 2-6, 16, 19, 26, 33, 35, 102-04, 106, 111. See also subject matter
scientific method, xxi, 51, 52, 54, 64, 66-67, 75, 80, 85, 119
scientism, 122
self-knowledge, 9, 87, 96
self-understanding, xvi, xx, 8-12, 19, 52, 65, 72, 82, 87, 96-97, 125
sensus communis, xx, 75, 78-79
social sciences, 57, 122
Socrates, xv, xvi, xx, 5, 8-16, 18, 20-21, 37, 85, 109, 111, 116
Socratic, xvii-xviii, xxi, 1-3, 6-8, 10-11, 14-16, 22, 26, 31, 37, 45, 88, 95, 109, 111, 122
solidarity, xvi, xviii, 6, 18, 22-23, 48, 56, 58, 61-64, 104-05, 108, 110, 114, 122, 126-27

sophism, xvii, 1, 6, 8, 10
sophist(s), 1, 3-4, 6, 8, 10, 16, 18, 21, 35, 42, 103, 109, 115, 117
subject matter, 2, 3, 5, 6-7, 15, 31, 35, 103-104, 111. See also *Sache, die*

taste, xx, 75, 79, 80
techne, xix, 26-31, 34, 57, 67-68, 76, 123
technique, 3, 16, 48, 58-63
technological, 61, 110, 121
telos, 41, 45, 126
tension, xiv-xvi, xviii-xx, xxii, 2, 7, 12, 18, 19, 23, 26-27, 36-38, 42-46, 47, 68, 70, 72, 78, 82, 86, 95, 99-100, 126
theoria, xv-xvi, xviii-xxi, 23, 25-32, 34, 36-37, 42-61, 63-67, 69, 70-71, 86, 94, 113, 119, 123. See also theory
theory, xxi, 43-44, 47-50, 52, 55, 57, 58, 62, 65, 67-68, 70, 91, 99, 119, 121. See also *theoria*
tradition, 56, 60, 62-63, 81, 82, 89-92, 101, 102, 113
transcendence, xviii, 14, 18, 20, 22-23, 27, 38, 44, 46, 116-117, 120-22, 126-27
transcendent, xiv, 18, 22, 32, 56, 69, 77, 79, 81, 124, 126-27. See also the good as transcendent
transformation into structure, xx, 75-76, 82-83, 86
truth: coherence theories of, 4, 73-74; correspondence theories of, 4, 73-74, 96. See also event of truth

understanding. See self-understanding and event of understanding
universal. See *allgemein* and *Universalität*
Universalität, 77
universality of hermeneutical consciousness, 66, 69
utopia, 43, 60, 61, 116

Vattimo, Gianni, 47, 75, 99n2, 101

Wachterhauser, Brice, xvn7, 3-5, 70,
   74, 74n6, 88-89, 115n20, 116
Warnke, Georgia, 48n2, 82n10, 107-08,
   110
West, Cornel, 113